Privacy Law Fundamentals

Daniel J. Solove
John Marshall Harlan Research Professor of Law
George Washington University Law School
and
Senior Policy Advisor
Hogan Lovells
and
President and CEO
TeachPrivacy, LLC

&

Paul M. Schwartz
Jefferson E. Peyser Professor of Law
U.C. Berkeley School of Law
and
Director
Berkeley Center for Law & Technology
and
Special Advisor
Paul Hastings LLC

An IAPP Publication

Cover design by -ing designs, llc.
Book design and layout by Tammy F. Sneddon Design.

ISBN 978-0-9885525-7-9

ABOUT PRIVACY LAW FUNDAMENTALS

"Two giants of privacy scholarship succeed in distilling their legal expertise into an essential guide for a broad range of the legal community. Whether used to learn the basics or for quick reference, *Privacy Law Fundamentals* proves to be concise and authoritative."

– Jules Polonetsky, Future of Privacy Forum

"There are no better-qualified authors than Professor Schwartz and Solove to summarize the current state of privacy law and, as a result, there is no better compact privacy law resource than *Privacy Law Fundamentals*."

– Christopher Wolf, Hogan Lovells US LLP

"This book is my go-to reference for when I need quick, accurate information on privacy laws across sectors and jurisdictions. Solove and Schwartz masterfully make complex privacy law more accessible and understandable for anyone, from the most experienced practitioner to first year law student."

– Nuala O'Connor, Center for Democracy & Technology

"Professors Solove and Schwartz pack an enormous amount of privacy knowledge into a slim volume in *Privacy Law Fundamentals*. In our fast-paced practice, there's nothing better than a compact and accessible work that is curated by two of the great thinkers of the field. It is a gem."

– Kurt Wimmer, Covington & Burling LLP

"The go-to privacy law reference that you will keep going to. Professors Schwartz and Solove manage to distill without distorting and to outline without obscuring. Part reference, part primer and part pathfinder, *Privacy Law Fundamentals* is the ultimate privacy law resource."

– Tom Counts, Paul Hastings LLP

"This is the essential primer for all privacy practitioners. Professors Solove and Schwartz have done a remarkable job of keeping this volume current in the fast-changing environment of new technology, case law and legislation."

– David A. Hoffman, Intel Corporation

ABOUT THE AUTHORS

Daniel J. Solove is the John Marshall Harlan Research Professor of Law at the George Washington University Law School. He is also a senior policy advisor at Hogan Lovells and the President and CEO of TeachPrivacy, http://teachprivacy.com, a company that provides privacy and data security training to organizations in a wide array of industries. One of the world's leading experts in privacy law, Solove is the author of numerous books, including *Nothing to Hide: The False Tradeoff Between Privacy and Security* (Yale 2011), *Understanding Privacy* (Harvard 2008), *The Future of Reputation: Gossip and Rumor in the Information Age* (Yale 2007; winner of the 2007 McGannon Award), and *The Digital Person: Technology and Privacy in the Information Age* (NYU 2004). Professor Solove is also the co-author (with Paul Schwartz) of a textbook, *Information Privacy Law*, with Aspen Publishing Co., now in its fourth edition. Additionally, he is the author of several other textbooks, including *Privacy and the Media* (1st edition, Aspen Publishing Co. 2009) and *Privacy, Information, and Technology* (3nd edition, Aspen Publishing Co. 2012), all with Paul Schwartz. He has published nearly 40 articles and essays.

Solove has testified before the U.S. Congress and has been involved as an expert and consultant in a number of high-profile privacy cases. He has been interviewed and featured in several hundred media broadcasts and articles in publications and on networks including *The New York Times, The Wall Street Journal, The Washington Post, Chicago Tribune, USA Today, Associated Press, Time, Newsweek, People, Reader's Digest*, ABC, CBS, NBC, CNN, NPR and C-SPAN's "Book TV."

For more information about Professor Solove's work go to www.danielsolove.com. He can also be followed on Twitter at http://twitter.com/DanielSolove. As one of a select group of LinkedIn "Influencers," Professor Solove blogs at LinkedIn, http://www.linkedin.com/today/post/articles/2259773, on privacy and data security issues. His blog has more than 850,000 followers.

Paul M. Schwartz is Jefferson E. Peyser Professor of Law at the University of California–Berkeley Law School and a director of the Berkeley Center for Law & Technology. A leading international expert on informational privacy and information law, he has published widely on these topics. In the U.S., his articles and essays have appeared in periodicals such as the *Harvard Law Review, Yale Law Journal, Stanford Law Review, California Law Review, N.Y.U. Law Review,* and *Chicago Law Review.* With Daniel Solove, he has published the leading casebook, *Information Privacy Law* (Aspen, 5th ed., 2015) and other books.

Schwartz has testified as an expert before congressional committees in the United States and provided legal reports to the Commission of the European Community and Department of Justice, Canada. He has assisted numerous corporations in the United States and abroad with information privacy issues. A member of the American Law Institute, Schwartz has received scholarships and grants from the American Academy in Berlin, where he was a Berlin Prize Fellow; the Alexander von Humboldt Foundation; German Marshall Fund; Fulbright Foundation; the German Academic Exchange, and the Harry Frank Guggenheim Foundation. He is a member of the American Law Institute and the organizing committee of the Privacy Law Salon.

Schwartz belongs to the editorial boards of *International Data Privacy Law,* the *International Journal of Law* and *Information Technology,* and the *Zeitschrift für Datenschutz* (Data Protection Journal).

Schwartz received a JD degree from Yale Law School, where he was a senior editor on *The Yale Law Journal,* and a BA degree from Brown University. His homepage is www.paulschwartz.net.

DEDICATION

To Pamela and Griffin—DJS

To Steffie, Clara and Leo—PMS

PREFACE

This book provides a concise guide to privacy law. *Privacy Law Fundamentals* is designed to serve as a primer of the essential information that one needs to know about the field. For the student of privacy law or the beginning privacy professional, the book will provide an overview that can be digested readily. For the more seasoned and experienced, the book will serve as a handy reference guide, a way to refresh one's memory of key components of privacy laws and central cases. It will help close gaps in knowledge and inform on areas of the field about which one wants to know more.

In writing this book, we have aimed to avoid the "too-much-information" problem by singling out the essential provisions of law, regulations and judicial decisions. A frequent risk in law books is that key definitions, provisions and concepts will become lost in a litany of very long and dense statutes and in a mass of cases. We have endeavored to distill the field down to its fundamentals and present this information in as clear and useful a manner as possible. Wherever possible, we have developed charts and lists to convey the material.

The book is organized in thirteen chapters:

- Chapter One—a review of the key privacy developments since the last edition of this book.

- Chapter Two—an overview of privacy law in all its varied types and forms and a timeline with key points in the development of privacy law.

- Chapter Three—privacy law involving the media, including the privacy torts, defamation and the First Amendment.

- Chapter Four—the law of domestic law enforcement, focusing on the Fourth Amendment and the statutes regulating electronic surveillance.

- Chapter Five—national security law, including the Foreign Intelligence Surveillance Act.

- Chapter Six—the laws and regulations that pertain to health and genetic data, including HIPAA.

- Chapter Seven—government records and laws, such as the Privacy Act and the Freedom of Information Act.

- Chapter Eight—the laws concerning financial information, including the Fair Credit Reporting Act and the Gramm-Leach-Bliley Act.

- Chapter Nine—legal regulation of the privacy of consumer data and business records, involving statutes, tort protections and FTC enforcement actions.

- Chapter Ten—data security law, including the varying laws in a majority of the states.

- Chapter Eleven—school privacy, including the Family Educational Rights and Privacy Act.

- Chapter Twelve—the regulation of employment privacy, including the different rules for government and private-sector employees.

- Chapter Thirteen—international privacy law, including the EU Data Protection Directive, the OECD Guidelines, the APEC Privacy Framework and rules of international data transfers.

For his suggestions on our chapter about school privacy, we wish to thank Steven McDonald. This book also benefitted greatly from the research assistance of Henry Becker, Benedikt Burger, Sarah Chai, Leah Duranti, Yan Fang, Bill Friedman, Thad Houston, Jesse Koehler, Lea Mekhneche, Devon Mongeluzzi, Joseph Mornin, and Lourdes Turrecha.

For further references, including books, websites, statutes and other sources of news and legal materials, visit our website (http://informationprivacylaw.com), and for our casebooks, click on the "resources" tab at the top.

We look forward to keeping this book up to date and to finding additional ways to make it as useful as possible. Please feel free to contact us with any suggestions and feedback about the book.

Daniel J. Solove
Washington, DC
dsolove@law.gwu.edu

Paul M. Schwartz
Berkeley, CA
pschwartz@law.berkeley.edu

TABLE OF CONTENTS

New Developments

In this chapter, we have identified leading developments in information privacy since the 2013 edition. This chapter contains a detailed overview of key recent developments. Only the most important of these developments—those serving as turning points or milestones in the law—are also included in the relevant chapters of this book.

POLICY INITIATIVES AND OTHER GENERAL DEVELOPMENTS

FTC Reports

What's the Deal? A Federal Trade Commission Study on Mobile Shopping Apps (August 2014)
FTC survey concludes that many mobile-shopping apps do not provide consumers with sufficient notice. Mobile-shopping apps should give consumers clear notice prior to download and implement sound data security practices.

Of Data Brokers: A Call For Transparency and Accountability: A Report of the Federal Trade Commission (May 2014)
FTC Report concludes that all data brokers "operate with a fundamental lack of transparency" and calls on Congress to enact legislation to regulate the industry.

Mobile Cramming: A Federal Trade Commission Staff Report (July 2014)
FTC Report on "Mobile Cramming" (the practice of placing charges for third-party goods and services in mobile phone bills) calls on mobile carriers to give

consumers the right to block third-party charges, to ensure that advertising and marketing practices for these services are not deceptive, to clearly display third-party charges on bills, to create effective processes for resolving disputes, and to seek express, informed consent before charging consumers.

Mobile Privacy Disclosures: Building Trust Through Transparency: A Federal Trade Commission Staff Report (February 2013)
FTC Staff Report recommends that companies involved in the mobile marketplace ensure that users get timely, easy-to-understand disclosures about what data they collect and how that data is used, including specific recommendations targeted to mobile platforms, app developers, advertising networks, and app developer trade associations.

Other Notable Reports

Executive Office of the President, *Big Data: Seizing Opportunities, Protecting Values* (May 2014)
Concludes that Big Data can be very beneficial but can also perpetuate discrimination and violate existing privacy standards. The report recommends that privacy values should be maintained by protecting personal information in the data marketplace. It also calls for prevention of new forms of discrimination enabled by Big Data as well as reform of education privacy law.

United Nations High Commissioner for Human Rights (UNHCHR), *The Right to Privacy in the Digital Age* (June 2014)
This report notes many positive benefits of the Internet, such as making it easier to publicize human rights abuses. At the same time, the Internet has made broad electronic surveillance much less expensive. National laws, policies, and practices relating to surveillance should be reviewed to ensure their compliance with international human rights laws, including the right to privacy. The UNHCHR recommends more transparency in surveillance laws and programs, the establishment of independent oversight regimes and practices, and continued multi-stakeholder engagement and analysis to provide further practical guidance for countries on how to comply with international human rights laws.

Studies and Surveys

PEW Internet and American Life Project, *Teens, Social Media, and Privacy* (May 2013)
Provides an overview of teens' social media use, including the demographics of Facebook and Twitter users, the size of their online networks, and the kinds of information that they post. Also exploring teens' social media privacy practices and reputation management.

PEW Internet and American Life Project, *Teens and Mobile Apps Privacy* (August 2013)
Analyzing how teen users of apps manage their privacy on mobile devices, including the nature of the steps that they take to uninstall or avoid apps due to privacy concerns.

Notable Scholarship: Books

J.C. Cannon, *Privacy in Technology: Standards and Practices for Engineers and Security and IT Professionals* (2014)
Discusses how to embed privacy in IT systems.

Michelle Finneran Dennedy, Jonathan Fox, & Thomas R. Finneran, *The Privacy Engineer's Manifesto* (2014)
A detailed and concrete discussion about Privacy by Design and how to implement privacy in the development of technology.

Frank Pasquale, *The Black Box Society: The Secret Algorithms That Control Money and Information* (2014)
Argues that the detailed profiles that companies are creating about people have profound implications for their reputations and opportunities as well as for society. The algorithms used to make automated decisions based on personal data are often hidden, and they should be more transparent. The law should also ensure that important decisions be made fairly and in a non-discriminatory manner.

Neil Richards, *Intellectual Privacy: Rethinking Civil Liberties in the Digital Age* (2015)
Argues that surveillance—by both the government and private-sector entities —threatens freedom of speech, belief, and intellectual exploration.

Eduardo Ustaran, *The Future of Privacy* (2013)
Discussing the challenging balancing necessary to protect privacy and enable the benefits of information flow. Offers public policy suggestions for reform.

Notable Scholarship: Articles and Other Sources

Alessandro Acquisti, Leslie John & George Loewenstein, *What is Privacy Worth?*, 42 J. Legal Stud. 2 (2013)
Experiments reveal that individuals assign different values to their privacy based on (1) how much money they would accept to disclose otherwise private information, or how much they would pay to protect otherwise public information; and (2) the order in which they consider different offers for that data.

Danielle Keats Citron & Frank Pasquale, *The Scored Society: Due Process for Automated Predictions, 89 Wash. L. Rev. 1 (2014)*
From credit scores to background checks, data mining is increasingly used to rank people. This article argues that the due process right should guarantee opportunities to challenge algorithmic decision-making.

Julie E. Cohen, *What Privacy Is For,* 126 Harv. L. Rev. 1904 (2013)
Privacy has a reputation for being old-fashioned and anti-progressive. Cohen argues that this perception is wrong; rather than protecting the liberal self, privacy "shelters dynamic, emergent subjectivity from the efforts of commercial and government actors to render individuals and communities fixed, transparent, and predictable."

Chris Jay Hoofnagle & Jennifer M. Urban, *Alan Westin's Privacy Homo Economicus,* 49 Wake Forest L. Rev. 261 (2014)
Critiquing Alan Westin's famous polls of people's privacy attitudes and demonstrating via empirical data that people do not behave according to Westin's model.

Paul Ohm, *The Underwhelming Benefits of Big Data,* 161 U. Pa. L. Rev. Online 339 (2013)
Arguing that the oft-touted benefits of Big Data should receive closer scrutiny. For instance, Google Flu Trends was touted as a major advance in public health, but its development did not include public conversation about such a use of its users' search data.

Scott Peppet, *Regulating the Internet of Things: First Steps Towards Managing Discrimination, Privacy, Security and Consent,* 93 Tex. L. Rev.— (forthcoming Nov. 2014).
This paper looks at difficult regulatory issues created by the emerging Internet of Things (IoT), including how to address when data collected by a device is used for other purposes, how to manage the challenges in de-identifying data collected by devices, how to deal with data security risks, and how to provide for consumer notice and consent.

Neil M. Richards, *The Perils of Social Reading,* 101 Geo. L.J. 689 (2013)
"The sharing of our reading habits is special," says Richards. "Such sharing should be conscious and only occur after meaningful notice."

Daniel J. Solove, *Privacy Self-Management and the Consent Dilemma,* 126 Harv. L. Rev. 1879 (2013)
Current approaches to privacy in law and policy rely on "privacy self-management"—providing people with notice about how their data is being collected and used, and then allowing people a choice about whether or not to consent

to such collection and use. Privacy self-management, however, cannot succeed alone because a range of cognitive and structural problems make it nearly impossible for people to weigh the costs and benefits of various uses of their personal data.

Lior Jacob Strahilevitz, *Toward a Positive Theory of Privacy Law,* **126 Harv. L. Rev. 2010 (2013)**
Privacy law leads to some people winning but other people losing. In order to formulate privacy rules, we must understand how they create winners and losers. Strahilevitz draws on public choice theory and median voter models to construct a positive account of why U.S. privacy law looks the way it does.

Omer Tene & Jules Polonetsky, *A Theory of Creepy,* **16 Yale J. L. & Tech. 59 (2013)**
Arguing that the increasing collection and use of personal data can create the potential for interpersonal spying and data collection, popularly termed as "creepy" behavior. The article sets forth strategies for avoiding creepiness without interfering with private innovation.

Yang Wang, Pedro Giovanni Leon, Xiaoxuan Chen, Saranga Komanduri, Gregory Norcie, Kevin Scott, Alessandro Acquisti, Lorrie Faith Cranor & Norman Sadeh, *From Facebook Regrets to Facebook Privacy Nudges,* **74 Ohio St. L. J. 6 (2013)**
Reporting an empirical study about what people regret posting on social networks. It discusses whether users can avoid these incidents while still deriving value from the platforms they use.

PRIVACY AND THE MEDIA

New Laws of Note

Revenge Porn Statutes
Non-consensual pornography, known as "revenge porn," occurs when people post nude or sexual images or videos of another person without their consent (often motivated by vengeance). In 2004, New Jersey adopted the first criminal invasion of privacy statute prohibiting the disclosure of someone's sexually explicit images without that person's consent. See N.J. Stat. Ann. § 2C:14-9. More recently, several other states have passed statutes criminalizing revenge porn.

Notable Scholarship: Books

Lori Andrews, *I Know Who You Are and I Saw What You Did:*
Social Networks and the Death of Privacy (2013)
Discusses the privacy risks that emerge from the use of online social media.
Proposes governing principles for social media.

Danielle Citron, *Hate Crimes in Cyberspace (2014)*
A discussion of how the Internet provides a platform for systematized targeting
of individuals (most frequently women and minorities) for repeated cyber-attacks. These attacks are vicious and threatening, and they create severe emotional
distress and other harm in victims. Currently, legislators and policymakers
frequently underestimate the need for adequate legal proscriptions and punishments
of this behavior. Recommends the use of civil rights law to combat the problem.

Danah Boyd, *It's Complicated: The Social Lives of Networked Teens* (2014)
Examines how teens interact with online social media. Argues for less paternalism
about how teenagers use the Internet.

Notable Scholarship: Articles and Other Sources

Danielle Keats Citron & Mary Anne Franks, *Criminalizing Revenge Porn,*
49 Wake Forest L. Rev. 345 (2014)
Argues for the criminalization of nonconsensual pornography because civil
remedies are inadequate.

Woodrow Hartzog & Frederic Stutzman, The Case for Online Obscurity,
101 Cal. L. Rev. 1 (2013)
Arguing that obscurity is a key component of privacy but often lacking in legal
protection. Proposes four indicia that define obscurity for the purposes of
protecting it.

Eugene Volokh, *Tort Law vs. Privacy,* 113 Colum. L. Rev 879 (2014)
A discussion of which legal institutions—juries, judges, or legislatures—should
resolve the privacy vs. safety questions that routinely arise within tort law.

PRIVACY AND LAW ENFORCEMENT

Fourth Amendment

Florida v. Jardines, 133 S. Ct. 1409 (2013)
A dog sniff at the front door of a house conducted by the police is a search
under the Fourth Amendment because it constitutes a physical trespass

on property. The majority did not express an opinion as to whether a dog sniff on the front porch of a home would also violate the occupant's reasonable expectation of privacy.

Florida v. Harris, 133 S. Ct. 1050 (2013)
Whether a trained narcotic dog's alert constitutes probable cause for a further search depends on whether a reasonable person, looking with common sense at all of the surrounding facts, would expect the search to reveal contraband or evidence of a crime. The reliability of the dog in detecting contraband in controlled settings is an important fact to be considered in making the probable cause assessment.

Riley v. California, 134 S. Ct. 2473 (2014)
A warrant is required to search digital information on a cell phone seized pursuant to an individual's arrest because cell phones are qualitatively different from other physical "papers and effects" found on the arrestee's person. Law enforcement must either obtain a warrant or fall within the exigent circumstances exception.

In re Application of the United States for Historical Cell Site Data, 724 F.3d 600 (5th Cir. 2013)
The Fifth Circuit held that government can access cell site records without a warrant. Court orders under the Stored Communications Act compelling cell phone providers to disclose historical cell information are not per se unconstitutional in contravention of the Fourth Amendment.

United States v. Davis, No. 12–12928, 2014 WL 4358411 (11th Cir. Sept. 4, 2014)
In disagreement with the Fifth Circuit's decision in In re Application, the Eleventh Circuit concluded that an individual has a reasonable expectation of privacy in his or her cell site records, and that the government must therefore first obtain a warrant in order to access such information.

Notable Scholarship: Books

Julia Angwin, *Dragnet Nation* (2014)
A journalist explores how the government and private sector implement inescapable dragnets that indiscriminately collect personal information. Her study emphasizes the harm that results when a state of constant surveillance is internalized and accepted as status quo.

Heidi Boghosian, *Spying on Democracy* (2014)
Exploring the pervasiveness of government surveillance, its intersection with corporate information gathering, and the resulting implications for American civil liberties.

Glenn Greenwald, *No Place to Hide; Edward Snowden, the NSA, and the U.S. Surveillance State* (2014)
Detailed chronicle of the leaks about NSA surveillance made by Edward Snowden. Written by the journalist who originally broke the story.

Notable Scholarship: Articles and Other Sources

Derek E. Bambauer, *Privacy Versus Security,* 103 J. Crim. L. & Criminology 667 (2013)
Arguing for different approaches to punishing violations of privacy and security. Bambauer proposes that privacy is a concept involving society's normative choices about access to and use of personal information, and security is one that implements and mediates between competing privacy principles.

David Gray & Danielle Citron, *The Right to Quantitative Privacy*, 98 Minn. L. Rev. 62 (2013)
Information privacy law has recognized the privacy implications of large datasets containing personally identifiable information. However, Fourth Amendment law—from the third-party doctrine to NSA surveillance—recognizes only limited interests in quantitative privacy.

Neil M. Richards, *The Dangers of Surveillance,* 126 Harv. L. Rev. 1934 (2013)
Apart from vague Orwellian threats, we lack a clear sense of the dangers of government surveillance. Richards explores the boundaries of legitimate surveillance activities, proposing principles to guide the future of surveillance law.

Orin S. Kerr, *The Next Generation Communications Privacy Act*, 162 U. Pa. L. Rev. 373 (2014)
Because the Electronic Communications Privacy Act is nearly three decades old, Kerr develops the communications privacy act of the future; it focuses on access, particularity, minimization, and a territorial rule that distinguishes between users located in the U.S. and abroad.

NATIONAL SECURITY AND FOREIGN INTELLIGENCE

The Fourth Amendment

Clapper v. Amnesty Intern. USA, 133 S. Ct. 1138 (2013)
Lawyers, journalists, human rights advocates, and others challenged Section 702 of the Foreign Intelligence Surveillance Act. In a 5-4 opinion, the Supreme Court held that the challengers lacked standing because they could not demonstrate a threatened injury that was "certainly impeding." Plaintiffs could point only to a "speculative chain of possibilities."

Foreign Intelligence Surveillance Act (FISA)

In re Application of the Fed. Bureau of Investigation for an Order Requiring the Production of Tangible Things from [Redacted], No. 13-80, 2013 WL 5460137 (F.I.S.C. Apr. 25, 2013)
Compelling Verizon to disclose bulk telephony metadata records.

In re Prod. of Tangible Things, No. 08-13, 2009 WL 9157881 (F.I.S.C. Jan. 28, 2009)
The FISC found that the NSA had violated the court's earlier orders on several occasions. It ordered the NSA to seek the court's approval each time that it sought to query its database of telephony metadata.

In re Fed. Bureau of Investigation, No. 13-109, 2013 WL 5307991 (F.I.S.C. Aug. 29, 2013)
After the Snowden leaks, the court continued to grant the NSA's request. In this order, the FISC explained its reading of Section 215 and Fourth Amendment doctrine.

Notable Reports

President's Review Group on Intelligence and Communications Technologies, *Liberty and Security in a Changing World: Report and Recommendations* (2013)
In the wake of the Snowden revelations, President Obama convened a group of experts to review the government's surveillance activities. This report contains 46 recommendations. The recommendations include limiting collection of bulk telephony meta-data; increasing transparency regarding telephone, Internet, and other providers; and enhancing privacy protections of non-U.S. persons.

President's Civil Liberties & Oversight Board (PCLOB), *Report on the Telephone Records Program Conducted under Section 215 of the USA PATRIOT Act and on the Operations of the Foreign Intelligence Surveillance Court* (Jan. 23, 2014)
PCLOB reached negative conclusions about the NSA's bulk collection of telephone metadata conducted under Section 215 of the USA PATRIOT Act. It called for an end to the program because it did not meet the "strong showing of efficacy" required of a government program with such "serious implications for privacy and civil liberties." Short of this recommendation, the PCLB also called for immediate changes to the program, including reducing the retention period for bulk telephone records from five years to three and restricting the number of "hops" used in contact chaining from three to two.

President's Civil Liberties & Oversight Board (PCLOB), *Report on the Surveillance Program Operated Pursuant to Section 702 of the Foreign Intelligence Surveillance Act* (July 2, 2014)
PCLOB's Report on NSA bulk data collection program that drew on Internet Service Providers and the Internet's basic infrastructure and was justified under Section 702, FISA. PCLOB found the program to be legal under Section 702. While the report noted that components of the program "push the program close to the line of constitutional reasonableness," it concluded that the program was useful for gathering intelligence, reasonable under the Fourth Amendment, and authorized by Congress.

Notable Scholarship: Articles and Other Sources

Susan Landau, *Making Sense from Snowden: What's Significant in the NSA Surveillance Revelations, IEEE Security & Privacy* (2013); and *Making Sense of Snowden, Part II: What's Significant in the NSA Revelations,* IEEE Security & Privacy (2014)
In these two articles, security researcher Susan Landau summarizes key points of NSA surveillance activities revealed by Edward Snowden's disclosures regarding the NSA. The first article discusses the leaked materials, the scope of the government's powers, and the NSA's international spying activities. The second article discusses wiretap law, the NSA's collection of communications metadata and content, and the government's ability to undermine widely used security technologies.

Joseph D. Mornin, *NSA Metadata Collection and the Fourth Amendment,* 29 Berkeley Tech. L. J. 985 (2014)
Through an analysis of leaked and publicly disclosed documents, this article pieces together a legal and technical narrative of the NSA's surveillance activities since 9/11. It also reviews the government's statutory and constitutional arguments and analyzes whether the NSA's activities are consistent with the Fourth Amendment.

HEALTH PRIVACY

Health Insurance Portability and Accountability Act (HIPAA)

HHS Omnibus Rule
On January 25, 2013, the Department of Health and Human Services (HHS) announced a final rule responding to modifications of HIPAA through the HITECH Act (2009). New requirements expand HHH's enforcement powers beyond health care providers to include providers' business associates, such as contractors and subcontractors. Penalties for noncompliance are increased

in proportion to severity of the violation, with a maximum of $1.5 million per violation. Breach notification requirements and individual protections are also expanded.

OCR HIPAA Enforcement Actions

OCR has reached several resolution agreements with HIPAA-regulated entities for violations of the HIPAA Privacy and Security Rules. The cases are summarized in a chart in Chapter 6.

Notable Scholarship: Treatises

Lisa M. Boyle, *HIPAA: A Guide to Health Care Privacy and Security Law* (2013)
A 1400-page volume on HIPAA.

Khaled El Emam, *Guide to the De-Identification of Personal Health Information* (2013)
Detailed discussion about why and how to de-identify PHI.

Khaled El Emam & Luk Arbuckle, *Anonymizing Health Data: Case Studies and Methods to Get You Started* (2013)
Practical and concrete discussion of how to de-identify PHI.

Rebecca Herold & Kevin Beaver, *The Practical Guide to HIPAA Privacy and Security Compliance* (2014)
A detailed guide to HIPAA and how to develop an effective compliance program.

Notable Scholarship: Books

Khaled El Emam, editor, *Risky Business: Sharing Health Data While Protecting Privacy* (2013)
This collection of essays focuses on balancing the benefits of use of medical data for research and other purposes with the costs to privacy. The book discuses de-identification of data extensively.

GOVERNMENT RECORDS

DNA Databases

Maryland v. King, 133 S. Ct. 1958 (2013)
Following an arrest supported by probable cause for a serious offense, the government may bring the suspect to the station to be detained in custody and also take and analyze a cheek swab of the arrestee's DNA without violating the Fourth Amendment.

Notable Scholarship: Articles and Other Sources

Erin Murphy, License, *Registration, Cheek Swab: DNA Testing and the Divided Court*, 127 Harv. L. Rev. 161 (2013)
Criticizes Maryland v. King and argues that the Supreme Court broadly embraced expansive forensic DNA testing without meaningful oversight.

FINANCIAL DATA

Notable Reports and Documents

FTC, *40 Years of Experience with the Fair Credit Reporting Act:*
An FTC Staff Report With Summary of Interpretations (2011)
The report officially withdraws the 1990 FTC commentary on FCRA and updates its substantive components in light of legislation that transferred the authority to issue interpretive guidance under FCRA to the Consumer Financial Protection Bureau (CFPB). It provides an overview of FTC's role in enforcing and interpreting FCRA since 1970 and a section-by-section summary of the agency's interpretations of the FCRA.

Memorandum of Understanding (MOU) Between the Consumer Financial Protection Bureau and the Federal Trade Commission (2012)
MOU jointly issued by FTC and CFPB in light of the grant of FCRA enforcement power to CFPB in the Dodd-Frank Act. The agencies have agreed to meet regularly to coordinate enforcement actions, inform the other agency before initiating enforcement actions to avoid duplicative enforcement efforts, consult on rulemaking and guidance initiatives, cooperate on consumer education efforts and to share consumer complaints.

New CFPB Rulemaking

Consumer Financial Protection Bureau (CFPB), Amendment to the Annual Privacy Notice Requirement Under Gramm-Leach-Bliley (Regulation P), 12 CFR Part 1016 (2014)
The CFPB amended Regulation P to allow certain financial institutions that meet its new requirements to post privacy policies on their website rather than engage in an annual mailing of such privacy policies to their customers. Financial institutions must still mail annual notices, however, to any customer who requests them by telephone. To be eligible for this alternative method of providing notice, the financial institution must (1) not have information sharing practices that trigger opt-out rights under GLBA; (2) not have included in its annual privacy notice the notice and opt-out rights of FCRA section 603; (3) not share information with an affiliate and previously provided notice and

opt-out rights pursuant to FCR section 624 in the annual notice; (4) have information in the privacy notice that has not changed since the last notice was sent; and (5) utilize the model form provided in Regulation P. This CFPB Rule is not applicable to an entity that is subject to the GLBA regulations of the FTC, the Securities and Exchange Commission, or the Commodities Futures Trading Commission.

Notable FTC FCRA Enforcement Actions

InfoTrack Information Services, Inc., and Steve Kaplan (FTC 2014)

InfoTrack sells background screening reports to employees to assist in hiring and employment-related issues. These reports include criminal records and sex offender registries. By doing so InfoTrack qualifies as a "consumer agency and is thus subject to FCRA. The FTC alleged that the company violated FCRA by not following "reasonable procedures to assure maximum possible accuracy." FCRA at § 1681e(b). As an example, if InfoTrack's search identified multiple individuals with a searched first and last name who had a record in the National Sex Offender Registry, it would forward the report as a "possible match" to employers. The company also failed to follow FCRA requirements for "furnishers" and for affected consumers. Under the terms of the FTC settlement, InfoTrack agreed to (1) pay civil penalties, (2) cease its allegedly illegal practices, (3) take reasonable steps to ensure maximum possible accuracy of information in consumer reports, and (4) provide consumer notice in cases where adverse effects are likely to occur.

Instant Checkmate, Inc. (FTC 2014)

Instant Checkmate offers an online service allowing any person to request background reports on individuals. According to the FTC's complaint, Instant Checkmate promoted its service as "a factor in establishing a person's eligibility for employment or housing." These were "consumer reports," as the FCRA defines the term, and Instant Checkmate was a "consumer reporting agency" (CRA). Although acting as a CRA, Instant Checkmate failed to follow required procedures, including limiting "the furnishing of consumer reports to purposes listed under" the FCRA. Instant Checkmate also failed to follow "reasonable procedures to assure maximum possible accuracy." FCRA at § 1681e(b). The FTC settlement required Instant Checkmate to verify that the person seeking a CRA from it had a "permissible purpose" to obtain it, to check the accuracy of data used, to provide user notices, and to file compliance reports to the FTC upon request. The FTC also required Instant Checkmate to pay a $525,000 fine.

TeleCheck Services, Inc. (FTC 2014)

TeleCheck is a leading check authorization service company. It provides recommendations to merchants as to whether or not to accept checks from consumers. In its complaint, the FTC argued that the check authorization recommendations of TeleCheck were consumer reports under the FCRA. Although its practices were regulated by this statute, TeleCheck violated FCRA by failing to follow its procedures for disputed information, including reinvestigations of the information and providing FCRA-required notice to consumers. It was also alleged to have failed to follow reasonable procedures to assure the maximum possible accuracy of the information that it provided to merchants. TeleCheck agreed to a $3.5 million penalty, the second largest obtained by the FTC in an FRCA case. TeleCheck also agreed to follow all FCRA requirements, including those for reinvestigations of disputes and notice to consumers.

Time Warner Cable, Inc. (FTC 2013)

In its first enforcement case under the Risk-Based Pricing Rule (finalized in 2011), the FTC alleged that Time Warner Cable (TWC) violated this rule and FCRA. The FTC alleged that it failed to provide consumers with a risk-based pricing notice to consumers receiving "materially less favorable terms" in the granting of credit. When reviewing a consumer's request for service, TWC retrieved a consumer's credit report and based on information in it decided whether or not to require the prospective customer to pay a deposit or pay the first month's bill in advance. This behavior triggered the detailed requirements of the risk-based pricing notice, which TWC failed to provide. In the settlement, TWC agreed to a $1.9 million civil penalty and to provide a full Risk-Based Pricing Notice to consumers.

Certegy Check Services, Inc. (FTC 2013)

According to the FTC's complaint, Certegy, a leading check authorization service company, was also a consumer reporting agent (CRA) under the FCRA. Moreover, the FTC alleged that Certegy was also a "nationwide specialty consumer reporting agency" with additional responsibilities under the FCRA section 603(x). Certegy violated the Fair Credit Reporting Act by failing: (1) to follow proper reasonable procedures to assure maximum possible accuracy of consumers' report information; (2) to reinvestigate disputed information; and (3) to provide consumers with an annual file disclosure as required by law. Certegy agreed to a $3.5 million civil penalty and to follow required procedures for tracking the handling of customer disputes and correcting inaccuracies in a credit report.

Filiquarian Publishing, LLC, Choice Level, LLC, and Joshua Linsk (FTC 2013)

This settlement was the first FCRA case involving mobile apps. Filiquarian, Choice Level, and CEO Linsk (respondents) were responsible for a mobile app that compiled and sold criminal record reports from specific states. It advertised its service as allowing individuals to conduct a "quick criminal background check for convictions" in specific states. It also had provided a disclaimer in its "terms and conditions" stating that its products were not to be considered "screening products" for employment, credit, and certain other purposes. Its disclaimer also stated that the company was not compliant with FCRA and that any person using its product for FCRA purposes would assume sole responsibility for compliance with this statute and any other applicable laws. Despite this disclaimer, the FTC alleged that Filiquarian was a consumer reporting agency and had violated the law by failing to comply with required FCRA procedures. Its disclaimers could not be used to avoid FCRA liability because the company had advertised that its reports could be used by customers for employment purposes and could expect such use of its reports. Under the terms of the settlement, the respondents agreed to follow the FCRA and only to furnish reports to persons who have a "permissible purpose" under the statute and "maintain reasonable procedures to assure the maximum possible accuracy" of information.

CONSUMER DATA

Personally Identifiable Information

Apple, Inc. v. Krescent, 292 P.3d 883 (Cal. 2013)
Online digital media retailer did not violate provision of the Song-Beverly Credit Card Act prohibiting merchants from requesting and recording "personal identification information" concerning the cardholder. The California Supreme Court found that the overall statutory scheme of the Song-Beverly Act indicated a legislative desire to balance privacy protection and fraud protection. For electronically downloadable products, online merchants faced limitations on their anti-fraud activities that brick-and-mortar retailers did not face for their own anti-fraud activities. The California Court was unwilling to assume that the Legislature that enacted Song-Beverly in 1990 would have extended its prohibitions to electronically downloadable products.

Standing

Clapper v. Amnesty International, 133 S. Ct. 1138 (2013)
Although this is a case involving a constitutional challenge to the Foreign Intelligence Surveillance Act (FISA), it has relevance for standing in consumer privacy cases. The U.S. Supreme Court held that plaintiffs failed to allege a legally cognizable injury when they challenged a provision of FISA that permits the government to engage in surveillance of their communications. The plaintiffs claimed that there was an "objectively reasonable likelihood" that their communications would be monitored, and as a result, they had to take "costly and burdensome measures to protect the confidentiality of their international communications." The Supreme Court concluded that the plaintiffs were speculating and that "allegations of possible future injury are not sufficient" to establish an injury. According to the Court, "fears of hypothetical future

harm" cannot justify the countermeasures the plaintiffs took. "Enterprising" litigants could establish an injury "simply by making an expenditure based on a nonparanoid fear."

In re Google, Inc. Cookie Placement Consumer Privacy Litigation, 988 F. Supp. 2d 434 (D. Del. 2013)
Plaintiffs alleged that Google "'tricked' their Apple Safari and/or Internet Explorer browsers into accepting cookies, which then allowed defendants to display targeted advertising." The court held that the plaintiffs couldn't prove harm because they couldn't demonstrate that Google interfered with their ability to "monetize" their personal data.

Torts

Fraley v. Facebook, 830 F. Supp. 2d 785 (2011)
In August 2013, the court in this case approved a $20 million settlement with Facebook. Court held that the plaintiffs successfully stated a claim for misappropriation under Cal. Civ. Code §3344.

Contracts

In re iPhone Application Litigation, 2013 WL 6212591 (N.D. Cal. Nov. 25, 2013)
Plaintiffs filed class action against Apple alleging, among other things, that Apple made misrepresentations about iPhone privacy. Court found that Plaintiffs did not present evidence of having read and understood any Apple privacy policy prior to purchasing an iPhone and therefore could not rely on it. The existence of Plaintiffs' iTunes accounts did not, by itself, demonstrate that Plaintiffs actually read and relied on any misrepresentations contained in the updated Privacy Policy.

Notable FTC Cases

In re Epic Marketplace (FTC 2012)
A behavioral advertising company, Epic engaged in "history sniffing." This practice involves a company accessing a user's browsing history to determine whether the user had previously visited a webpage. Epic then used this information within interest segments, including such sensitive categories as "Incontinence," "Arthritis," and "Pregnancy—Fertility Getting Pregnant." Once placed in such categories, the consumer would receive targeted ads based on this classification. The FTC settlement prohibited Epic from engaging in history sniffing and from misrepresenting its practices. It was also required to delete any information collected using history sniffing.

United States v. Path, Inc. (FTC 2013)

Social networking app involved users uploading personal data to a journal that they could share with friends in the Path network. The FTC charged that Path collected information from users' mobile device contacts when users did not consent to such collection. Path's privacy policy failed to disclose that it collected user data when users initially launched the app and each time users signed into their account.

In re DesignerWare, LLC and other Software and Rent-to-Own Companies (FTC 2013)

The FTC brought this action against seven rent-to-own companies (and a software company and others) for spying on consumers from computers they were renting. Without knowledge of the customers, software on the computer (called "Detective Mode") took screenshots of confidential and personal information, logged customers' computer keystrokes, and in certain cases, took webcam pictures of people in their own homes. The FTC settlement includes 20 years of auditing and a prohibition on the use of GPS information without consumer consent and notice. Information improperly gathered from consumers cannot be used by the companies to collect on accounts.

In re Aaron's (FTC 2013)

A follow-up to the DesignerWare and related settlements. Although Aaron's own stores did not license or use the contested DesignerWare product, Aaron's knew that some of its franchisee's had done so. It also knew, according to the FTC's complaint, that "Detective Mode captured confidential and personal information from consumer computer users without notice to those users." Under the terms of the FTC settlement, Aaron's will be prohibited from utilizing "monitoring technology to gather data or information from or about a consumer from any computer rented to a consumer." The order also prohibits it from "[r]eceiving, storing, or communicating" data gathered from a computer rented to a consumer using monitoring technology.

In re Snapchat (FTC 2014)

Company made misrepresentations about its privacy and security practices to consumers in contrast to how their app actually operated. Snapchat collected names and phone numbers of all the contacts in their users' mobile device address books without any prior notice and secretly transmitted geolocation information from users. Snapchat will be required to implement a comprehensive privacy program that will be monitored by an independent privacy professional for the next 20 years.

In re Goldenshares Technologies, LLC (FTC 2014)

A company offered "Brightest Flashlight Free," a popular Android mobile application. Users had downloaded it tens of millions of time. The flashlight app transmitted user geolocation data and persistent device identifiers from Android mobile devices to third parties, including advertising networks. The FTC alleged that Brightest Flashlight's Privacy Policy did not adequately disclose this fact. Although the EULA presented a choice to "Accept" or "Refuse" the terms of the Agreement, the app was already collecting and sending information to third parties before a consumer was presented with this choice. The settlement required improved notice and also for "just-in-time" notice and affirmative consent when geolocation data is collected.

Children's Online Privacy Protection Act (COPPA)

FTC Amendments to the COPPA Rule (July 2013)
In 2013, the FTC adopted final amendments to COPPA, which include an expansion of the list of personal information covered by this statute to include location data, photos, and videos; new ways to obtain parental consent; expansion of COPPA to cover persistent identifiers such as IP addresses and mobile device IDs; a requirement that covered entities release children's data to companies that are able to keep it secure; and other requirements.

FTC COPPA Cases

United States v. Path, Inc. (FTC 2013)
Social networking app involved users uploading personal data to a journal that they could share with friends in the Path network. The app collected birth date information during user registration, including about 3000 children under the age of 13. Parental consent was not obtained. The settlement requires Path to pay an $800,000 penalty, to establish a comprehensive privacy program, and be audited every other year for the next 20 years.

In re Apple Inc. (FTC 2014)
Apple failed to notify parents that by entering a password they were approving 15 minutes of unlimited purchases their children could make when using apps. FTC settlement required Apple to obtain express informed consent before billing them, and consumers who consent to future charges must be allowed to withdraw consent at any time. Apple must provide refunds to consumers, for a minimum total of $32.5 million.

Video Privacy Protection Act (VPPA)

In re Hulu Privacy Litigation, 2014 WL 1724344 (N.D. Cal. 2014)
Class action brought by viewers of Hulu's on-line video content alleged that Hulu wrongfully disclosed to third parties their video viewing selections and other data linked to their unique identifiers. The court held that the classification of information as PII under VPPA does not require disclosure of a person's actual

name—all that is required is "identification of a specific person tied to a specific transaction." Anonymized IDs alone are not PII "but context could render it not anonymous and the equivalent of the identification of a specific person." Certain disclosures made by Hulu were thus not PII but other disclosures, such as sending cookies that could "show the Hulu user's identity on Facebook" would constitute the disclosure of PII. To be liable under VPPA, Hulu would have to know that it was "transmitting both an identifier and the person's video watching information," and facts remained in dispute about intent, and thus Hulu's motion to dismiss was denied.

Telephone Consumer Protection Act (TCPA)

Gager v. Dell, 727 F.3d 265 (3rd Cir. 2013)
Consumer brought action against creditor, alleging that creditor violated the TCPA by calling her through an automated telephone dialing system after prior express consent to be contacted had been revoked. The Third Circuit held that a contractual relationship between consumer and creditor does not exempt the creditor from TCPA requirements and that the creditor violated the TCPA.

Electronic Communications Privacy Act (ECPA)

In re Google, Inc. Gmail Litigation, 2013 WL 5366963 (N.D. Cal. 2013)
Google violated state and federal anti-wiretapping laws in its operation of Gmail, because non-Gmail users had not explicitly or implicitly consented to Google's interceptions and were not subject to Google's Privacy Policies or Terms of Service. Court also found that data transmitted via Wi-Fi is not a "radio communication" that is "readily accessible to the general public" and exempt from the Wiretap Act.

Joffe v. Google, Inc., 746 F.3d 920 (9th Cir. 2013)
Internet user brought action against Google for intercepting private communications, passwords, medical records, and financial information, of millions of users. Court held that the collection of data via Wi-Fi networks did not meet ECPA exemptions for radio or publicly readily available communications.

Notable Scholarship: Books

Neil Richards, *Intellectual Privacy: Rethinking Civil Liberties in the Digital Age* (2015)
Argues that surveillance—by both the government and private-sector entities —threatens freedom of speech, belief, and intellectual exploration.

Notable Scholarship: Articles and Other Sources

Chris Jay Hoofnagle & Jan Whittington, *The Price of 'Free': Accounting for the Cost of the Internet's Most Popular Price*, 61 UCLA L. Rev. 606 (2014)
Suggesting that the FTC should help consumers realize the true nature of online services by clarifying that the consumer's personal information is the basis of a bargain and will be used for secondary purposes.

Andrea M. Matwyshyn, *Privacy, The Hacker Way*, 87 S. Cal. L. Rev. 1 (2013)
Examines relationship between contract law and promises of privacy by challenging commonly held misconceptions in privacy literature (propertization fatalism, economic value fatalism and displacement fatalism). Argues in favor of contracts to protect consumer privacy.

Ariel Porat & Lior Jacob Strahilevitz, *Personalizing Default Rules and Disclosure with Big Data*, 112 Mich. L. Rev. 1417 (2014)
Big Data's rise makes the effective personalization of default rules and disclosure far easier than it would have been during earlier eras. The article demonstrates how personalization might improve existing approaches to the law of consumer contracts, medical malpractice, organ donation, inheritance, landlord-tenant relations, and labor law.

Joel Reidenberg et al., *Disagreeable Privacy Policies: Mismatches Between Meaning and Users' Understanding*, 30 Berkeley Tech. L. J.— (forthcoming 2015)
This paper investigates the differences in interpretation among expert, knowledgeable users, and typical users and explores whether these groups can understand the practices described in privacy policies at a level sufficient to support rational decision-making. Based on their findings, the authors conclude that the gap in interpretation among the groups indicates that privacy policies may be misleading the general public and that those policies could be considered legally unfair and deceptive.

Ira S. Rubinstein & Nathaniel Good, *Privacy by Design: A Counterfactual Analysis of Google and Facebook Privacy Incidents*, 28 Berkeley Tech. L. J. 1333 (2013)
Carrying out the first comprehensive analysis of engineering and usability principles specifically relevant to privacy. Based on a review of the technical literature, it proposes a small number of relevant principles and illustrates them by reference to ten recent privacy incidents involving Google and Facebook.

DATA SECURITY

FTC Enforcement Under Section 5 of the FTC Act: Leading Case

FTC v. Wyndham Worldwide Corp., 2014 WL 1349019 (D.N.J. 2014)
District court upheld FTC's authority to bring cases against companies with inadequate data protection practices. Prior FTC Act actions constitute sufficient notice to companies as to what adequate and inadequate data protection practices are. FTC's allegation that Wyndham's inadequate data security practices led to theft of personal data was sufficient consumer harm to grant standing under FTC Act.

Notable FTC Data Security Enforcement Actions

In re Snapchat (FTC 2014)
Failure to secure "Find Friends" feature resulted in a breach permitting attackers to compile a database of 4.6 million Snapchat usernames and phone numbers. Snapchat failed to verify user phone numbers during registration, resulting in users sending "snaps" to strangers who registered phone numbers belonging to them.

In the Matter of TRENDnet, Inc. (FTC 2014)
FTC entered into 20-year consent decree with manufacturer of webcams marketed as secure, but the feed from which could be accessed over the Internet without properly secured login credentials. TRENDnet allegedly ignored numerous notifications from third parties that its devices were not secure, stored user login credentials as unsecured text, and generally did not implement adequate security practices. This case is notable as the first FTC enforcement action related to the "Internet of Things."

In the Matter of Credit Karma (2014)
In the Matter of Fandago (2014)
Credit Karma provided a website and mobile app that allowed consumers to monitor and evaluate their credit and financial status. Its mobile app was alleged to have failed to validate SSL certificates, which left it vulnerable to "man-in-the-middle attacks." This spoofing technique took place on a public Wi-Fi network in which an attacker presents an invalid certificate to the app. Moreover, until the staff of the FTC contacted Credit Karma, it did not perform an adequate security review of the Credit Karma mobile app and did not provide adequate oversight of its service providers' security practices. Fandango provided a website and mobile app that allowed consumers to purchase movie tickets and view showtimes. Like Credit Karma, it allegedly failed to validate SSL certificates, which also left it vulnerable to "man-in-the-middle attacks." Moreover, Fandago failed to have a "clearly publicized and effective channel for

receiving security vulnerability reports" and misrepresented the security that it provided to consumers. Under the terms of the respective settlements with the two companies, the FTC required the companies to establish and maintain comprehensive security programs designed to address security risks and to cease misrepresenting their privacy or security. The companies also agreed to submit to independent biennial security assessments for 20 years.

Notable Cases

Resnick v. AvMed, Inc., 693 F.3d 1317 (11th Cir. 2012)
Class action against healthcare company that had two unencrypted laptops stolen with customers' personal information on them. The 11th Circuit granted standing where named plaintiffs alleged sufficient injury-in-fact by demonstrating they had their identities stolen after the data breach, paid for identity-theft protection services, and had never had their identities stolen prior to the breach.

PATCO Construction Co. v. People's United Bank, 684 F.3d 197 (1st Cir. 2012)
Under Article 4A of the Uniform Commercial Code, a bank is generally held not liable for losses if it followed commercially responsible security procedures to verify the transaction. The defendant bank had not used commercially reasonable security procedures in light of its "collective failures, taken as a whole" measured against security knowledge at the time of the transaction. As an example, it failed to implement additional procedures despite its knowledge of ongoing fraud involving keylogging malware.

New Laws

AB 1710, Amendments to California Data Breach Notification Law (2014)
On September 30th, 2014, California governor Jerry Brown signed AB 1710, which amends California's data breach notification statute. AB 1710 requires California businesses that are the source of a data breach to provide at least one year of credit monitoring and identity theft prevention services to customers whose social security numbers or driver's license numbers are breached. The law also prohibits the sale of social security numbers unless they are released as part of a legitimate transaction.

Notable Reports

California Office of Privacy Protection, *Recommended Practices on Notice of Security Breach Involving Personal Information* (2012)
This report recommends best practices for entities that collect personal information. It groups its recommendations into three categories. First, organizations should take steps to protect data and prevent intrusion. Second, organizations should develop incident response plans. Third, if a data breach

occurs, organizations should act quickly and transparently to notify the people whose information may have been affected.

Congressional Research Service, *Data Breach Notification Laws* (2012)
This report summarizes state data breach notification laws that apply to entities that interact with personal information. The report also describes federal requirements, such as those in HIPAA and GLBA.

California Attorney General, *Data Breach Report for 2012* (2012)
The California Attorney General's office describes the 131 data breach incidents reported in the state in 2012. Among its key findings, the report notes that data breaches affected 2.5 million Californians in 2012 alone, and that more than half of those affected would not have been at risk if the breached data had been encrypted. The report makes several recommendations, including wider adoption of encryption, tighter internal security controls, and legislation to require notification of a wider range of breaches.

California Attorney General, *Data Breach Report for 2013* (2014)
In the year 2013, the California AG's office had 167 data breach notifications, involving more than 18.5 million records of Californians that were compromised—up from 2.5 million in 2012. California has 38.5 million residents. The increase in number is due in significant part to two large-scale data breaches (one of which was the Target breach). Without these breaches, the numbers would have been more consistent with 2012. More than 50% of the breaches were caused by malware and hacking and 18% were caused by physical theft and loss. The "most frequently compromised data type" was the SSN. The average out-of-pocket costs "to a consumer who falls victim to the fraudulent use of a credit card account is $63, debit card $170, checking account $222 and Social Security number $289."

***Verizon, Data Breach Investigations Report* (2014)**
The Verizon Report termed 2013 the "year of the retailer" breach. The 2014 Report collected data on over 63,000 security incidents occurring in 95 countries. This report is the latest installment in a ten-year project, which has surveyed data breaches involving more than 1 billion compromised records. It provides a detailed analysis of the range of threats and their effects. Regarding Point-of-Sale Intrusions, the Verizon Report recommended the following controls for all companies: restrict remote access; enforce password policies; do not permit use of social activities, such as browsing the web, on POS systems; deploy anti-virus software.

Notable Scholarship: Treatises

Ronald Weikers, *Data Security and Privacy Law* (2014)
2200-page treatise on data security and privacy law.

Notable Scholarship: Books

P.W. Singer and Allan Friedman, *Cybersecurity and Cyberwar: What Everyone Needs to Know* (2014)
In an FAQ format, this book discusses cybersecurity with many stories and anecdotes.

Notable Scholarship: Articles and Other Sources

Derek E. Bambauer, *Ghost in the Network*, 162 U. Penn. L. Rev. 1011 (2014)
Bambauer argues that cyberattacks are inevitable. Rather than focus solely on preventing data breaches, there is a need for increased regulation to address cybersecurity's market failures. In addition, organizations should design their systems to mitigate the effects of known cyberattack techniques, and regulation should increase government's access to markets for zero-day attacks.

Sasha Romanosky, David Hoffman & Alessandro Acquisti, *Empirical Analysis of Data Breach Litigation*, 11 J. Empirical Legal Stud. 74 (2014)
The article empirically explores data breach litigation. Despite the fact that the law is strongly against plaintiffs in data breach class actions, about 50% of cases settle. A firm is 3.5 times more likely to be sued when data breach causes individuals financial harm, but 6 times less likely when the firm provides free credit monitoring. There were 86 different types of causes of action in the cases they studied, the most common being State Unfair Business Practice statutes, the federal Fair Credit Reporting Act, breach of contract, negligence, the federal Privacy Act, and the privacy torts.

EDUCATION PRIVACY

New State Student Data Collection, Use, and Disclosure Laws

Alabama: State Board of Education Policy (2013)
In October 2013, the Alabama State Board of Education adopted a new policy on student data that allows the state to share student data with the federal government only in aggregate form. The policy also calls on school districts to adopt their own policies on the collection and sharing of student data.

California, Student Online Personal Information Protection Act (2014)

New law restricting companies from selling or disclosing personal information about students from kindergarten through high school. The statute specifically targets operators of Internet web sites, online services, online applications, or mobile applications. These companies are prohibited from knowingly engaging in targeted advertising to students or their parents, from using covered information to amass student profiles, from selling students' information, or from disclosing covered information. The law also requires an operator to implement and maintain reasonable security procedures and practices appropriate to the nature of the covered information.

Georgia, Executive Order (2013)

Executive Order prohibiting the state from collecting or sharing personally identifiable data on students and prohibiting student data from being collected for the development of commercial products or services.

Iowa, Executive Order (2013)

Student data in Iowa should be collected in accordance with state and federal privacy laws, and only aggregate student data is to be provided to the federal government.

Texas, H.B. 2268 (2013)

Texas law enforcement officials must obtain a warrant before accessing email and other communications content.

New Social Media Account Access Statutes

Numerous states are enacting statutes forbidding educational institutions from requesting social media account information from students or prospective students. Some examples are below.

Louisiana, Personal Online Account Privacy Protection Act (2014)

This law prohibits educational institutions, such as primary and secondary schools and universities, from requiring students or prospective students from disclosing authorizing information to personal online accounts. The educational institution may place conditions, however, on the use of the school's equipment or online services.

Illinois, Right to Privacy in the School Setting Act (2013)

This law prohibits post-secondary educational institutions from requiring students or their parents or guardians to provide passwords or other account information in order to gain access to a student's account or profile on social networking websites. The law does not prohibit a covered school from monitoring use of the school's equipment or services and does not include email within the meaning of "social networking website." An elementary or secondary school may request or require account information when there is reasonable cause to believe the account contains evidence that the student violated a school rule or policy, but the school must notify the student and his or her parents or guardians.

New Mexico, Senate Bill 422 (2013)

This law prohibits post-secondary educational institutions from requesting or requiring students or potential students to provide passwords in order to gain access to a social networking website account or profile. Post-secondary educational institutions are further prohibited from taking adverse action against a student or potential student for refusing to grant access to a social networking website account or profile.

Oregon, S.B. 344 (2013)

This bill prohibits a public or private educational institution from requiring, requesting or otherwise compelling a student or prospective student to disclose or to provide access to a personal social media account.

Other Developments

Student Privacy Pledge (2014)

Drafted by the Future of Privacy Forum, this pledge involves companies declaring that they will refrain from selling information on K-12 students, refrain from using students' data to target them with advertisements; and refrain from compiling personal profiles of students unless authorized by schools or parents. Although not contractually binding, this pledge creates a public commitment for the companies of the kind that could lead to enforcement actions by the FTC should these privacy promises be violated.

Notable Scholarship: Articles and Other Sources

Joel Reidenberg et al., *Privacy and Cloud Computing in Public Schools*, Fordham Center on Law and Information Policy (2013)

This study examines how school districts address privacy when they transfer student information to cloud computing service providers. To conduct this study, Fordham's Center on Law and Information Policy selected a national sample of school districts from every geographic region of the country and requested from each selected district all of the district's cloud service agreements, notices to parents, and computer use policies for teachers.

New NLRB Cases

Three D, LLC (Triple Play), 361 NLRB No. 31 (2014)

Several employees at a non-union employer—a bar and restaurant—posted comments to a Facebook post by a former employee criticizing the employer for a tax withholding issue among other things. Some current employees and others commented on post, including a statement that the employer believed to be defamatory. One employee called the employer an "asshole." One employee hit the Like button. The employee who called the employer an "asshole" and the employee who "Liked" the post were fired. The NLRB concluded that the comment and Like were related to the post about the tax issue, which involved workplace terms and conditions. Just because there is a comment or a Like does not mean that these employees endorse everything in a discussion thread. The employer's social media policy prohibiting "engaging in inappropriate discussions about the company, management, and/or co-workers" was too vague and chilled employee NLRA rights.

Hoot Winc, LLC d/b/a/ Hooters of Ontario Mills, Case No. 31-CA-104872 (2014)

NLRB deemed employer confidential information policy overbroad and chilling of Section 7 activity. Employer policy prohibited unauthorized disclosure of "sensitive Company operating materials or information" that "includes but is not limited to, recipes, policies, procedures, financial information, manuals or any other information in part or in whole as contained in any Company records." Some of this information could involve employment terms and conditions, and there was no exemption in the policy for protected activities.

Lily Transportation Corp., Case CA-108618 (2014)

Confidentiality policy that prohibited the disclosure of "confidential information, including Company, customer information and employee information maintained in confidential personnel files," was overbroad because information about wages and other matters involving terms and conditions of employees could be included. Social media policy that employees refrain from "disparaging, negative, false or misleading" information about the company" failed to make clear the zone of NLRA-protected speech.

Durham School Services, L.P., 360 NLRB No. 85 (2014)

Employer, a company operating school busses, had a social media policy requiring employees to keep "communication with coworkers ... professional and respectful, even outside of work hours" and threatened to punish employees who share with the public "unfavorable" information about the company, its employees, or customers. This policy was overbroad and failed to define what "respectful" or "unfavorable" information was, and risked chilling NLRA-protected speech.

Laurus Technical Institute, 360 NLRB No. 133 (2014)

Employer policy prohibited "gossip about the company, an employee, or customer." The policy defined gossip as "[n]egative or untrue or disparaging comments" about others or "repeating" a "rumor" or "information that can injure a person." The NLRB deemed the policy overbroad and ambiguous.

Professional Electrical Contractors of Connecticut, Inc., Case No. 34-CA-071532 (2014)

Employer policy prohibiting "using personal computers in any manner that may adversely affect company business interests or reputation" was overbroad because it failed to exclude NLRA-protected activities.

State Criminal Background Check "Ban the Box" Laws

More than 10 states and many localities have passed "Ban the Box" laws and or-dinances. The term "Ban the Box" originated in a campaign by various advocacy groups to stop the check box on hiring applications asking applicants about whether they have a criminal record. Examples of recent laws include:

D.C. Fair Criminal Record Screening Amendment Act (2014)

Restricts employers from using criminal background checks during the applica-tion process. Once employers make a conditional employment offer, they are then permitted to consult criminal background check information. Employers "cannot make any inquiry or require an applicant to disclose or reveal any criminal con-viction until after making a conditional offer of employment." Conditional offers may be withdrawn for a "legitimate business reason" and must be reasonable. When such an offer is withdrawn, applicants can request all records considered by the employer. There is no private right of action, but people can file complaints with the DC Office of Human Rights. Penalties range between $1000 to $5000, with half going to the complaining individual. Exemptions include courts, the federal government, when any law requires consideration of criminal history, or when the position involves "direct care to minors or vulnerable adults."

Illinois Job Opportunities for Qualified Applicants Act (2014)

Employers with 15 or more employees may not inquire about the criminal history of an applicant until the applicant has been selected for an interview and notified about such selection. For hiring without interviews, inquiries into criminal history cannot occur until after a conditional employment offer is made. Exemp-tions include public-sector employers as well as when laws exclude employees with criminal convictions from certain jobs. No private right of action, and first offenses receive a warning. Subsequent violations are punished with fines.

San Francisco Police Code Article 49 and Administrative Code Article 12 (2014)

Employers with 20 or more employees within the City are prohibited from inquiring into or considering arrests that did not lead to conviction, expunged or voided convictions, juvenile justice system convictions, convictions older than 7 years, among other things. "Inquiry" is defined as "any direct or indirect conduct intended to gather information from or about an applicant." Convictions older than 7 years or unresolved arrest can be considered if they have "a direct and specific negative bearing on that person's ability to perform the duties or responsibilities necessarily related to the employment position." Notice must be provided to an applicant or employee before the employer takes adverse action based upon conviction history.

Rhode Island Fair Employment Practices Law (2014)

Employers of 4 or more people are restricted from inquiring into the criminal backgrounds of applicants prior to the first interview. The law applies to both private sector and government employers.

New Employer Access to Employee Social Media Account Laws

Louisiana Personal Online Account Privacy Protection Act (2014)

Prohibits employer from requesting or requiring employees or applicants to give information such as account names or passwords giving access to a personal online account. This statute explicitly does not extend to information necessary to operate devices or online services provided by the employer, nor prohibit an employer from searching public information on an employee's or applicant's online account. Inadvertently obtaining account information does not create liability, but an employer may not act upon, keep or in any way distribute such information. The law extends a similar framework to the university-student relationship.

New Hampshire Use of Social Media and Electronic Mail (2014)

Barring employers from requesting or requiring employee or applicant login information, requesting that an employer add contacts or change settings to a personal account, or disciplining employees accordingly. Inadvertently obtaining account information does not create liability, but an employer may not act upon, keep or in any way distribute such information. The act does not explicitly restrict employers from monitoring provided services and equipment, or conducting investigations under requirements of state and federal statutes.

Utah, Internet Employment Privacy Act, H.B. 100 (2013)

Enacting protections for personal Internet accounts. The Act includes provisions such as permitting or prohibiting certain actions by an employer and providing a private right of action.

Wisconsin Senate Bill 223 (2013)

As a condition of employment, employees may not require employees to provide access to a personal Internet account, or discriminate against an employee refusing to give such information. Employers are also prohibited from refusing to hire an applicant because the applicant will not disclose information to gain access to a personal Internet account. Exceptions apply when the employee uses a device or service at least partially provided for by the employer. An employer may request to view a personal Internet account during an investigation following a reasonable belief that the employee transferred the employer's proprietary information. Under such circumstances, however, the employer can only request to view the account, not require the information to access the account.

Notable Scholarship: Treatises

Matthew W. Finkin, *Privacy in Employment Law* (4th ed. 2013)

Analysis of the law of privacy in the employment context with coverage of recent developments such as employer access to applicant and employee social media accounts.

Robert Sprague, ed. *Workplace Data: Law and Litigation* (2013)

Analysis of legal issues relating to "electronically stored information" relating to employees with a special focus on discovery issues.

INTERNATIONAL PRIVACY LAW

OECD Privacy Guidelines

The Organization for Economic Co-operation and Development (OECD) is a group of 34 leading industrial countries concerned with global economic and democratic development. Its privacy guidelines were adopted in 1980 and revised in 2013. The new Guidelines do not replace, but merely supplement the 1980 Guidelines. Like the 1980 guidelines policy document, the 2013 new Guidelines are not legally binding on OECD member countries.

The 2013 Guidelines seek to promote global interoperability by encouraging transborder-cooperation between enforcement authorities. The 2013 Guidelines also emphasize the need for multifaceted national privacy strategy, privacy management programs, and data security breach notification. Regarding accountability, a concept already present in the 1980 Guidelines, the 2013 Guidelines provide further details about this idea. Finally, the new Guidelines simplify and consolidate the 1980 document's earlier Guidelines' approach to transborder data flows.

ECHR Cases

Von Hannover v. Germany (no. 3), 8772/10 ECHR 835, (September 19, 2013)
Holding that the German Federal Court of Justice's refusal to grant an injunction prohibiting any further publication of von Hannover's photograph did not violate Article 8 of the Convention. The ECHR found that the German court sufficiently took the ECHR's rulings into consideration when balancing the right to respect for private life against the right to freedom of expression. Given that it lies in the discretion of the Member States to ensure the rights given by Article 8, the ECHR declared that the German court's rulings did not constitute a breach of von Hannover's privacy rights as enshrined in Article 8. The ECHR also accepted the German court's findings that the photographs contributed to a debate of general interest.

New Max Mosley Cases

LG Hamburg, Decision of January 24, 2014 [Mosley v. Google],
Az. 324 0 264/11
In 2014, Mosley won a decision against Google in the Regional Court of Hamburg. Mosley had informed Google of a violation of Mosley's personality right caused by publication of certain images. The Regional Court in Hamburg found that Google had an obligation to prevent future similar violations by making the offending images inaccessible at its site. Google's legal duty was to use filtering software to stop its search engine's future distribution of these images.

Max Mosley v. Google Inc. et Google France, TGI Paris, 17e ch.,
RG 11/07970 (November 6, 2013)
In 2013, Mosely won a similar judgment in France. The court found that Google had an obligation to automate a procedure for blocking nine images that courts had found to represent a significant violation of Mosley's privacy.

EU Data Protection Directive

Google Spain v. AEPD, C-131/12 (May 13, 2014)
The European Court of Justice (ECJ) required that Google remove from its search results links to a 1998 newspaper article about his foreclosed house. According to the ECJ, under what has become known as the "right to be forgotten," EU citizens have a right to the deletion of certain personal data under the EU Data Protection Directive. Operators of search engines must remove links to third party webpages when such links violate people's fundamental privacy rights.

Notable National Caselaw relating to Search Engines

Google Autocomplete, **German Federal Court of Justice BGH VI ZR 269/12 (May 14, 2013)**
In May 2013, Germany`s Federal Court of Justice found that Google's Autocomplete function was capable of violating an individual's personality rights and that an autocomplete suggestion was Google's own content. The Federal Court of Justice held that although the operator of a search engine was not generally required to check Autocomplete suggestions in advance for privacy violations, it did have responsibility once it acquired knowledge of a legal violation of a right to personality. In such case, search engines were required to prevent their software from generating a result that would lead to the privacy violation.

EU Proposed Data Protection Regulation

On March 12, 2014 the Parliament voted in favor of the proposed regulation. The Parliament, the Council of the European Union and the Commission will now negotiate a final text for the Regulation. Once adopted, the Regulation will establish a unified data protection law for Europe and be immediately and directly enforceable within all Member States.

Important aspects of the proposed regulation include:

Limits on Data Processing
Data may only be processed if, and as long as, the purposes of the processing could not be fulfilled by other means. There is a requirement of data minimization, meaning data has to be adequate, relevant, and limited to the minimum necessary in relation to the purposes for which the data is processed.

The Right to Erasure
Right to obtain erasure of personal data from the data controller where legitimate interests of controller are overridden by the individual's privacy rights. Data controller is responsible for taking all reasonable steps to inform third parties who are processing the personal data that a request for erasure has been made.

Stricter Consent
The Proposed Regulation heightens the consent requirement by shifting the burden of proof to a controller to show that individuals agreed to the processing of their personal data.

Limits on Processing of Sensitive Data and Automated Decision-making
Reinforces the Directive's concept of consent by placing "the burden of proof" on a "controller" to show that individuals agree to the processing of their personal data.

Monetary Fines

High penalties for violations are set out in Article 79. In the version of the Draft Regulation adopted by the European Parliament's Committee on Civil Liberties, Justice and Home Affairs, for example, fines can amount to up to 5 percent of a company's worldwide turnover or $100 million Euros, whichever is greater.

Consistency Mechanism

The Proposed Regulation creates a new institution, the European Data Protection Board (EDPB), which provides a forum for national supervisory authorities. It also grants great power to the commission to issue a wide range of "delegating" and "implementing" acts.

The US-EU Safe Harbor Arrangement

European Commission, *Restoring Trust in EU-US Data Flows* (November 2013)

On November 27, 2013, the European Commission released a number of reports on the functioning of the EU-US Safe Harbor as well as the PNR agreement and Terrorist Finance Tracking Program. It called for actions in six areas: (1) swift adoption of the EU's data protection reform; (2) improving the Safe Harbor; (3) strengthening data protection safeguards in the law enforcement area; (4) using the existing Mutual Legal Assistance and Sectoral agreements to obtain data; (5) addressing European concerns in the on-going U.S. reform process; and (6) promoting privacy standards internationally.

Regarding the Safe Harbor, the European Commission issued thirteen recommendations. These pertain to the need to make the Safe Harbor Framework more transparent, to embed Alternative Dispute Resolution mechanisms in the Framework, to increase enforcement and audits of the Safe Harbor, and to make clear the circumstances under which U.S. authorities may access EU personal data. It called on relevant U.S. authorities to respond to these recommendations and remedy these issues.

EU Parliament Votes Non-Binding Resolution to Suspend Safe Harbor (March 2014)

In March 2014, the EU Parliament passed a resolution calling for "immediate suspension" of the Safe Harbor Framework. It did so because of its view that the Safe Harbor did not adequately protect European citizens. This resolution does not affect the current validity of the Framework, which is negotiated by the European Commission. It also called for Parliament to withhold consent to any Transatlantic Trade and Investment Partnership (TTIP) with the U.S. unless such a deal fully respected EU fundamental rights to data protection.

FTC Enforcement of the Safe Harbor Agreement (FTC 2014)
In January 2014, the FTC settled Safe Harbor charges with twelve companies. According to the FTC, these companies had deceptively claimed that they held current certifications under the Safe Harbor. In three of the complaints, the FTC alleged that the companies had also deceptively claimed certifications under the U.S.-Swiss Safe Harbor. Among the companies settling with the FTC were two teams in the National Football League, a provider of P2P file sharing, and a DNA testing lab.

Schrems v. Data Protection Commissioner, IECH 310
(Irish High Court, June 18, 2014)
Assessing a claim that the Snowden revelations demonstrated that there is "no effective data protection regime in the United States" and that, therefore, the Safe Harbor did not provide "adequate" data protection. The litigant would have the Data Protection Commissioner of Ireland exercise his statutory authority and stop Facebook Ireland from transferring any personal information to its parent company in the U.S. The Irish High Court found that the Safe Harbor agreement, which authorized these transfers, was a matter of EU law and pre-empted Irish data protection law. As a matter of EU law, the Irish Court then certified these issues to the European Court of Justice: did the Snowden revelations and the entry into force of Article 8 of the Charta of Human Rights require re-evaluation of (1) the 1995 EU Directive on Data Protection and (2) the 2000 Commission decision that the Safe Harbor provided adequate data protection?

EU Data Retention Directive

ECJ, Joined Cases C-293/12 and C-594/12 - *Digital Rights Ireland and Seitlinger and Others* (April 8, 2014)
On April 8, 2014, the European Court of Justice declared the Data Retention Directive 2006/24/EC (2006) invalid. It held that it did not meet the principle of proportionality. The Data Retention Directive lacked sufficient safeguards to protect the fundamental rights of respect for private life and of protection for personal data. The Court also found that data retention generally served a legitimate and general interest by protecting public security and would be permissible if subject to clear and precise conditions.

New Developments: Canada

R. v. Chehil, 2013 SCC 49 (2013)
Use of a properly deployed drug detection dog is a search that is reasonable based merely on "reasonable suspicion." Because dog sniffs are minimally intrusive, narrowly targeted, and can be highly accurate, these searches may be conducted without prior judicial authorization. Even though indicia like a dog's

past performance and the risk of cross-contamination can be relevant to determining a dog's reliability, no specific evidentiary requirements will apply mechanically to every case. The prosecution does not have to prove that the dog is infallible, just as it does not have to prove that an informer's tip is infallible.

R. v. Vu, 2013 SCC 60 (2013)

The privacy interests at stake when computers are searched require that these devices be treated, to a certain extent, as a separate place. Therefore, police must obtain a specific search warrant to search a computer; police must satisfy the authorizing justice that reasonable grounds exist to believe that any computer they discover will contain the information things for which they are searching.

R. v. Telus Communications Co., 2013 SCC 16 (2013)

Canada's Supreme Court found police were required to comply with rules regarding interception set out in the Criminal Code if they want to secure the prospective and continuous production of text messages from a mobile carrier. It found that the police cannot merely obtain a general warrant but must obtain an intercept order and comply with the conditions needed to intercept voice communications if they want to copy text messages.

New Developments: Singapore

Personal Data Protection Act ("Singapore PDPA") (2012)

The Act follows the general structure of the EU-Data-Protection Directive. The Singapore PDPA's rules regarding the transfer of data also follow the provisions set out in the EU-Directive, so that the standard of protection in the receiving country is of crucial importance. Unlike the EU model, however, it contains no extra definition for sensitive data and most provisions do not apply to business information. Regardless of its size, organizations subject to the Singapore PDPA must designate a data protection officer. Currently there is no requirement for an organization to register its use of personal information with the data protection authority. The PDPA also establishes a national Do Not Call (DNC) Registry to allow individuals to register their telephone numbers and to opt out of receiving marketing phone calls, mobile text messages and faxes from organizations.

Notable Scholarship: Treatises

Simon Chesterman, ed., Data Protection Law in Singapore (2014)

A series of essays exploring Singapore's Personal Data Protection Act (2012) and other aspects of privacy law in Singapore. Essays also explore Malaysia's Data Protection Law and draws comparisons with other Asian jurisdictions.

Axel von dem Bussche & Markus Stamm,
Data Protection Law in Germany (2013)
Concise treatise on the Federal Data Protection Act and its requirements. Coverage of issues such as customer and supplier data protection, employee data protection, and international transfer of personal data.

Christopher Kuner, *Transborder Data Flows and Data Privacy Law* (2013)
Examining the transfer of personal data across national borders under data protection law. Coverage includes the EU and other global regulatory regimes, such as the APEC Privacy Framework, Organization of American States, and World Trade Law.

Chris Millard, ed., *Cloud Computing Law* (2013)
A wide-reaching examination of the European law of cloud computing, including the issues of public sector cloud procurement and the privacy of personal data in clouds.

Eduardo Ustaran, editor, *European Privacy:*
Law and Practice for Data Protection Professionals (2012)
Detailed guide to EU privacy law.

Notable Scholarship: Articles and Other Sources

Kenneth A. Bamberger & Deirdre K. Mulligan, *Privacy in Europe:*
Initial Data on Governance Choices and Corporate Practices,
81 Geo. Wash. L. Rev. 1529 (2013)
The authors examine the ground-level practices of corporations and other private entities and make suggestions to policymakers in the EU.

Dennis D. Hirsch, *Going Dutch? Collaborative Dutch Privacy Regulation and the Lessons It Holds for U.S. Privacy Law,* 2013 Mich. St. L. Rev. 83 (2013)
Argues that the Dutch model of collaboration between regulators and industry in rule drafting offers an effective solution to the challenges of crafting effective privacy law. US policymakers can learn from the 20-plus years of Dutch experience using this collaborative model.

Christopher Kuner et. al, *The Proposed EU Data Protection Regulation Two Years Later,* 13 PVLR 1 (Jan. 6, 2014)
Analyzing the current status of the Proposed Regulation with attention to the amendment adopted by the European Parliament and on progress made in the Council of the EU towards enactment of this document.

Paul Ohm, *Sensitive Data*, 88 S.Cal. L. Rev.—(forthcoming 2015)
Developing a taxonomy for defining sensitive data based on a concept of "information that can be used to enable privacy or security harm when placed in the wrong hands."

Joel Reidenberg, *The Data Surveillance State in Europe and the United States*, 49 Wake Forest L. Rev. 583 (2014)
US law has generally focused on access restraints for government to obtain privately held information, ignored the collection and storage of data. In contrast, the EU focuses more on restricting the collection and retention of data and less on government access. This article recommends stricter retention limits combined with stronger access controls, increased transparency of government access to personal information, and personal liability of government officials for overreaching.

Ira Rubinstein, *Big Data: The End of Privacy or a New Beginning?*, 3 Int'l Data Privacy L. 74 (2013)
Europe is presently considering a General Data Protection Regulation that would replace the aging Data Protection Directive. The Proposed Regulation creates new individual rights and imposes new accountability measures on organizations that collect or process data. But the Big Data tsunami is likely to overwhelm these reform efforts. Thus, this article argues that a supplementary approach should use codes of conduct. In particular, the article stresses that regulators should encourage businesses to adopt new business models premised on consumer empowerment by offering incentives such as regulatory flexibility and reduced penalties.

Ira Rubinstein, Gregory Nojeim & Ronald Lee, *Systematic Government Access to Personal Data: A Comparative Analysis*, 4 Int'l Data Privacy L. (2014)
Drawing on the analysis of the law and practices in 13 countries in an earlier volume of this journal, this article develops both (1) a descriptive framework for comparing national laws on surveillance and government access to data held by the private sector, and (2) a normative framework based on factors derived from constitutional and human rights law. The article calls for a robust, global debate on the standards for government surveillance premised on greater transparency about current practices.

Paul M. Schwartz, *Information Privacy in the Cloud*, 161 U. Pa. L. Rev. 1623 (2013)
Comparative analysis of U.S. and EU privacy regulations of cloud services and the current uncertainty around many established privacy doctrines, including the definition of personal information and jurisdiction issues. Identifying weaknesses in how both systems regulate cloud companies and developing proposals for both legal systems.

Paul M. Schwartz, *The EU-U.S. Privacy Collision: A Turn to Institutions and Procedures*, 126 Harv. L. Rev. (2013)
Exploring the path that the U.S. has taken in its information privacy law and the reasons for the relative lack of American influence on worldwide information privacy regulatory models. This Article also analyzes the likely impact of the Proposed Data Protection Regulation and how it may destabilize the current privacy policy equilibrium.

Paul M. Schwartz & Daniel J. Solove, *Reconciling Personal Information in the United States and European Union*, 102 Cal. L. Rev. 877 (2014)
The privacy law of the US and EU greatly differ in their definitions of personal information. The US approach is narrow and inconsistent, while the EU approach is overly broad. Schwartz and Solove propose a tiered risk-based approach to bridge the gaps between US and EU privacy law—"PII 2.0"—which focuses on whether data identifies a person, whether the data is identifiable, or whether there is a minimal risk that the data is identifiable. The article suggests that more Fair Information Practice Principles (FIPPs) be applied the risk of identification increases.

CHAPTER 2

An Overview of Privacy Law

ESSENTIAL POINTS

- Information privacy law is a relatively youthful area of law. New developments are still shaping it and changing its form. For example, data breach notification statutes in the United States date only to 2003.

- The development of privacy law in the United States may also be viewed as a dialogue between the courts and the legislature about the scope and application of the legal concept of privacy. In some matters, courts will define new privacy rights. In others, the courts will leave the job to the legislature.

- Privacy problems occur in particular contexts, and different types of problems involve different trade-offs and concerns.

- Technology plays an especially important role in shaping the kinds of privacy concerns that society faces and the role of the law.

- In Europe and most of the rest of the world, this area is called data protection law. International developments have played a highly visible and important part in shaping the role of privacy professionals and the privacy dialogue within the United States.

TYPES OF PRIVACY LAW

Torts

In the United States, tort law is primarily state law. As a result, the particular boundaries of this area of law will differ from state to state—sometimes dramatically. For example, some states recognize all four privacy interests, but Minnesota accepts only three of the four. It does not recognize the false light tort. *Lake v. Wal-Mart*, 582 N.W.2d 231 (Minn. 1998).

TORTS MOST COMMONLY INVOLVED IN PRIVACY CASES

- **Invasion of Privacy** (a collective term for the four privacy torts)
  – Public disclosure of private facts
  – Intrusion upon seclusion
  – False light
  – Appropriation of name or likeness

- **Breach of Confidentiality**

- **Intentional Infliction of Emotional Distress**

- **Defamation**
  – Libel
  – Slander

- **Negligence**

ORIGINS OF THE PRIVACY TORTS

Samuel Warren & Louis Brandeis, *The Right to Privacy*, 4 Harv. L. Rev. 193 (1890)
This foundational article, which inspired the development of privacy law in the twentieth century, argued that privacy was protected by the common law as "the right to be let alone."

William Prosser, *Privacy*, 48 Cal. L. Rev. 383 (1960)
The legendary torts scholar William Prosser surveyed all the common law privacy tort cases and identified the central four interests protected. His formulations of the privacy torts remain in widespread use today. The states have widely adopted Prosser's four privacy torts.

Contract/Promissory Estoppel

Confidentiality or other privacy protections can be an express or implied contractual term in a relationship. Promises to protect privacy might be enforced through promissory estoppel.

Criminal Law

Many privacy laws have criminal penalties. Many states have criminalized blackmail, "Peeping Tom" activity or the surreptitious capture of nude images.

Evidentiary Privileges

In evidence law, many privileges protect the confidentiality of information shared within certain relationships, such as attorney-client and patient-physician.

Federal Constitutional Law

WAYS THE U.S. CONSTITUTION PROTECTS PRIVACY

- The First Amendment right to speak anonymously

- The First Amendment freedom of association, which protects privacy of one's associations

- The Third Amendment's protection of the home from the quartering of troops

- The Fourth Amendment's protection against unreasonable searches and seizures

- The Fifth Amendment's privilege against self-incrimination

- The constitutional right to privacy

- The constitutional right to information privacy

State Constitutional Law

A number of states have directly provided for the protection of privacy in their constitutions. For example, Cal. Const. art. I, § 1 stipulates: "All people are by their nature free and independent and have inalienable rights. Among these are enjoying and defending life and liberty, acquiring, possessing, and protecting property, and pursuing and obtaining safety, happiness and privacy."

Federal Statutory Law

- Fair Credit Reporting Act of 1970, 15 U.S.C. §§ 1681 *et seq.*—provides citizens with rights regarding the use and disclosure of their personal information by consumer reporting agencies.

- Bank Secrecy Act of 1970, Pub. L. No. 91-508—requires banks to maintain reports of people's financial transactions to assist in government white-collar investigations.

- Privacy Act of 1974, 5 U.S.C. § 552a—provides individuals with a number of rights concerning their personal information maintained in government record systems, such as the right to see one's records and to ensure that the information in them is accurate.

- Family Educational Rights and Privacy Act of 1974, 20 U.S.C. §§ 1221 note, 1232g—protects the privacy of school records.

- Right to Financial Privacy Act of 1978, 12 U.S.C. §§ 3401–3422—requires a subpoena or search warrant for law enforcement officials to obtain financial records.

- Foreign Intelligence Surveillance Act of 1978, 15 U.S.C. §§ 1801–1811—regulates foreign intelligence gathering within the U.S.

- Privacy Protection Act of 1980, 42 U.S.C. § 2000aa—restricts the government's ability to search and seize the work product of the press and the media.

- Cable Communications Policy Act of 1984, 47 U.S.C. § 551—mandates privacy protection for records maintained by cable companies.

- Electronic Communications Privacy Act of 1986, 18 U.S.C. §§ 2510–2522, 2701–2709—updates federal electronic surveillance law to respond to the new developments in technology.

- Computer Matching and Privacy Protection Act of 1988, 5 U.S.C. § 552a—regulates automated investigations conducted by government agencies comparing computer files.

- Employee Polygraph Protection Act of 1988, 29 U.S.C. §§ 2001–2009—governs the use of polygraphs by employers.

- Video Privacy Protection Act of 1988, 18 U.S.C. §§ 2710–2711—protects the privacy of videotape rental information.

- Telephone Consumer Protection Act of 1991, 47 U.S.C. § 227—provides certain remedies from repeat telephone calls by telemarketers.

- Driver's Privacy Protection Act of 1994, 18 U.S.C. §§ 2721–2725—restricts the states from disclosing or selling personal information in their motor vehicle records.

- Communications Assistance for Law Enforcement Act of 1994, Pub. L. No. 103-414—requires telecommunication providers to help facilitate government interceptions of communications and surveillance.

- Personal Responsibility and Work Opportunity Reconciliation Act of 1996, Pub. L. No. 104-193—requires the collection of personal information (including Social Security numbers, addresses and wages) of all people who obtain a new job anywhere in the nation. The resulting information is placed into a national database to help government officials track down deadbeat parents.

- Health Insurance Portability and Accountability Act of 1996—gives the Department of Health and Human Services the authority to promulgate regulations governing the privacy of medical records.

- Identity Theft and Assumption Deterrence Act of 1998, 18 U.S.C. § 1028—criminalizes the transfer or use of fraudulent identification with the intent to commit unlawful activity.

- Children's Online Privacy Protection Act of 1998, 15 U.S.C. §§ 6501–6506—restricts the use by Internet websites of information gathered from children under age 13.

- Gramm-Leach-Bliley Act of 1999, 15 U.S.C. §§ 6801–6809—requires privacy notices and provides opt-out rights when financial institutions seek to disclose personal data to other companies.

- USA Patriot Act of 2001—amends a number of electronic surveillance statutes and other statutes to facilitate law enforcement investigations and access to information.

- CAN-SPAM Act of 2003—provides penalties for the transmission of unsolicited e-mail.

- Video Voyeurism Prevention Act of 2004, 18 U.S.C § 1801—criminalizes the capturing of nude images of people (when on federal property) under circumstances where they have a reasonable expectation of privacy.

State Statutory Law

Much of privacy law is found in state law. Privacy tort law and data breach notification statutes are all state law. In addition, numerous federal statutes permit state laws to exceed their specifications. This issue is regulated under the rubric of "preemption." In Chapter 9 we provide a chart that lists the federal statutes that preempt state laws and those that do not. The U.S. regulation of privacy is best thought of as a dual federal-state system for information privacy law.

Areas of State Legislation on Privacy

Substantial state legislation on privacy exists in the following areas:

Law Enforcement
- Wiretapping and electronic surveillance

Medical and Genetic Information
- Confidentiality of medical information
- Genetic privacy

Government Records
- Public records
- State agency use and disclosure of personal information

Financial Privacy
- Banking privacy
- Consumer reports
- Security freeze

Consumer Data and Business Records
• Spam
• Spyware and phishing
• Telecommunications privacy
• Pretexting
• Use of Social Security numbers
• Data disposal
• Video privacy
• RFID and tracking devices
• Restrictions on ISPs
• Unauthorized access to computers and networks

Data Security
• Identity theft
• Data security breach notification

Employment
• State employee personal information
• Restrictions on employment application questions

For a more detailed analysis of these laws, consult Andrew B. Serwin's *Information Security and Privacy* (2014).

International Law

Around the world, numerous countries have endeavored to protect privacy in their laws. There are two general approaches toward protecting privacy:

1. *Omnibus*: A comprehensive approach to protecting privacy that covers personal data across all industries and most contexts. Sometimes a single omnibus law will also regulate the public and private sectors.

2. *Sectoral*: Regulates information on a sector-by-sector basis. Different industries receive different regulation, and some contexts are not regulated at all. Different statutes regulate the public and private sectors.

The world's first comprehensive information privacy statute was a state law; the Hessian Parliament enacted this statute in Wiesbaden, Germany, on September 30, 1970. Like most European data protection laws, this statute is an omnibus law.

In contrast, the United States has generally relied on regulation of information use on a sector-by-sector basis. For example, the Children's Online Privacy Protection Act provides privacy protection for children on the Web, but there is no such law that generally regulates privacy for adults on the Web.

Outside of Europe and the United States, there are many information privacy statutes in the rest of the world. Most countries have adopted the omnibus approach.

There are also important international and transnational accords, guidelines, treaties, directives and agreements. These include:

- Organisation of Economic Co-operation and Development (OECD) Guidelines (1980), with additional, supplemental OECD Guidelines (2013)

- The Safe Harbor Privacy Principles (2000) established between the United States and the European Commission

- Asia-Pacific Economic Cooperative (APEC) Privacy Framework (2004)

THE CHIEF PRIVACY OFFICER

The chief privacy officer (CPO) is becoming a mainstay at many large organizations. Among other things, a CPO ensures that the organization is complying with the law, that employees are trained about privacy and security practices and that the organization has an effective privacy policy.

In the public sector, the Homeland Security Act of 2002 established a privacy officer within the Department of Homeland Security. 6 U.S.C. § 142. This statute created the first explicit legal requirement in a federal law for a privacy officer in the United States government. Previously, the Clinton administration had appointed a chief counselor for privacy and located this position in the Office of Management and Budget's Office of Information and Regulatory Affairs (OIRA).

In 2002, Congress also enacted the E-Government Act, which requires administrative agencies to conduct Privacy Impact Assessments (PIAs).

In the private sector, regulations enacted pursuant to the Health Insurance Portability and Accountability Act of 1996 (HIPAA) require "a covered entity" to "designate a privacy official who is responsible for the development and implementation of the policies and procedures of the entity." 45 C.F.R. 164.30(a)(1)(i).

As part of its role implementing the Gramm-Leach-Bliley Act, the Federal Trade Commission issued a Safeguards Rule that requires designation of an employee or employees to coordinate the company's information security program. This requirement can encourage introduction of a chief privacy officer position at organizations that do not yet have one. 16 C.F.R. Part 314.4(a), 67 Federal Register 36484 (2002).

In addition, the Safe Harbor Agreement, negotiated by the U.S. Department of Commerce with the European Commission, calls for U.S. companies to engage in either "self-assessment or outside compliance review" of their privacy practices. By mandating these requirements, the Safe Harbor creates the obligation for a certain amount of compliance work and an incentive for U.S. organizations that register under it to designate a CPO to take care of these tasks.

It is fair to say that most large companies that handle personal data now have a CPO.

THE DEVELOPMENT OF PRIVACY LAW: A TIMELINE

ANTIQUITY

400 B.C.   Hippocratic Oath provides the first recorded expression of a duty of medical confidentiality.

1000 – 1699

1361   England's Justices of the Peace Act criminalizes eavesdropping and Peeping Toms.

1604   *Semayne's Case*, 77 Eng. Rep. 194 (K.B. 1604) declares that "the house of everyone is to him as his castle and fortress."

1700 – 1799

1763   *Wilkes v. Wood*, 98 Eng. Rep. 489 (K.B.), repudiates the use of a general warrant to search for documents relating to a pamphlet involving seditious libel. Influential in the creation of the Fourth Amendment.

1765   *Entick v. Carrington*, 95 Eng. Rep. 807 (K.B.), is another repudiation of general warrants in a seditious libel case. Influential in the creation of the Fourth Amendment.

1789   U.S. Constitution—First, Third, Fourth, and Fifth Amendments.

1800 – 1899

1860   U.S. Census becomes more inquisitive. Public outcry for greater census privacy.

1877   *Ex Parte Jackson*, 96 U.S. 727 (1877)—U.S. Supreme Court holds that the Fourth Amendment protects sealed letters in the mail.

1886   *Boyd v. United States*, 116 U.S. 616 (1886)—U.S. Supreme Court holds that the government cannot compel people to turn over documents.

1890   Samuel Warren & Louis Brandeis, *The Right to Privacy*, 4 Harv. L. Rev. 193 (1890). This article inspires the recognition during the twentieth century of privacy torts in the majority of the states.

1900 – 1959

1903   States begin to recognize privacy torts. New York enacts law creating Warren and Brandeis tort of appropriation. N.Y. Civ. Rts. L. §§ 50-51. Georgia Supreme Court recognizes appropriation tort. *Pavesich v. New England Life Insurance Company*, 50 S.E. 68 (Ga. 1905).

1908   FBI is formed. Originally called the Bureau of Investigation.

1928   *Olmstead v. United States*, 277 U.S. 438 (1929). In a decision later overruled, the U.S. Supreme Court holds that Fourth Amendment protections do not extend to wiretapping. Now on the Supreme Court, Justice Louis Brandeis writes a famous dissent to the majority opinion.

1934   In response to *Olmstead*, Congress enacts § 605 of the Federal Communications Act of 1934 to limit wiretapping.

1936   Social Security system begins. Creation of the Social Security number, which is not intended to be used in other programs or as a form of identification.

1947   Central Intelligence Agency (CIA) is created.

1948   The Universal Declaration of Human Rights is adopted by the UN, protecting a right to privacy in Article 12.

1949   Publication of George Orwell's 1984. Birth of "Big Brother."

1950   European Convention on Human Rights (ECHR) is adopted, protecting the right to privacy in Article 8.

1952   President Truman creates the National Security Agency (NSA).

1953   Origins of the "right of publicity" tort in *Haelan Laboratories v. Topps Chewing Gum, Inc.*, 202 F.2d 866 (2d Cir. 1953).

1960 – 1979

1960   William L. Prosser, *Privacy*, 48 Cal. L. Rev. 383 (1960).

1961   In *Mapp v. Ohio*, 367 U.S. 643 (1961), the U.S. Supreme Court holds that the exclusionary rule for Fourth Amendment violations applies to the states.

1965   In *Griswold v. Connecticut*, 381 U.S. 479 (1965), the U.S. Supreme Court prevents the government from banning contraceptives. The Griswold Court finds that the Constitution protects a right to privacy through the "penumbras" of many of the 10 amendments of the Bill of Rights.

1966	Congress enacts the Freedom of Information Act (FOIA).
1967	In *Katz v. United States*, 389 U.S. 347 (1967), the U.S. Supreme Court reverses Olmstead. The concurrence in the case by Justice John Marshall Harlan articulates the "reasonable expectation of privacy test," the current approach for determining the Fourth Amendment's applicability.
1967	Alan Westin publishes *Privacy and Freedom*.
1968	Title III of the Omnibus Crime and Control and Safe Streets Act is passed, a major revision of electronic surveillance law. Title III is now known as the Wiretap Act.
1970	In Wiesbaden, Germany, the Hessian Parliament enacts the world's first comprehensive information privacy statute.
1970	The Fair Credit Reporting Act.
1973	According to *Roe v. Wade*, 410 U.S. 113 (1973), the right to privacy "encompass[es] a woman's decision whether or not to terminate her pregnancy."
1973	The U.S. Department of Health, Education and Welfare (HEW) issues a report, *Records, Computers, and the Rights of Citizens*, articulating the FIP.
1974	The Privacy Act.
1974	The Family Educational Rights and Privacy Act.
1975	Congress's Church Committee conducts a thorough investigation of surveillance abuses by the government.
1975	In *Cox Broadcasting v. Cohn*, 420 U.S. 469 (1975), the U.S. Supreme Court recognizes some First Amendment limitations on the privacy torts.
1976	In *United States v. Miller*, 425 U.S. 435 (1976), the U.S. Supreme Court holds that financial records possessed by third parties are not protected by the Fourth Amendment. The Court articulates the "third party doctrine"—people lack a reasonable expectation of privacy in information conveyed to third parties.
1977	The Supreme Court recognizes the constitutional right to information privacy—the "individual interest in avoiding disclosure of personal matters" in *Whalen v. Roe*, 429 U.S. 589 (1977) and *Nixon v. Administrator of General Services*, 433 U.S. 425 (1977).
1977	German Federal Data Protection Act.

1978	French Data Protection Act.

1979	In *Smith v. Maryland*, 442 U.S. 735 (1979), the U.S. Supreme Court rules that the Fourth Amendment does not apply to a pen register (the telephone numbers a person dials) because of the third party doctrine— people cannot expect privacy in their phone numbers since they expose the information to the phone company.

1980 – 1989

1980	Organisation of Economic Co-operation and Development (OECD) Guidelines.
1981	Israel's Protection of Privacy Law.
1986	Congress passes the Electronic Communications Privacy Act (ECPA), creating the contemporary statutory approach to regulating the electronic surveillance of communications.
1986	Computer Fraud and Abuse Act (CFAA).
1988	Australia passes the Privacy Act, which is based on the OECD Guidelines.
1988	Video Privacy Protection Act (VPPA).

1990 – 1999

1992	The UK begins implementing its CCTV video surveillance system.
1992	Switzerland's Federal Law on Data Protection.
1992	Israel's Basic Law on Human Dignity and Freedom provides for a right to privacy.
1994	Driver's Privacy Protection Act (DPPA).
1995	Communications Decency Act (CDA).
1996	Congress passes the Health Insurance Portability and Accountability Act (HIPAA). Title II of HIPAA requires the establishment of national standards for electronic data exchange and addresses issues concerning the privacy and security of healthcare information.
1996	The European Union promulgates the EU Data Protection Directive.
1996	Hong Kong Personal Data Ordinance.
1998	The FTC begins to bring actions against companies that violate their privacy policies.

1998	Children's Online Privacy Protection Act (COPPA).
1998	The UK Human Rights Act.
1998	The UK Data Protection Act.
1998	Sweden's Personal Data Act.

2000 – 2009

2000   The Safe Harbor Agreement is established between the U.S. and EU for data sharing under the EU Data Protection Directive.

2000   Argentina becomes the first country in South America to adopt a comprehensive data protection statute: the Law for the Protection of Personal Data. The EU Data Protection Directive strongly influences the Argentinean statute.

2001   USA Patriot Act.

2001   Personal Information Protection and Electronic Documents Act (PIPEDA) takes effect in Canada.

2001   In *Kyllo v. United States*, 523 U.S. 27 (2001), the U.S. Supreme Court holds that the Fourth Amendment requires a warrant and probable cause before the government can use thermal sensors to detect activity in people's homes.

2002   Department of Health and Human Services issues final modifications to the HIPAA Privacy Rule.

2003   Japan enacts the Personal Data Protection Act.

2004   Asia-Pacific Economic Cooperation (APEC) Privacy Framework.

2004   The European Court of Human Rights decides *Von Hannover v. Germany*, ECHR 294 (2004), recognizing privacy rights in certain public settings.

2005   ChoicePoint, one of the largest data brokers, announces that it sold personal data on more than 145,000 people to fraudulent companies established by a ring of identity thieves. Subsequently, numerous companies and organizations began disclosing data security breaches. A vast majority of states enacted data security breach notification legislation in response.

2009   HITECH Act, enacted as part of the American Recovery and Reinvestment Act of 2009, establishes a breach notification requirement for "covered entities" under HIPAA. It also extends HIPAA's requirements for privacy and information security to the business associates of covered entities.

2010 – Present

2010   32nd International Conference of Data Protection and Privacy Commissioners held in Jerusalem. One adopted resolution, proposed by the Information and Privacy Commissioner of Ontario (Canada), calls for adoption of Privacy by Design within organizations in order to make privacy a default mode of operation.

2010   Mexico enacts the Federal Law for the Protection of Personal Data.

2011   In *United States v. Jones*, 131 S. Ct. 1207 (2011), the U.S. Supreme Court finds that law enforcement's installation of a GPS device to a car without a warrant is a search under the Fourth Amendment.

2012   Commission proposes EU General Data Protection Regulation.

2013   HHS issues HIPAA Omnibus Final Rule.

2013   Edward Snowden leaks classified documents detailing numerous broad surveillance programs by the NSA.

2013   In *Clapper v. Amnesty Intern. USA*, 133 S. Ct. 1138 (2013), the U.S. Supreme Court denies standing to challengers to NSA surveillance lacked standing to bring their case.

2013   FTC issues Amendments to the COPPA Rule (July 2013).

2013   Supplemental, additional OECD Privacy Guidelines released.

2014   FTC celebrates 100th birthday.

2014   Several prominent large data security breaches are announced by major retailers including Target, Neiman Marcus, Home Depot, Kmart and others.

2014   In *Riley v. California,* 134 S. Ct. 2473 (2014), the U.S. Supreme Court holds that a warrant is generally required to search digital information on a cell phone seized pursuant to an individual's arrest.

2014   InBloom closed (in part) due to privacy concerns. Numerous states enact new privacy laws for K-12 students.

2014   In *Google Spain v. AEPD*, C-131/12 (ECJ, May 13, 2014), the European Court of Justice (ECJ) requires a search engine to remove a link to a search result that violates the "right to be forgotten."

(2014) FTC announces Safe Harbor settlements with twelve U.S. companies.

FOR FURTHER REFERENCE

Treatises

Kristin J. Matthews, *Proskauer on Privacy* (2006)
(originally created and edited by Christopher Wolf).

Andrew B. Serwin, *Information Security and Privacy* (2009)

Lisa Sotto, *Privacy and Data Security Law Deskbook* (2010)

General Sources

Anita L. Allen, *Uneasy Access: Privacy for Women in a Free Society* (1988)
Provides a valuable overview of philosophical accounts of privacy's
definition and value.

Kenneth A. Bamberger & Deirdre K. Mulligan, *Privacy on the
Books and on the Ground*, 63 Stan. L. Rev. 247 (2011)
An insightful study comprised of interviews of chief privacy officers.

Colin Bennett & Charles Raab, *The Governance of Privacy* (2003)
A thoughtful study of the political landscape of privacy policymaking
around the world.

Michelle Finneran Dennedy, Jonathan Fox, & Thomas R. Finneran,
The Privacy Engineer's Manifesto (2014)
A detailed and concrete discussion about Privacy by Design and how to
implement privacy in the development of technology.

Viktor Mayer-Schönberger, *Delete: The Virtue of Forgetting in the
Digital Age* (2009)
A powerful depiction of the legal, social and cultural implications of a world
that no longer remembers how to forget. Advocates, among other solutions,
an expiration date for information in different settings and contexts.

Helen Nissenbaum, *Privacy in Context: Technology, Policy, and the
Integrity of Social Life* (2009)
An illuminating theory for understanding privacy in its social context.

Frank Pasquale, *The Black Box Society: The Secret Algorithms That Control Money and Information* (2014)
Argues that the detailed profiles that companies are creating about people have profound implications for their reputations and opportunities as well as for society. The algorithms used to make automated decisions based on personal data re often hidden, and they should be more transparent. The law should also ensure that important decisions be made fairly and in a non-discriminatory manner.

Richard A. Posner, *The Right of Privacy*, 12 Ga. L. Rev. 393 (1978)
One of the most compelling critiques of privacy.

Robert C. Post, *The Social Foundations of Privacy: Community and Self in the Common Law Tort*, 77 Cal. L. Rev. 957 (1989)
A valuable argument about how privacy is a social value, not just an individual right.

Priscilla M. Regan, *Legislating Privacy: Technology, Social Values, and Public Policy* (1995)
Illuminating study of how and why Congress has passed certain privacy laws.

Neil Richards, *Intellectual Privacy: Rethinking Civil Liberties in the Digital Age* (2015)
Argues that surveillance—by both the government and private-sector entities—threatens freedom of speech, belief, and intellectual exploration.

Jeffrey Rosen, *The Unwanted Gaze: The Destruction of Privacy in America* (2000)
Views privacy as protecting "a space for negotiating legitimately different views of the good life" and examines the loss of private spaces in modern life.

Paul M. Schwartz, *Privacy and Democracy in Cyberspace*, 52 Vand. L. Rev. 1609 (1999)
An account of the importance of protecting the privacy of digital communications.

Daniel Solove, *Understanding Privacy* (2008)
A theory of what privacy is and why it is valuable.

Alan Westin, *Privacy and Freedom* (1967)
An early classic work about information privacy, providing an insightful account of the value privacy contributes to individuals and society.

CHAPTER 3

Privacy and the Media

ESSENTIAL POINTS

- Most states recognize the privacy torts.

- The privacy torts and other related torts have wide applicability in a variety of contexts.

- The First Amendment creates significant restrictions on the privacy torts. These reach their apex when public figures or information of public concern are at stake.

THE PRIVACY TORTS

The four privacy torts are:

1. Public disclosure of private facts
2. Intrusion upon seclusion
3. False light
4. Appropriation of name or likeness

Public Disclosure of Private Facts

The public disclosure of private facts tort creates a cause of action for one who publicly discloses a private matter that is "highly offensive to a reasonable person" and "is not of legitimate concern to the public." Restatement (Second) of Torts § 652D (1977). "Publicity" requires widespread disclosure in most jurisdictions. The last element—"not of legitimate concern to the public"— is known as the "newsworthiness test" and is designed to protect free speech interests.

Approaches to the Newsworthiness Test

Courts use at least three newsworthiness tests:

1. *The "Leave It to the Press" Approach*—defer to editorial judgment

2. *The "Community Customs" Approach*—focus on social norms

3. *The "Nexus" Approach*—require a "logical nexus" between the person whose privacy was invaded and a matter of legitimate public interest

Leading Cases

Sipple v. Chronicle Publishing Co., 201 Cal. Rptr. 665
(Cal. Ct. App. 1984)
A newspaper column that "outed" as gay the hero who thwarted an assassination attempt on President Gerald Ford was newsworthy. Among the reasons for such newsworthiness: The report revealed potential bias by Ford in not publicly thanking the hero.

Sidis v. F-R Publishing Corp., 113 F.2d 806 (2d Cir. 1940)
An article about a child prodigy who retreated from the public spotlight for many years was newsworthy because it is of public interest to give a status report on people who were once well known.

Intrusion Upon Seclusion

The intrusion upon seclusion tort provides a remedy when one intrudes "upon the solitude or seclusion of another or his private affairs or concerns" if the intrusion is "highly offensive to a reasonable person." Restatement (Second) of Torts § 652B (1977).

"The intrusion itself makes the defendant subject to liability even though there is no publication or other use of any kind of the photograph or information outlined." Id. Comment (b).

Leading Cases

Nader v. General Motors Corp., 255 N.E.2d 765 (N.Y. Ct. App. 1970)
Although generally people don't have an expectation of privacy in public, "overzealous surveillance" in public can be actionable when the "information sought is of a confidential nature" and the defendant's conduct is "unreasonably intrusive" (beyond the "normal inquiry of observation").

Dietemann v. Time, Inc., 449 F.2d 245 (9th Cir. 1971)
Entering a person's home under false pretenses and secretly recording his activities is actionable.

WHAT CONSTITUTES A PRIVACY INTEREST?

In the public disclosure and intrusion upon seclusion torts, a key element involves whether the plaintiff had a privacy interest.

PRIVACY INTEREST

Involuntary exposure in public—Involuntary exposure in public—certain kinds of involuntary exposure in public, especially involuntary nudity. *Daily Times Democrat v. Graham*, 162 So.2d 474 (Ala. 1964).

Overzealous surveillance in public—surveillance in public that reveals confidential data. *Nader v. General Motors Corp.*, 255 N.E.2d 765 (N.Y. Ct. App. 1970).

Inside the home—activities occurring within people's houses. *Dietemann v. Time, Inc.*, 449 F.2d 245 (9th Cir. 1971).

Known to a certain social group—data known to a discrete social group not likely to circulate it to outsiders. *Y.G. v. Jewish Hospital*, 795 S.W.2d 488 (Mo. Ct. App. 1990).

Extensive harassment in public—*Linehan v. Linehan*, 285 P.2d 326 (Cal. App. 1955).

Photos of corpses of loved ones —*Sellers v. Henry*, 329 S.W.2d (Ky. 1959); Catsouras v. Department of the California Highway Patrol, 104 Cal. Rptr. 3d 352 (Cal. App. 2010).

NO PRIVACY INTEREST

Public view—anything exposed to public view. *Gill v. Hearst Publishing Co.*, 253 P.2d 441 (Cal. 1953).

Public domain—any information available in a public record. *Reece v. Grissom*, 267 S.E.2d 838 (Ga. App. 1980).

Republication—restating facts already publicized. *Heath v. Playboy Enterprises*, Inc., 732 F. Supp. 1145 (S.D. Fla. 1990).

Known by others—information shared with many people. *Fisher v. Ohio Dep't of Rehabilitation and Correction*, 578 N.E.2d 901 (Ohio Ct. Cl. 1988).

In the public disclosure, intrusion upon seclusion and false light torts, a key element involves whether the violation is highly offensive to a reasonable person. Courts are not always consistent in their holdings, but generally, the following things have been found either highly offensive or not highly offensive.

HIGHLY OFFENSIVE	NOT HIGHLY OFFENSIVE
Peeping into home windows. *Pritchett v. Board of Com'rs of Knox County*, 85 N.E. 32 (N.D. Ga. 1951).	**Disclosure of reputation-enhancing information.** *Wood v. National Computer Systems, Inc.*, 643 F. Supp. 1092 (W.D. Ark. 1986).
Harassing telephone calls. *Rogers v. Loews L'Enfant Plaza Hotel*, 526 F. Supp. 523 (D.D.C. 1981).	**Disclosure of union membership.** *International Union v. Garner*, 601 F. Supp. 187 (M.D. Tenn. 1985).
Snooping into mail. *Doe v. Kohn Nast & Graf, P.C.*, 866 F. Supp. 190 (E.D. Pa. 1994).	**Disclosure of non-embarrassing information.** *Bisbee v. John C. Conover Agency, Inc.*, 452 A.2d 689 (N.J. App. Div. 1982).
Secretly recording conversations. *Fischer v. Hooper*, 732 A.2d 396 (1999).	**Disclosure of minor injury.** Restatement (Second) of Torts § 652D comment (c).
Illegally accessing credit card records. *Pulla v. Amoco Oil Co.*, 882 F. Supp. 836 (S.D. Iowa 1994).	**Disclosures causing "minor and moderate annoyance."** Restatement (Second) of Torts § 652D comment (c).
Distribution of nude photos. *Taylor v. K.T.V.B., Inc.*, 525 P.2d 984 (Idaho 1974).	
Disclosure of autopsy photos. *Reid v. Pierce County*, 961 P.2d 333 (1998).	
Disclosure of confidential medical data. *Crippen v. Charter Southland Hosp., Inc.*, 534 So.2d 286 (Ala. 1988).	
Identifying a rape victim. *Nappier v. Jefferson Standard Life Ins. Co.*, 322 F.2d 502 (4th Cir. 1963).	
Disclosure of debts. *Brents v. Morgan*, 299 S.W. 967 (Ky. 1927).	

False Light

The false light tort creates a cause of action when one publicly discloses a matter that places a person "in a false light" that is "highly offensive to a reasonable person." Restatement (Second) of Torts § 652E (1977).

Leading Case

Time Inc. v. Hill, 385 U.S. 374 (1967)
The U.S. Constitution's First Amendment permits liability in false light cases only if the plaintiff publicly discloses the matter with a reckless disregard for the truth or with actual knowledge of falsity.

Appropriation of Name or Likeness

A plaintiff has a remedy against one "who appropriates to his own use or benefit the name or likeness" of the plaintiff. Restatement (Second) of Torts § 652C (1977). From the right against appropriation, courts have also developed a "right of publicity" that provides famous people an exclusive right to exploit the value of their identity as celebrities.

Leading Cases

Carson v. Here's Johnny Portable Toilets, 698 F.2d 831 (6th Cir. 1983)
A right of publicity protects against an unauthorized commercial exploitation of celebrity identity. An unauthorized use of a famous phrase, "Here's Johnny," that is associated with a celebrity appropriates his identity as celebrity and violates his right of publicity.

Finger v. Omni Publications International, Ltd., 566 N.E.2d 141 (N.Y. Ct. App. 1990)
A photograph of plaintiffs, used to illustrate a magazine article without their permission, does not violate their privacy interests so long as there is a "real relationship" between their photograph and the topic of the article.

OTHER TORTS

Intentional Infliction of Emotional Distress

The tort of intentional infliction of emotional distress can also serve as a remedy for certain privacy invasions. This tort provides a remedy when one "by extreme and outrageous conduct intentionally or recklessly causes severe emotional distress to another." Restatement (Second) of Torts § 46 (1977). Since privacy invasions can often result in severe emotional distress, this tort may provide a remedy. However, it is limited by the requirement of "extreme and outrageous conduct."

Breach of Confidentiality

The tort of breach of confidentiality provides a remedy when a professional (i.e., doctor, lawyer, banker) divulges a patient's or client's confidential information. A plaintiff must prove that the defendant owed the plaintiff a duty of confidentiality and that the defendant breached that duty. Unlike the tort of public disclosure, the breach of confidentiality tort does not require the tests of "highly offensive," publicity or newsworthiness.

PUBLIC DISCLOSURE TORT vs. BREACH OF CONFIDENTIALITY TORT	
PUBLIC DISCLOSURE	**BREACH OF CONFIDENTIALITY**
Publicity—widespread disclosure	Breach of a duty of confidentiality—need not be widespread disclosure
Private matter	Confidential information
Highly offensive to a reasonable person	N/A
Not of legitimate concern to the public	N/A

OTHER PRIVACY LAWS OF NOTE

Video Voyeurism Prevention Act (VVPA), 18 U.S.C. § 1801 (2004)
Prohibits capturing images or videos of people's private parts. Provides protection when a reasonable person expects to be able to disrobe without being photographed or recorded as well as when a person expects his or her private parts not to be publicly visible "regardless of whether that person is in a public or private area." The statutory jurisdiction of this federal law is limited to the special maritime and territorial jurisdiction of the U.S.

State Video Voyeurism Statutes
Many states have laws prohibiting the capturing of photos or videos of people's private parts. Some of these include criminal penalties. *See*, e.g., California Penal Code § 647(k); Fla. Stat. Ann. § 810.145; La. Rev. Stat. Ann. § 14:283; N.J. Stat. Ann. § 2C:18-3; N.Y. Penal Law § 250.45; Washington, RCW 9A.44.115.

"Peeping Tom" Laws

A number of states criminalize peeping into people's homes or other places where they expect privacy. Many state statutes require that the perpetrator trespass onto private property in order to peep or that the perpetrator see the victim wholly or partially nude. Other states lack such restrictions. For example, Hawaii makes it a crime when one "[p]eers or peeps into a window or other opening of a dwelling or other structure adapted for sojourn or overnight accommodations for the purpose of spying on the occupant thereof or invading the privacy of another person with a lewd or unlawful purpose, under circumstances in which a reasonable person in the dwelling or other structure would not expect to be observed." Haw. Rev. Stat. § 711-1111.

Blackmail Laws

Blackmail laws address threats to expose discreditable secrets unless a person pays money. Example: "A person extorts if he purposely threatens to: ... (c) expose or publicize any secret or any asserted fact, whether true or false, tending to subject any person to hatred, contempt or ridicule, or impair his credit or business repute." N.J. Stat. Ann. §2C:20-5.

California Anti-Paparazzi Act, Cal Civ. Code § 1708.8

The first anti-paparazzi law in the United States. Among other things, it prohibits capturing images, video or audio with enhancing devices. Although it is similar to the tort of intrusion upon seclusion, the statute only requires that the violation be offensive rather than highly offensive, and the statute provides for treble damages.

Revenge Porn Statutes

Non-consensual pornography, known as "revenge porn," occurs when people post nude or sexual images or videos of another person without their consent (often motivated by vengeance). In 2004, New Jersey adopted the first criminal invasion of privacy statute prohibiting the disclosure of someone's sexually explicit images without that person's consent. See N.J. Stat. Ann. § 2C:14-9. More recently, several other states have passed statutes criminalizing revenge porn.

DEFAMATION LAW

Libel and Slander

Defamation: A person is liable for defamation if he makes "a false and defamatory statement concerning another" to a third party with the applicable fault standard. Restatement (Second) of Torts § 558. A "defamatory" statement "tends so to harm the reputation of another as to lower him in the estimation of the community or to deter third persons from associating or dealing with him." Restatement (Second) of Torts § 559.

Libel vs. Slander: Defamation law consists of two torts—libel and slander. Libel is defamation in tangible form—written or broadcast via TV or radio. Slander is defamation spoken directly to other people.

Republication: "[O]ne who repeats or otherwise republishes defamatory matter is subject to liability as if he had originally published it." Restatement (Second) of Torts § 578.

Distribution: One who distributes, transmits or broadcasts on television or radio defamatory material is also liable if she knows or would have reason to know of its defamatory character. Restatement (Second) of Torts § 581.

First Amendment Restrictions

New York Times Co. v. Sullivan, **376 U.S. 254 (1964)**
Libel law must be constrained by the First Amendment to ensure speech is "uninhibited, robust and wide-open." A public official must prove "actual malice" to prevail.

Actual Malice

"Actual malice" involves making a statement "with knowledge that it was false or with reckless disregard of whether it was false or not." *New York Times Co. v. Sullivan,* 376 U.S. 254 (1964).

Curtis Publishing Co. v. Butts, **388 U.S. 130 (1967)**
Public figures, in addition to public officials, must prove actual malice to prevail in a defamation case.

Gertz v. Robert Welch, Inc., **418 U.S. 323 (1974)**
Private figures do not need to establish actual malice in order to prevail in a defamation lawsuit.

Public vs. Private Figures

1. **All-Purpose Public Figures**—people who have "general fame or notoriety." Deemed a public figure for all issues.

2. **Limited Public Figures**—people who are involved in a particular controversy. They are deemed public figures with regard to stories about the context or controversy that makes them public figures, but for everything else, they remain private.

Dun & Bradstreet, Inc. v. Greenmoss Builders, Inc., 472 U.S. 749 (1985)
For matters of purely private concern, such as providing a report on one's financial condition for use by another person or company, actual malice is not required by the First Amendment, nor any other limitations on the defamation torts.

DEFAMATION: FAULT STANDARDS		
	PUBLIC FIGURE (includes public officials)	**PRIVATE FIGURE**
Speech of Public Concern	*Curtis Publishing Co. v. Butts* Compensatory Damages = Malice Punitive Damages = Malice Presume Damages = Malice	*Gertz v. Robert Welch, Inc.* Compensatory Damages = Negligence Punitive Damages = Malice Presumed Damages = Malice
Speech of Private Concern	Unclear. Probably same as above, but might be *Gertz* rule.	*Dun & Bradstreet v. Greenmoss Builders* Compensatory Damages = Negligence Punitive Damages = Negligence Presumed Damages = Negligence (or possibly strict liability for all forms of damages)

Communications Decency Act (CDA) § 230(c) (1996)

"No provider or user of an interactive computer service shall be treated as the publisher or speaker of any information provided by another information content provider." Immunizes ISPs, blogs, social network sites and others from liability for the content posted by users.

Leading Cases

Zeran v. America Online, Inc., **129 F.3d 327 (4th Cir. 1997)**
The CDA § 230 immunizes an ISP that fails to remove a defamatory posting by a user even after the ISP knows it is defamatory.

Carafano v. Metrosplash.com, **339 F.3d 1119 (9th Cir. 2003)**
Dating website immune under CDA § 230 for false profile of plaintiff posted by a third party.

Batzel v. Smith, **333 F.3d 1018 (9th Cir. 2003)**
Listserv operator who forwarded defamatory e-mail was immune under CDA § 230 because a third party authored the e-mail.

Fair Housing Council of San Fernando Valley v. Roommates.com, LLC, **521 F.3d 1157 (9th Cir. 2008)**
Roommates.com not immune under CDA § 230 when it created questions and answer choices for users to select. By providing "pre-populated answers, Roommates becomes much more than a passive transmitter of information provided by others; it becomes the developer, at least in part, of the information."

FIRST AMENDMENT

The First Amendment provides restrictions to tort liability for the disclosure of true and false information:

- For content-based restrictions on the disclosure of true information, the First Amendment requires strict scrutiny when the data pertains to a matter of public significance. When the data involves a private matter, the Supreme Court has not indicated what, if any, First Amendment restrictions would be involved.

- For false information, the First Amendment follows the rules set forth in its line of cases involving defamation, generally requiring actual malice for public figures.

- For the enforcement of contract or promissory estoppel that involves restrictions on the disclosure of information, the First Amendment does not provide restrictions.

Leading Cases

Cox Broadcasting Corp. v. Cohn, 420 U.S. 469 (1975)
If the information is released in court records by the government, the tort of public disclosure cannot apply (even if the information is private and not newsworthy).

The Florida Star v. B.J.F., 491 U.S. 524 (1989)
"[I]f a newspaper lawfully obtains truthful information about a matter of public significance then state officials may not constitutionally punish publication of the information, absent a need to further a state interest of the highest order."

Bartnicki v. Vopper, 532 U.S. 514 (2001)
A provision in the federal Wiretap Act prohibits one from intentionally disclosing the contents of a communication "knowing or having reason to know that the communication was obtained" in violation of the wiretap law. The Supreme Court held that the First Amendment prevents the application of the statute when the illegally obtained communication involves a matter of public concern.

Time, Inc. v. Hill, 385 U.S. 374 (1967)
Actual malice rule applies to the false light tort. After *Gertz,* it appears the actual malice rule would apply to cases brought only by public figures.

Hustler Magazine v. Falwell, 485 U.S. 46 (1988)
Public figures must prove actual malice to recover for intentional infliction of emotional distress.

Snyder v. Phelps, 131 S. Ct. 1207 (2011)
For speech of public concern, plaintiffs must prove actual malice in order to prevail under the intentional infliction of emotional distress tort. The First Amendment also restricts intrusion upon seclusion liability for picketing near a funeral.

Zacchini v. Scripps-Howard Broadcasting Co., 433 U.S. 562 (1977)
Actual malice rule does not apply to the appropriation tort.

Cohen v. Cowles Media Co., 501 U.S. 663 (1991)
The First Amendment does not limit contracts and promissory estoppel when they involve restrictions on speaking.

Public Disclosure of Private Facts	The First Amendment requires strict scrutiny if the information is truthful and involves a matter of public concern. *The Florida Star v. B.J.F.*, 491 U.S. 524 (1989); *Bartnicki v. Vopper*, 532 U.S. 514 (2001).
Intrusion Upon Seclusion	Intrusion upon seclusion tort action used improperly to impose liability on protesting near a funeral violates the First Amendment. *Snyder v. Phelps*, 131 S. Ct. 1207 (2011). When the tort does not involve direct restrictions on speech, it will likely have no First Amendment problems.
False Light	Actual malice required. *Time, Inc. v. Hill,* 385 U.S. 374 (1967). It is likely that the same standards apply as in defamation law.
Appropriation of Name or Likeness	No actual malice required. *Zacchini v. Scripps-Howard Broadcasting Co.*, 433 U.S. 562 (1977).
Intentional Infliction of Emotional Distress	Actual malice required for public figures. *Hustler Magazine v. Falwell*, 485 U.S. 46 (1988).
Breach of Confidentiality	No U.S. Supreme Court First Amendment case yet. If seen as akin to tort, then might be treated akin to the public disclosure tort. But if seen as akin to contract or promissory estoppel, then no First Amendment limitation. *Cohen v. Cowles Media Co.*, 501 U.S. 663 (1991).
Defamation Torts	See the Defamation: Fault Standards chart on page 63.

Anti-SLAPP

When lawsuits implicate a defendant's speech, 30 states and the District of Columbia provide special anti-SLAPP protections.

A SLAPP lawsuit – or a "strategic lawsuit against public participation"—is a lawsuit designed to censor or retaliate against a person for their speech. Fearing significant legal defense costs, defendants might retract their speech or stop engaging in new speech about a matter. SLAPP suits can successfully silence people engaging in protected speech even when the suit is without merit because the costs of getting the suit dismissed can still be significant.

Anti-SLAPP legislation typically has the following elements, which include: (1) requirements that the plaintiff demonstrate early that the case has merit; (2) provisions that allow the defendant to seek an expedited hearing; (3) limits on long costly discovery; (4) the right of a prevailing defendant to recover attorney fees and costs.

ANONYMOUS SPEECH

The First Amendment protects anonymous speech. Unless narrowly tailored to a compelling government interest, a law or regulation cannot:

• Require people to include their true identities on handbills and pamphlets. *Talley v. State of California*, 362 U.S. 60 (1960); *McIntyre v. Ohio Elections Commission*, 514 U.S. 334 (1995).

• Require individuals handing out petitions to wear name tags. *Buckley v. ACLF*, 525 U.S. 182 (1999).

• Force solicitors of private residences to obtain a permit requiring they supply their identities. *Watchtower Bible & Tract Society v. Village of Stratton*, 536 U.S. 150 (2002).

Standards for Unmasking Anonymous Speakers

Courts have articulated several different standards for a plaintiff to find out the identity of an anonymous speaker:

1. *The Motion to Dismiss Standard.* The plaintiff must show the case can survive a motion to dismiss in order to ascertain the identity of the anonymous speaker. *Columbia Ins. Co. v. Seescandy.Com,* 185 F.R.D. 573 (N.D. Cal. 1999).

2. *The Prima Facie Case Standard.* The plaintiff must produce evidence showing a prima facie case on all elements and must demonstrate that revealing the identity of the anonymous speaker will not severely harm the speaker's free speech or privacy rights and will be "necessary to enable plaintiff to protect against or remedy serious wrongs." *Highfields Capital Mgmt., LP v. Doe,* 385 F. Supp. 2d 969 (N.D. Cal. 2005); *Dendrite Int'l v. Doe No. 3,* 775 A.2d 756 (N.J. Super. App. Div. 2001).

3. *The Summary Judgment Standard.* The plaintiff must prove the case could survive a motion for summary judgment. *Doe v. Cahill,* 884 A.2d 451 (Del. 2005); *Sinclair v. TubeSockTedD,* 596 F.Supp.2d 128 (D.D.C., 2009).

4. *The Variable Standard.* The standard varies depending on the nature of the speech, with commercial speech being protected by a much lower standard than noncommercial speech. *In re Anonymous Online Speakers,* 611 F.3d 653 (9th Cir. 2010) (known as the "*Quixtar*" case).

PRIVACY OF READING AND INTELLECTUAL EXPLORATION

Stanley v. Georgia, 394 U.S. 557 (1969)
The First and Fourteenth Amendments prohibit making mere private possession of obscene material a crime.

Osborne v. Ohio, 495 U.S. 103 (1990)
The rule in Stanley does not apply to the possession of child pornography in the home.

Reporter's Privilege

In *Branzburg v. Hayes*, 408 U.S. 665 (1972), the Supreme Court held that there is no First Amendment reporter's privilege against grand jury requests for evidence. Following *Branzburg*, many federal circuit courts have recognized a qualified reporter's privilege. The reporter's privilege has fared much better in civil cases than in criminal ones.

In the states, the reporter's privilege has been recognized, with sources in state constitutions, state statutes, and common law. Forty-nine states and the District of Columbia have recognized it. In most states, there is a qualified reporter's privilege, which can be overridden if the government establishes that it has no alternative way to obtain the information and that there is a compelling interest to do so. About 13 states have an absolute privilege, which cannot be overridden.

Currently, the Federal Rules of Evidence do not recognize a reporter's privilege.

FOR FURTHER REFERENCE

Treatises

J. Thomas McCarthy, *The Rights of Publicity and Privacy* (2d ed. 2009)

Books

Huw Beverley-Smith, Ansgar Ohly & Agnès Lucas-Schloetter,
Privacy, Property, and Personality (2005)
A comparative look at tort privacy in European legal systems and in the U.S.

Danielle Citron, *Hate Crimes in Cyberspace* (2014)
A discussion of how the Internet provides a platform for systematized targeting of individuals (most frequently women and minorities) for repeated cyber-attacks. These attacks are vicious and threatening, and they create severe emotional distress and other harm in victims. Currently, legislators and policymakers frequently underestimate the need for adequate legal proscriptions and punishments of this behavior. Recommends the use of civil rights law to combat the problem.

Lawrence M. Friedman, *Guarding Life's Dark Secrets: Legal and Social Controls Over Reputation, Propriety, and Privacy* (2007)
An illuminating history of gossip and reputation, with a focus on the Victorian Age.

Saul Levmore & Martha C. Nussbaum, eds., *The Offensive Internet: Speech, Privacy, and Reputation* (2010)
A compilation of pieces from distinguished scholars connecting the absence of legal oversight of the Internet with harassment and discrimination.

Don R. Pember, *Privacy and the Press: The Law, the Mass Media, and the First Amendment* (1972)
A good historical account of the development of the privacy torts, with an extensive discussion of how the torts evolved in each decade following Warren and Brandeis' seminal 1890 article on privacy.

Daniel Solove, *The Future of Reputation: Gossip, Rumor, and Privacy on the Internet* (2008)
A discussion of how new forms of social media are transforming the nature of gossip and rumor in troubling ways.

Articles and Other Sources

Danielle Citron, *Cyber Civil Rights*, 89 Boston U. L. Rev. 61 (2009)
An insightful account of how civil rights laws can regulate offensive online speech directed toward attacking women and minorities.

Amy Gajda, *Judging Journalism: The Turn Toward Privacy and Judicial Regulation of the Press*, 97 Cal. L. Rev. 1039 (2009
Describes and explains the weakening judicial deference to the media in privacy cases.

Woodrow Hartzog & Frederic Stutzman, *The Case for Online Obscurity*, 101 Cal. L. Rev. 1 (2013)
Arguing that obscurity is a key component of privacy but often lacking in legal protection. Proposes four indicia that define obscurity for the purposes of protecting it.

William Prosser, *Privacy*, 48 Cal. L. Rev. 383 (1960)
An influential article organizing the privacy tort into four categories.

Daniel J. Solove & Neil M. Richards, *Rethinking Free Speech and Civil Liability*, 109 Colum. L. Rev. 1650 (2009)
Examines why the First Amendment generally restricts civil liability for tort but not for contract or property law.

Lior Strahilevitz, *A Social Networks Theory of Privacy*,
72 U. Chi. L. Rev. 919 (2005)
Examines how social network theory can resolve the question of when
privacy expectations are eliminated by disclosure of secrets to other people.

Eugene Volokh, *Freedom of Speech and Information Privacy:*
The Troubling Implications of a Right to Stop People from Speaking
About You, 52 Stan. L. Rev. 1049 (2000)
A strong critique of civil liability for the disclosure of true personal
information.

Eugene Volokh, *Tort Law vs. Privacy*, 113 Colum. L. Rev 879 (2014)
A discussion of which legal institutions—juries, judges, or legislatures—
should resolve the privacy vs. safety questions that routinely arise within
tort law.

Samuel Warren & Louis Brandeis, *The Right to Privacy*,
4 Harv. L. Rev. 193 (1890)
The article that inspired the privacy torts and that has been called the most
influential law review publication ever.

Diane L. Zimmerman, *Requiem for a Heavyweight: A Farewell to*
Warren and Brandeis's Privacy Tort, 68 Cornell L. Rev. 291 (1983)
A powerful attack on the Warren and Brandeis privacy torts.

CHAPTER 4

Privacy and Law Enforcement

ESSENTIAL POINTS

- There are fundamental distinctions between how the law regulates access by law enforcement to personal information and how it treats that of intelligence agencies. This chapter examines the former; the next chapter, the latter.

- The Fourth Amendment provides protection whenever a person has a reasonable expectation of privacy. Generally, though subject to numerous exceptions, the Fourth Amendment requires a warrant supported by probable cause in order for law enforcement officers to conduct a search.

- Even if the Fourth Amendment does not apply, federal statutory law may require safeguards and impose process requirements on the governmental party seeking the information. The following federal statutes may apply:
  1. Electronic Communications Privacy Act (ECPA), consisting of the
     - Wiretap Act
     - Stored Communications Act
     - Pen Register Act
  2. Privacy Protection Act (PPA)
  3. Right to Financial Privacy Act (RFPA)

- States also have statutes that regulate electronic surveillance and access to computers. In some states, these laws provide stricter privacy protections than their federal counterparts.

- Highly intricate electronic surveillance law regulates the government's access to personal data. This area of law draws complex and sometimes confusing distinctions based on different types of communications ("wire communications," "oral communications" and "electronic communications").

- Many electronic surveillance laws apply to the private sector and not just to the government.

- Under certain federal statutes, companies can be liable for disclosing data to law enforcement officials if the companies do not comply with legal standards.

- The government has a number of tools to access private-sector records. These include:
  - Statutes with reporting requirements (e.g., Bank Secrecy Act)
  - National Security Letters (NSLs)
  - Subpoenas

- The Fourth Amendment does not apply to much government information gathering because of the third-party doctrine. Even if a company promises privacy, a customer lacks an expectation of privacy under the Fourth Amendment.

- Many federal privacy statutes provide for government access to records through a court order or subpoena, which have loose standards for access, much lower than probable cause.

FOURTH AMENDMENT

The Fourth Amendment to the U.S. Constitution
"The right of the people to be secure in their persons, houses, papers, and effects, against unreasonable searches and seizures, shall not be violated, and no Warrants shall issue, but upon probable cause, supported by Oath or affirmation, and particularly describing the place to be searched, and the persons or things to be seized."

How the Fourth Amendment Works

In Fourth Amendment cases, a court must answer two important questions:

1. Is the Fourth Amendment applicable?
The government must engage in a "search" or "seizure" in order to trigger Fourth Amendment protection. A search occurs whenever the government activity invades a person's reasonable expectation of privacy. A seizure occurs when government officials exercise control over a person or thing.

2. If the Fourth Amendment applies, is the search reasonable?
A search with a warrant supported by probable cause is generally reasonable, with only a few rare exceptions.

Probable cause exists when a reasonable person would believe that the place to be searched will turn up evidence of a crime or that the person arrested committed a crime.

A search without a warrant and probable cause is often deemed unreasonable, but there are many exceptions to the warrant and probable cause requirements, such as exigent circumstances, plain view, automobile searches, searches incident to arrest, stop and frisk and the special needs doctrine.

Evidence obtained in violation of the Fourth Amendment is generally to be excluded from trial. But there are a number of exceptions to this rule.

Leading Cases

Katz v. United States, 389 U.S. 347 (1967)
Overrules *Olmstead v. United States*, 277 U.S. 438 (1929). The Katz Court agreed with Justice Louis Brandeis' dissent in *Olmstead* and found that the Fourth Amendment applies to wiretapping. Justice Harlan's concurrence in *Katz* established the "reasonable expectation of privacy test," which the majority of the Supreme Court later adopted as its governing standard to determine whether a search falls under the scope of the Fourth Amendment. Under this test: (1) a person must exhibit an "actual (subjective) expectation of privacy" and (2) "the expectation [must] be one that society is prepared to recognize as 'reasonable.'"

Terry v. Ohio, 392 U.S. 1 (1968)
A police officer can "stop" an individual if the officer has "reasonable suspicion" that criminal activity is afoot. During the stop, the officer may "frisk" an individual for weapons if the officer has reasonable suspicion that the person is armed and dangerous.

Smith v. Maryland, 442 U.S. 735 (1979)

The Supreme Court held that no reasonable expectation of privacy exists in the numbers that a person dials when the police record them with a pen register. The court reached this conclusion because (1) the numbers do not involve the "content" of the communications and (2) when a person conveys information to another (the phone company), that person must assume the risk that the company will reveal the information to others.

Florida v. Riley, 488 U.S. 445 (1989)

The Fourth Amendment is not triggered by the police flying a helicopter over a greenhouse and peering from above through the greenhouse's missing roof panels. There is no reasonable expectation of privacy if something is visible from a vantage point accessible to the public.

Kyllo v. United States, 523 U.S. 27 (2001)

Use of a thermal imaging device to monitor activities in a home triggers Fourth Amendment protection because of the importance of protecting privacy at home and the fact that the thermal imaging device "is not in general public use."

United States v. Jones, 132 S. Ct. 945 (2012)

Law enforcement's installation of a GPS device in a car without a warrant is a search under the Fourth Amendment because it represents a trespass on a person's property. Concurring opinions also argue that the use of extensive long-term surveillance violates a reasonable expectation of privacy.

Riley v. California, 134 S. Ct. 2473 (2014)

A warrant is required to search digital information on a cell phone seized pursuant to an individual's arrest because cell phones are qualitatively different from other physical "papers and effects" found on the arrestee's person. Law enforcement must either obtain a warrant or fall within the exigent circumstances exception.

Key Fourth Amendment Doctrines

1. *Third Party Doctrine:* If a person exposes information to a third party, she can no longer expect privacy in that information. *United States v. Miller*, 425 U.S. 435 (1976) (bank records); *Smith v. Maryland*, 442 U.S. 735 (1979) (phone numbers).

2. *Misplaced Trust Doctrine:* A person has no Fourth Amendment protection against being betrayed by an informant or undercover agent because the person assumes the risk of betrayal. *Hoffa v. United States*, 385 U.S. 293 (1966).

3. *Plain View Doctrine:* If something is seen in plain view, it is not a search and does not trigger any Fourth Amendment protection. *Harris v. United States*, 390 U.S. 234 (1968).

4. *Special Needs Doctrine:* Under certain circumstances, typically when searches are by non-law-enforcement government officials (school officials, government employers), a search need only be "reasonable." *O'Connor v. Ortega*, 480 U.S. 709 (1987).

FOURTH AMENDMENT REASONABLE EXPECTATION OF PRIVACY

YES	NO
• Wiretapping private conversation. *Katz v. United States*, 389 U.S. 347 (1967).	• Obtaining phone numbers dialed from a phone company. *Smith v. Maryland*, 442 U.S. 735 (1979).
• Searching a home. *Minnesota v. Olson*, 495 U.S. 91 (1990).	• Obtaining financial records from a bank. *United States v. Miller*, 425 U.S. 435 (1976).
• Using sense enhancement not in general use to reveal activities in the home. *Kyllo v. United States*, 523 U.S. 27 (2001).	• Dog sniff for drugs. *Illinois v. Caballes*, 543 U.S. 405 (2005).
• Tracking device that monitors a person's movements at home. *United States v. Karo*, 468 U.S. 705 (1984).	• Search of trash left on the curb for collection. *California v. Greenwood*, 486 U.S. 35 (1988).
• Searching a bag or container. *Arkansas v. Sanders*, 422 U.S. 753 (1979).	• Viewing a person's property overhead from a helicopter. *Florida v. Riley*, 488 U.S. 445 (1989).
• Searching a personal computer. *Trulock v. Freeh*, 275 F.3d 391 (4th Cir. 2001).	• Using sense enhancement technology in general public use. *Dow Chemical Co. v. United States*, 476 U.S. 227 (1986).
• Opening a sealed letter. *Ex Parte Jackson*, 96 U.S. 727 (1877).	• Tracking device that monitors a person's movements in public. *United States v. Knotts*, 460 U.S. 276 (1983).

YES	NO
• Searching an office desk. *O'Connor v. Ortega*, 480 U.S. 709 (1987).	• Requiring a person to provide a voice sample. *United States v. Dionisio*, 410 U.S. 1 (1973).
	• Requiring a person to provide a handwriting sample. *United States v. Mara*, 410 U.S. 19 (1973).
	• Searching a workplace computer where the user was notified that the device is subject to monitoring. *United States v. Angevine*, 281 F.3d 1130 (10th Cir. 2002).

EXCEPTIONS TO THE WARRANT AND PROBABLE CAUSE REQUIREMENTS

NO WARRANT REQUIRED (BUT MUST HAVE PROBABLE CAUSE)

• **Exigent Circumstances**
No warrant is required if delay of obtaining it would endanger the public, permit escape, or allow destruction of evidence.

• **Plain View**
Objects may be seized if there is probable cause to believe they are contraband or evidence of a crime.

• **Vehicle Searches**
Mobile vehicles can be searched if there is probable cause to believe they contain evidence of criminal activity.

• **Arrests**
A person can be arrested without a warrant outside of her home.

• **Searches Incident to Arrest**
If there is probable cause to arrest, a search for weapons or evidence on the arrestee and in the immediate area is permissible.

NO WARRANT OR PROBABLE CAUSE REQUIRED

• **Consent**
If permission is given for the search, no warrant or probable cause is needed.

• **Stop and Frisk**
A brief stop can be made with reasonable suspicion crime is afoot and a frisk can be done for weapons.

• **Special Needs**
Searches in schools or government workplaces must be reasonable under the circumstances.

• **Administrative Searches**
Searches of homes for code violations and of closely regulated businesses can be made without specific suspicion.

• **Checkpoints**
Certain kinds of checkpoints do not require a warrant or probable cause if reasonable.

• **Border Searches**
The special need to collect duties and intercept contraband coming into the U.S. often does not require probable suspicion.

ELECTRONIC COMMUNICATIONS

Electronic Communications Privacy Act (ECPA)
18 U.S.C. §§ 2510-2522, 2701-2711, 3121-3127 (1986)

The ECPA amended Title III (the Wiretap Act) and also included two new acts in response to developments in computer technology and communication networks. As a result, federal electronic surveillance law for domestic law enforcement agencies contains three parts:

1. Wiretap Act (updated version of Title III), 18 U.S.C. §§ 2510–2522
2. Stored Communications Act (SCA), 18 U.S.C. §§ 2701–2711
3. Pen Register Act, 18 U.S.C. §§ 3121–3127

Note: The next chapter discusses the legal regulations in place for intelligence agencies that seek to carry out electronic surveillance for the purpose of foreign intelligence gathering (as opposed to domestic law enforcement).

Types of Communications in ECPA

1. *Wire Communications:* A "wire communication" involves "aural transfers" (communications containing the human voice) that travel in part or whole through wire (i.e., telephone wires or cable wires) or a similar medium. 18 U.S.C. § 2510(1).

2. *Oral Communications:* An "oral communication" is a communication "uttered by a person exhibiting an expectation that such communication is not subject to interception under circumstances justifying such expectation." Such communications are typically intercepted through bugs or other recording or transmitting devices. 18 U.S.C. § 2510(2).

3. *Electronic Communications:* An "electronic communication" consists of all non-wire and non-oral communications (i.e., signals, images, data) that can be transmitted through a wide range of transmission mediums (wire as well as radio, electromagnetic, photoelectronic, etc.). E-mail is an example of electronic communication. 18 U.S.C. § 2510(12).

Wiretap Act
18 U.S.C. §§ 2510–2522

THE WIRETAP ACT	
Applies to	Interception of communications in flight.
Key Provisions	*Interception:* Provides strict controls on the interception of communications. "Interception" is the acquiring of the contents of a communication through an electronic, mechanical or other device while the communication is being transmitted.
Court Order	Application for court order to intercept must contain details justifying the interception and information about how the interception will occur and its duration. 18 U.S.C. § 2518. These statutory standards are stricter than those that the Supreme Court has identified in the Fourth Amendment. Hence, the Wiretap Act is said to require a "super warrant." The judge must find: 1. Probable cause 2. That alternatives to interception have failed, are unlikely to succeed or will be too dangerous Orders must require that interception be conducted to "minimize the interception of the communications not otherwise subject to interception." Only high-level government prosecutors can apply for orders. Orders are limited to certain felonies ("predicate offenses").
Exceptions	*Consent:* Title I does not apply if one party to the communication consents. 18 U.S.C. § 2511(2)(c). *Service Provider:* : Title I does not apply to the interception of communications by a communications service provider. 18 U.S.C. § 2511(2)(a)(i).
Exclusionary Rule	Yes, for wire and oral communications. No, for electronic communications.
Penalties	Damages (minimum $10,000 per violation). Up to five years imprisonment.

Stored Communications Act (SCA)
18 U.S.C. §§ 2701–2711

THE STORED COMMUNICATIONS ACT	
Applies to	1. Accessing communications in "electronic storage" 2. Records of ISPs
Key Provisions	*Stored Communications:* Requires the government to obtain via court order, subpoena or warrant. 18 U.S.C. § 2703. *ISP Records:* Requires the government to obtain a warrant or court order to access specified customer data held by ISPs, including name, address, length of service, means of payment, etc. 18 U.S.C. § 2703(c).
Court Order	*Communications Stored 180 Days or Less:* Government must obtain warrant supported by probable cause. 18 U.S.C. § 2703(a). *Communications Stored Over 180 Days (Prior Notice):* Government must provide prior notice to subscriber and obtain a subpoena or court order. Court order requires "specific and articulable facts showing that there are reasonable grounds" to believe communications are relevant to the criminal investigation. *Communications Stored Over 180 Days (No Prior Notice):* If government does not provide prior notice to subscriber, it must obtain a warrant. *ISP Records:* Government must obtain court order; same standard as that for communications stored over 180 days.
Exceptions	*Consent:* SCA does not apply if the subscriber consents. 18 U.S.C.§ 2702(b). *Service Provider:* SCA does not apply to the accessing of stored communications by communications service providers. 18 U.S.C. § 2701(c)(1).
Exclusionary Rule	No
Penalties	Damages (minimum $1,000 per violation). Up to one year imprisonment (if done for commercial gain).

Pen Register Act
18 U.S.C. §§ 3121–3127

THE PEN REGISTER ACT	
Applies to	Pen registers or trap and trace devices.
Key Provisions	Requires court order before installation of pen registers. A "pen register" is a "device or process" that records outgoing "dialing, routing, addressing or signaling information," but "such information shall not include the contents of any communication." 18 U.S.C. § 3127(3). A "trap and trace device" is a "device or process" that captures incoming "dialing, routing, addressing and signaling information" but "such information shall not include the contents of any communication." 18 U.S.C. § 3127(4).
Court Order	The government must obtain a court order to install pen register and trap and trace devices. The court shall grant the order if the government has demonstrated that "the information likely to be obtained by such installation and use is relevant to an ongoing criminal investigation." 18 U.S.C. § 3123(a).
Exceptions	*Service Provider:* The Pen Register Act does not apply to the use of a pen register or trap and trace device by a communications service provider relating to the provision of the service. 18 U.S.C. § 3121(b)(1). *Abuse Protection:* The act does not apply when a communications service provider records the existence of the communication to protect against unlawful or abusive use of the service. 18 U.S.C. § 3121(b)(2). *Consent:* The act does not apply if the user consents. 18 U.S.C. § 3121(b)(3).
Exclusionary Rule	No
Penalties	Fines. Up to one-year imprisonment. 18 U.S.C. § 3123(d).

United States v. Forrester, 512 F.3d 500 (9th Cir. 2008)

E-mail headers and IP addresses are akin to pen registers and have no Fourth Amendment protection. The Ninth Circuit notes in dicta that URLs "might be more constitutionally problematic" because a URL "identifies the particular document within a website that a person views and thus reveals much more information about the person's Internet activity."

United States v. Councilman, 418 F.3d 67 (1st Cir. 2005) (en banc)

An Internet bookseller provided e-mail service for its customers, and it intercepted all incoming communications from Amazon.com. The First Circuit concluded that "the term 'electronic communication' includes transient electronic storage that is intrinsic to the communication process, and, hence, interception of an e-mail message in such storage is an offense under the Wiretap Act."

Theofel v. Farey-Jones, 359 F.3d 1066 (9th Cir. 2004)

E-mail messages delivered to a recipient are still covered by the Stored Communications Act because they are stored as a "backup" for the user.

Fraser v. Nationwide Mutual Insurance Co., 352 F.3d 108 (3d Cir. 2003)

Same result as *Theofel.*

United States v. Warshak, 631 F.3d 266 (6th Cir. 2010)

Compelling an ISP to turn over the contents of a subscriber's e-mails violates a reasonable expectation of privacy—and hence violates the Fourth Amendment—even though the ISP itself may have access to the e-mails.

Key Facts About ECPA

1. The Wiretap Act provides the strongest level of protection, followed by the Stored Communications Act. The Pen Register Act provides the weakest level of protection.

2. ECPA applies not only to government officials, but also to everyone. Private-sector employers and regular citizens are regulated.

3. ECPA provides for an exclusionary rule only for Wiretap Act violations involving wire or oral communications.

4. ECPA does not regulate silent video surveillance or location-tracking devices.

5. ECPA is a one-party consent statute—surveillance is permissible when only one party to a communication consents. Most state electronic surveillance statutes are one-party consent, but several states have two-party consent statutes. In these states, all parties to the communication must consent to the surveillance.

	THE FOURTH AMENDMENT	FEDERAL ELECTRONIC SURVEILLANCE LAW
Applicability	The Fourth Amendment applies to electronic surveillance when there is a reasonable expectation of privacy. The Fourth Amendment applies only to government officials (subject to limited exceptions).	Federal electronic surveillance law applies to all interceptions of communications and to accessing stored communications (even if there is no reasonable expectation of privacy). Federal electronic surveillance law applies to pen registers and trap and trace devices (Pen Register Act). The Fourth Amendment does not apply to these devices. See *Smith v. Maryland*. Federal electronic surveillance law applies to government officials and to private parties.
Judicial Authority to Obtain Access	Subject to a number of exceptions, the Fourth Amendment requires a warrant supported by probable cause.	Federal electronic surveillance law contains a wide variety of forms of judicial authority, including subpoenas, court orders with varying levels of notice to the subject of the investigation, warrants and the super warrant required by the Wiretap Act.
Duration of Authority to Obtain Access	Fourth Amendment warrants authorize a single entry and prompt search. Warrants must be narrowly circumscribed.	Federal wiretap orders can have a broad duration. A judge can authorize 24-hour surveillance for a 30-day period.
Enforcement	The Fourth Amendment is enforced by the exclusionary rule. The Fourth Amendment can serve as the basis for a § 1983 or Bivens action.	Federal electronic surveillance law is enforced through the exclusionary rule only sometimes—for interceptions of wire or oral communications under the Wiretap Act. Federal electronic surveillance law also has civil and criminal penalties.

Communications Assistance for Law Enforcement Act (CALEA)
47 U.S.C. §§ 1001-1010, § 1021 (1994)

Primary Function: Requires "telecommunications carriers" to design their networks to make them compliant with authorized governmental requests for surveillance.

Facilitate Law Enforcement Access: Requires all telecommunications providers to be able to isolate and intercept electronic communications and be able to deliver them to law enforcement personnel.

Privacy and Security: Carriers must "facilitat[e] authorized communications interceptions and access to call-identifying information … in a manner that protects … the privacy and security of communications and call-identifying information not authorized to be intercepted." 47 U.S.C. § 1002(a)(4)(A).

Limitations: CALEA does not apply to "information services," an important and long-standing term of art in telecommunications law. It does apply to "telecommunication carriers." Drawing the distinction between the two categories can be quite complex, but it is an absolutely critical issue; information service providers fall outside of CALEA, which means that they need not design their networks to be accessible to law enforcement agencies.

Leading Case

American Council on Education v. FCC, 451 F.3d 266 (D.C. Cir. 2006)
The DC Circuit upheld the FCC's classification of broadband Internet access and voice over Internet protocol (VoIP) as "telecommunications carriers" under CALEA. As a consequence, broadband and VoIP providers must ensure that law enforcement officials can intercept communications that are transmitted over their networks.

STATE ELECTRONIC SURVEILLANCE LAW

The vast majority of states have electronic surveillance statutes. Many are quite similar to ECPA. The majority, like ECPA, permit surveillance if one party to a communication consents. But several states have all-party consent laws, requiring all parties to a communication to consent.

Many people unwittingly violate all-party consent statutes. If they secretly record a conversation between themselves and another person, they violate this kind of statute.

If a person records a call made from a one-party consent state to an all-party consent state, the law of the all-party consent state governs. *Kearney v. Salomon Smith Barney,* 137 P.2d 914 (Cal. 2006).

Recording Police Encounters

In some instances, people recording their encounters with police officers have been prosecuted under state electronic surveillance laws because the police officer did not consent. *Commonwealth v. Hyde,* 750 N.E.2d 963 (Mass. 2001) (upholding felony conviction under Massachusetts electronic surveillance law for recording a traffic stop with a police officer).

Some courts have held that the First Amendment prohibits the criminalization of secretly recording encounters with police when performing official duties. *ACLU v. Alvarez,* 679 F.3d 583 (7th Cir. 2012) (striking down application of Illinois electronic surveillance law when recording police officers).

ONE-PARTY CONSENT STATES

AL	Ala. Code §§ 13A-11-30 to -31
AK	Alaska Stat. § 42.20.310
AZ	Ariz. Rev. Stat. Ann. § 13-3005
AK	Ark. Code Ann. § 5-60-120
CO	Colo. Rev. Stat. §§ 18-9-301, 18-9-303
DE	Del. Code Ann. tit. 11, § 2402
DC	D.C. Code §§ 23-541, 23-542
GA	Ga. Code Ann. §§ 16-11-62, 16-11-66
HI	Haw. Rev. Stat. § 803-42
ID	Idaho Code Ann. § 18-6702
IN	Ind. Code § 35-33.5-1 et seq.
IA	Iowa Code § 727.8
KS	Kan. Stat. Ann. §§ 21-4001, 21-4002
KY	Ky. Rev. Stat. Ann. §§ 526.010 to .020
LA	La. Rev. Stat. Ann. § 15:1303
ME	Me. Rev. Stat. Ann. tit. 15, §§ 709-10
MI	Mich. Comp. Laws § 750.539c
MN	Minn. Stat. §§ 626A.01, .02
MS	Miss. Code Ann. § 41-29-501 et seq.
MO	Mo. Rev. Stat. § 542.402
NE	Neb. Rev. Stat. § 86-290
NJ	N.J. Stat. Ann. § 2A:156A-1 et seq.
NM	N.M. Stat. § 30-12-1
NY	N.Y. Penal Law §§ 250.00, .05
NC	N.C. Gen. Stat. § 15A-287
ND	N.D. Cent. Code § 12.1-15-02
OH	Ohio Rev. Code Ann. § 2933.51 et seq.
OK	Okla. Stat. tit. 13, § 176.1 et seq.
OR	Or. Rev. Stat. §§ 165.540, .543
RI	R.I. Gen. Laws § 11-35-21
SC	S.C. Code Ann. §§ 17-30-20, -30
SD	S.D. Codified Laws §§ 23A-35A-1
TN	Tenn. Code Ann. § 39-13-601
TX	Tex. Penal Code Ann. § 16.02
UT	Utah Code Ann. § 77-23a-1 et seq.
VA	Va. Code Ann. §§ 19.2-61, -62
WV	W. Va. Code § 62-1D-1 et seq.
WI	Wis. Stat. §§ 968.27, .31
WY	Wyo. Stat. Ann. §§ 7-3-701, -702

ALL-PARTY CONSENT STATES

CA	Cal. Penal Code § 630 et seq.
CT	Conn. Gen. Stat. § 52-570d
FL	Fla. Stat. §§ 934.01 to .03
IL	720 Ill. Comp. Stat. 5/14-1, -2
MD	Md. Code Ann. Cts. & Jud. Proc. § 10-402
MA	Mass. Gen. Laws ch. 272, § 99
MT	Mont. Code Ann. § 45-8-213
NV	Nev. Rev. Stat. §§ 200.610 to .620
NH	N.H. Rev. Stat. Ann. §§ 570-A:1, -A:2
PA	18 Pa. Cons. Stat. § 5701 et seq.
WA	Wash. Rev. Code § 9.73.030

No Electronic Surveillance Statute
VT

Source: Scott P. Cooper et al., *Practising Law Institute,* Proskauer on Privacy § 5:10.1 (2010)

GOVERNMENT ACCESS TO PERSONAL DATA

Fourth Amendment: Third-Party Doctrine

In several cases, the U.S. Supreme Court concluded that whenever a third party possesses a person's information, that person can no longer have a reasonable expectation of privacy in the data.

Couch v. United States, 409 U.S. 322 (1973)
The government could obtain documents that a person provided to his accountant without violating the Fourth Amendment.

United States v. Miller, 425 U.S. 435 (1976)
Financial records possessed by third parties are not protected by the Fourth Amendment because people lack a reasonable expectation of privacy in their bank records. This information is "voluntarily conveyed to the banks and exposed to their employees in the ordinary course of business."

Smith v. Maryland, 442 U.S. 735 (1979)
The court held that there is no reasonable expectation of privacy in the numbers a person dials that the police record with a pen register. The numbers do not involve the "content" of the communications, and when a person conveys information to another (the phone company), that person must assume the risk that the company will reveal the information to others.

Lower courts have applied the third-party doctrine widely, including to records about a person's Internet use held by ISPs. *United States v. Forrester*, 512 F. 3d 500 (9th Cir. 2008); *Guest v. Leis*, 255 F. 3d 325 (6th Cir. 2001).

Bank Secrecy Act (1970)

Recordkeeping: Requires the retention of bank records and creation of reports that would be useful in criminal, tax or regulatory investigations or proceedings. Requires that federally insured banks record the identities of account holders as well as copies of each check, draft or other financial instrument. Not all records and financial instruments must be maintained, only those that the secretary of the treasury designates as having a "high degree of usefulness." 12 U.S.C. § 1829b.

Reporting: The act authorizes the secretary of the treasury to promulgate regulations for the reporting of domestic financial transactions. 31 U.S.C. § 1081. The regulations require that a report be made for every deposit, withdrawal or other transfer of currency exceeding $10,000. 31 C.F.R. § 103.22. For transactions exceeding $5,000 into or out of the United States, the amount, the date of receipt, the form of financial instrument and the person who received it must be reported. 31 C.F.R. §§ 103.23, 103.25.

California Bankers Association v. Shultz, 416 U.S. 21 (1974)
Upholds the Bank Secrecy Act against a Fourth Amendment challenge.

Right to Financial Privacy Act (RFPA) (1978)
29 U.S.C. §§ 3401–3422

Primary Function: The RFPA prevents banks and other financial institutions from disclosing a person's financial information to the government unless the records are disclosed pursuant to a subpoena or search warrant.

Subpoenas

A subpoena is an order to obtain testimony or documents. Numerous statutes authorize federal agencies to issue subpoenas. "A subpoena may order the witness to produce any books, papers, documents, data or other objects the subpoena designates. The court may direct the witness to produce the designated items in court before trial or before they are to be offered in evidence. When the items arrive, the court may permit the parties and their attorneys to inspect all or part of them." Fed. R. Crim. P. 17(c)(1).

If the party served with the subpoena has an objection, she may bring a motion to quash or modify the subpoena. "[T]he court may quash or modify the subpoena if compliance would be unreasonable or oppressive." Fed. R. Crim. P. 17(c)(2).

Leading Case

United States v. Dionisio, 410 U.S. 1 (1973)
Concludes that a grand jury subpoena does not trigger any Fourth Amendment protection.

Gonzales v. Google, 234 F.R.D. 674 (N.D. Cal. 2006)
The government subpoenaed search records from Google to assist in examining the effectiveness of content filtering software. The court did not permit the government to obtain the search query information because "there is a potential burden as to Google's loss of goodwill if Google is forced to disclose search queries to the Government."

Federal Statutory Provisions for Government Access to Records
(see Chapter 5 for National Security Letter provisions)

Cable Communications Policy Act (CCPA), 47 U.S.C. § 551(h)
The government can obtain cable subscriber data pursuant to a court order justified by "clear and convincing evidence" that the subscriber is "reasonably suspected of engaging in criminal activity and that the information sought would be material evidence in the case." The subscriber must be notified and allowed to challenge the order.

Fair Credit Report Act (FCRA), 15 U.S.C. § 1681f
"[A] consumer reporting agency may furnish identifying information respecting any customer, limited to his name, address, former addresses, places of employment or former places of employment, to a governmental agency."

Health Insurance Portability and Accountability Act (HIPAA), 45 C.F.R. § 164.512(f)(1).
Law enforcement officials may access medical records with a warrant, court order or subpoena. Health information may also be disclosed "in response to a law enforcement official's request for such information for the purpose of identifying or locating a suspect, fugitive, material witness or missing person."

Pen Register Act, 18 U.S.C. § 3123(a)
To obtain pen register information, the government must obtain a court order by certifying that "the information likely to be obtained by such installation and use is relevant to an ongoing investigation."

Right to Financial Privacy Act (RFPA), 29 U.S.C. § 3407
The government must first obtain a warrant or subpoena in order to access financial information. The subpoena requires a "reason to believe that the records sought are relevant to a legitimate law enforcement inquiry."

Stored Communications Act (SCA), 18 U.S.C. § 2703
Requires the government to obtain a court order or warrant in order to access stored e-mail messages. The government must obtain a warrant or court order to obtain a customer's ISP records. The court order requires "specific and articulable facts showing that there are reasonable grounds" to believe communications are relevant to the criminal investigation.

Video Privacy Protection Act (VPPA), 18 U.S.C. § 2710(b)(2)(C)
Permits disclosure to a law enforcement agency pursuant to a warrant, court order or subpoena.

LAW ENFORCEMENT

SEARCHES AND SEIZURES OF MEDIA DOCUMENTS

Privacy Protection Act (PPA)
42 U.S.C. § 2000aa (1980)

Primary Function: Protects media documents and work product from government searches and seizures.

Key Provisions: During a criminal investigation, government officials cannot search or seize work product or documents that are "reasonably believed" to be intended to be disseminated to the public. These include a newspaper, book, broadcast or other similar form of public communication. 42 U.S.C. § 2000aa(a).

How the PPA Works: The effect of the PPA is to require law enforcement officials to obtain a subpoena in order to obtain such information. Unlike search warrants, subpoenas permit the party subject to them to challenge them in court before having to comply. Further, instead of law enforcement officials searching through offices or records, the persons served with the subpoena must produce the documents themselves.

Exceptions: The government can search or seize the work product or documents if they relate to a crime the possessor has committed, if necessary to prevent death or serious injury, or if the documents might be destroyed or concealed.

Leading Case

Zurcher v. The Stanford Daily, 4326 U.S. 547 (1978)
The Supreme Court held that the First and Fourth Amendments permit law enforcement to search media offices with a warrant supported by probable cause rather than a heightened standard. This holding led Congress to enact the PPA.

FOR FURTHER REFERENCE

Treatises

Thomas J. Clancy, *The Fourth Amendment: Its History and Interpretation* (2008)
A great resource on current Fourth Amendment law.

William J. Cuddihy, *The Fourth Amendment: Origins and Original Meaning*, 602–1791 (2009)
The most comprehensive intellectual history of the origins of the Fourth Amendment.

Wayne R. LaFave, Jerold H. Israel, Nancy J. King & Orin S. Kerr, *Criminal Procedure* (3d ed. 2009)
Leading multivolume treatise contains a detailed look at scope of the exclusionary rule and search and seizure issues, including electronic surveillance. Also available abridged in a hornbook format.

Books

Samuel Dash, *The Intruders: Unreasonable Searches and Seizures from King John to John Ashcroft* (2004)
A short, accessible history of the Fourth Amendment, filled with interesting stories about the key cases.

Jeffrey Rosen, *The Naked Crowd: Reclaiming Security and Freedom in an Anxious Age* (2004)
A sociological account of fear, liberty and security following the September 11 attacks.

Christopher Slobogin, *Privacy at Risk: The New Government Surveillance and the Fourth Amendment* (2007)
The government engages in both physical surveillance, through means such as CCTV, and transaction surveillance when it examines records of our daily activities. This book advocates that legislatures and courts create stronger constraints on such governmental activities.

Daniel J. Solove, *Nothing to Hide: The False Tradeoff Between Privacy and Security* (2011)
Argues that the current debate between privacy and security is skewed toward the security side based on faulty arguments.

Articles and Other Sources

Anthony G. Amsterdam, *Perspectives on the Fourth Amendment,*
58 Minn. L. Rev. 349 (1974)
A classic article about the Fourth Amendment and one of the most
influential on this topic.

Orin S. Kerr, *Fourth Amendment Seizures of Computer Data,*
119 Yale L.J. 700 (2010)
Analysis of what it means to "seize" computer data for Fourth Amendment
purposes and the kinds of police action that govern digital evidence
investigations.

Orin S. Kerr, *The Case for the Third Party Doctrine,* 107 Mich. L. Rev. 561 (2009)
The most extensive defense of the third-party doctrine in an academic article.

Orin S. Kerr, *The Fourth Amendment and New Technologies:
Constitutional Myths and the Case for Caution,* 102 Mich. L. Rev. 801 (2004)
Makes the provocative argument that courts should defer to legislatures in
Fourth Amendment cases involving new technologies.

Winston Maxwell & Christopher Wolf, *A Global Reality: Governmental
Access to Data in the Cloud* (2012)
White Paper compares protections against government access to data in
the cloud in ten industrialized nations and concludes that the protections
in other countries often do not exceed those in the U.S.

Neil. M. *Richards, The Dangers of Surveillance,* 126 Harv. L. Rev. 1934 (2013)
Apart from vague Orwellian threats, we lack a clear sense of the dangers
of government surveillance. Richards explores the boundaries of legitimate
surveillance activities, proposing principles to guide the future of
surveillance law.

Paul M. Schwartz, *Reviving Telecommunications Surveillance Law,*
75 U. Chi. L. Rev. 287 (2008)
Description of each of the main parts of statutory telecommunications
law and analysis of the extent to which numerical data is collected to track
the extent of governmental activity in these areas.

Christopher Slobogin, *Subpoenas and Privacy,* 53 DePaul L. Rev. 805 (2005)
A thorough examination of subpoenas and their implications for
accessing data.

Daniel J. Solove, *Digital Dossiers and the Dissipation of Fourth Amendment Privacy*, 75 S. Cal. L. Rev. 1084 (2002)
Argues that the Supreme Court has developed a flawed conception of the Fourth Amendment.

Daniel J. Solove, *Digital Dossiers and the Dissipation of Fourth Amendment Privacy*, 75 S. Cal. L. Rev. 1083 (2002)
A discussion of how the third-party doctrine eviscerates Fourth Amendment protection in the Information Age.

William J. Stuntz, *Privacy's Problem and the Law of Criminal Procedure*, 93 Mich. L. Rev. 1016 (1995)
Contends that the Fourth Amendment should focus on police coercion and violence rather than privacy.

CHAPTER 5

National Security and Foreign Intelligence

ESSENTIAL POINTS

- Although the Fourth Amendment regulates domestic criminal investigations and national security investigations, how the Fourth Amendment regulates foreign intelligence gathering within the United States remains an open question.

- The Foreign Intelligence Surveillance Act (FISA) is the main statute that regulates the government's electronic surveillance. It applies when foreign intelligence gathering is "a significant purpose" of the investigation.

- There are other legal authorities that permit the gathering of information for national security purposes, including National Security Letters and Patriot Act § 215 Orders.

THE FOURTH AMENDMENT

There is not much U.S. Supreme Court guidance about how the Fourth Amendment addresses national security issues and foreign intelligence gathering. The Court has distinguished between three categories of searches and surveillance:

- *Criminal Investigations*—ordinary Fourth Amendment protections apply.

- *Domestic National Security Investigations*—protected by the Fourth Amendment but may require different standards other than warrants and probable cause.

- *Foreign Intelligence Gathering*—no determination by the court as to whether the Fourth Amendment applies and, if so, what the standards are.

Leading Cases

***United States v. United States District Court*, 407 U.S. 297 (1972) (the "Keith" Case)**
Rejects Nixon administration argument that the Fourth Amendment does not apply when the president conducts electronic surveillance for domestic national security investigations. Notes that domestic security surveillance "may involve different considerations from the surveillance of 'ordinary crime'" and concludes that "[d]ifferent standards may be compatible with the Fourth Amendment if they are reasonable both in relation to the legitimate need of government for intelligence information and the protected rights of our citizens."

***United States v. Butenko*, 494 F.2d 593 (3d Cir. 1974)**
Concludes that the Fourth Amendment does not require a warrant for foreign intelligence gathering because "foreign intelligence gathering is a clandestine and highly unstructured activity, and the need for electronic surveillance often cannot be anticipated in advance."

***United States v. Truong Dinh Hung*, 629 F.3d 908 (4th Cir. 1980)**
Concludes that the Fourth Amendment does not require a warrant for foreign intelligence gathering.

FOREIGN INTELLIGENCE GATHERING

Foreign Intelligence Surveillance Act (FISA)
50 U.S.C. §§ 1801–1811 (1978)

Primary Function: FISA establishes standards and procedures for the government's use of electronic surveillance to collect "foreign intelligence" within the United States. FISA requires the government, if seeking evidence of domestic security violations, to follow the authorities granted by the usual criminal law.

Applies to: Applies when foreign intelligence gathering is "a significant purpose" of the investigation. 50 U.S.C. § 1804(a)(7)(B) and § 1823(a)(7)(B).

The Foreign Intelligence Surveillance Court (FISC): Requests for FISA orders are reviewed by a special court of 11 federal district court judges. The proceedings are ex parte, and the court meets in secret.

The Foreign Intelligence Surveillance Court of Review (FISCR): The government may appeal decisions of the FISC to a three-judge appellate court. This judicial entity is called the Foreign Intelligence Surveillance Court of Review.

Court Orders: FISA orders are granted when the FISC finds probable cause that the party to be monitored is a "foreign power" or "an agent of a foreign power." 50 U.S.C. § 1801. Therefore, unlike ECPA or the Fourth Amendment, FISA surveillance is not tied to any required showing of a connection to criminal activity. However, if the monitored party is a "United States person" (a citizen or permanent resident alien), the government must establish probable cause that the party's activities "may" or "are about to" involve a criminal violation. 50 U.S.C. § 1801(b)(2)(A). Under special limited circumstances, FISA authorizes surveillance without having to first obtain a court order.

The FISA Amendments Act (FAA) of 2008: The FAA explicitly permits collection of information from U.S. telecommunications facilities where it is not possible in advance to know whether a communication is purely international (that is, all parties to it are located outside of the United States) or whether the communication involves a foreign power or its agents. The collection of this information must be carried out in accordance with certain "targeting procedures" to ensure that the collection is directed at persons located outside the United States. The FISC is to review certifications and the targeting and minimization procedures adopted.

Leading Cases

Clapper v. Amnesty International USA, 133 S. Ct. 1138 (2013)
Lawyers, journalists, human rights advocates, and others challenged Section 702 of the Foreign Intelligence Surveillance Act. In a 5-4 opinion, the Supreme Court held that the challengers lacked standing because they could not demonstrate a threatened injury that was "certainly impeding." Plaintiffs could point only to a "speculative chain of possibilities."

In re Sealed Case, 310 F.3d 717 (FISCR 2002)
This case, the first published decision of the FISCR, concerns "Intelligence Sharing Procedures" implemented by Attorney General John Ashcroft. The court upheld the new Department of Justice procedures and concluded that the new regulations correctly interpreted applicable statutory requirements for information sharing between criminal enforcement officials and intelligence officials working on shared investigations. "FISA, as amended, does not oblige the government to demonstrate to the FISA court that its primary purpose in conducting electronic surveillance is not criminal prosecution." The FISCR also concluded that the Patriot Act's amendment to FISA does not violate the Fourth Amendment by making FISA applicable when foreign intelligence gathering is a "significant purpose" of the investigation.

In re Directives, 551 F.3d 1004 (FISCR 2008)
In its second published opinion, released only in redacted form, the FISCR identified a foreign intelligence exception to the Fourth Amendment warrant requirement. The exception applies to surveillance undertaken for national security purposes and directed at a foreign power or an agent of a foreign power reasonably believed to be located outside the United States. The court declared that "there is a high degree of probability that requiring a warrant would hinder the government's ability to collect time-sensitive information and, thus, would impede the vital national security interests that are at stake."

United States v. Duggan, 743 F.2d 59 (2d Cir. 1984)
Concludes that FISA (in its version prior to the Patriot Act changes) does not violate the Fourth Amendment because the Supreme Court in the Keith case had indicated that "the governmental interests presented in national security investigations differ substantially from those presented in traditional criminal investigations."

GOVERNMENT ACCESS TO PERSONAL DATA FOR NATIONAL SECURITY PURPOSES

National Security Letters (NSLs)

Several provisions of law provide for national security letters (NSLs), which allow the FBI to demand the production of information when relevant to foreign intelligence gathering or a terrorism investigation:

- Stored Communications Act, 18 U.S.C. § 2709—customer records of communications companies

- Right to Financial Privacy Act, 12 U.S.C. § 3414(a)(5)(A)—financial records

- Fair Credit Reporting Act, 15 U.S.C. § 1671u—credit records and consumer reports

USA Patriot Act § 215

Section 215 of the USA Patriot Act added a new section to FISA that gives the director of the FBI or her designee the authority to make "an application for an order requiring the production of any tangible things (including books, records, papers, documents and other items) for an investigation to protect against international terrorism or clandestine activities."

Section 215 orders cannot be directed toward an investigation of a "United States person" when "conducted solely upon the basis of activities" protected by the First Amendment.

Applications for a Section 215 order are to be made to a judge and to specify that the records are sought for an authorized investigation.

STATE SECRETS

The state secrets doctrine is an evidentiary privilege that protects information from discovery when its disclosure would harm national security. The doctrine first occurred in *Reynolds v. United States*, 345 U.S. 1 (1953). In this Cold War era case, the Supreme Court drew on English precedents regarding crown privilege to permit the Air Force to decline to share an accident investigation report with civilians who were suing the government under the Federal Tort Claims Act.

The state secrets doctrine has been used in numerous cases after 9/11. Private industry has also asserted state secrets in many cases, a strategy to provoke the federal government to join the litigation to prevent certain documents from being discovered or even to block the underlying lawsuit.

THE INTELLIGENCE COMMUNITY

Intelligence Agencies

Federal Bureau of Investigation (FBI)

Originally created in 1908 as the Bureau of Investigation, the FBI received its current name in 1935. Beyond its focus on domestic criminal investigations involving federal crimes, the FBI also has intelligence, counterintelligence and counterterrorism functions. It has a National Security Branch, established in 2005, which is run by an executive assistant director of the FBI.

Central Intelligence Agency (CIA)

Originally, the CIA's functions were handled by the Office of Strategic Services (OSS), created in 1942 by President Franklin D. Roosevelt. The OSS was eliminated at the end of World War II. President Harry Truman created the CIA with the National Security Act of 1947.

National Security Agency (NSA)

Located within the Department of Defense, the NSA was created by President Truman in 1952 to engage in cryptology—deciphering encryption codes used in foreign communications.

Additionally, there are intelligence agencies within the Department of Defense, the Department of Homeland Security, the Department of State and the Department of the Treasury, among others. Some of these entities include the Defense Intelligence Agency (DIA), the State Department's Bureau of Intelligence and Research (INR) and the Treasury Department's Office of Terrorism and Financial Intelligence.

Intelligence Reform and Terrorism Prevention Act (IRTPA), Pub. L. 108-458, 118 Stat. 3638 (codified as amended in scattered sections of the U.S.C.)

Primary Function: The IRTPA reorganized the intelligence community and implemented several recommendations of the 9/11 Commission. It created the position of the director of national intelligence and established the National Counterterrorism Center.

New Information Sharing: The act authorizes the creation of a new "Information Sharing Environment" to link federal and state entities as well as the private sector. 15 U.S.C. § 485(a)(2) (2006). It states that the president is to "create an information-sharing environment for the sharing of terrorism information in a manner consistent with national security and with applicable legal standards relating to privacy and civil liberties." 15 U.S.C. § 485(b)(1).

"Secure Flight," Biometrics and Identification: IRTPA contains provisions for "Secure Flight," which is a TSA passenger-screening system. It authorizes the creation of a biometric entry and exit data system to the United States, seeks improved pre-inspection of travelers to the United States at foreign airports, sets minimum standards for domestic birth certificates and driver's licenses, and prohibits the display of Social Security numbers on driver's licenses or motor vehicle registrations. IRTPA also requires the Secretary of Homeland Security to establish minimum standards for the identification documents required of domestic air travelers.

Privacy and Civil Liberties Oversight Board: IRTPA establishes a Privacy and Civil Liberties Board within the executive branch. Through subsequent amendments, the board is an independent agency and has subpoena power.

FOR FURTHER REFERENCE

Treatises

David S. Kris & J. Douglas Wilson, *National Security Investigations & Prosecutions* (2007)
A detailed description of how FISA works, the process for obtaining National Security Letters and other issues, such as the process for searches and seizures abroad.

Government Reports

President's Review Group on Intelligence and Communications Technologies, *Liberty and Security in a Changing World: Report and Recommendations* (2013)
In the wake of the Snowden revelations, President Obama convened a group of experts to review the government's surveillance activities. This report contains 46 recommendations. The recommendations include limiting collection of bulk telephony meta-data; increasing transparency regarding telephone, Internet, and other providers; and enhancing privacy protections of non-U.S. persons.

President's Civil Liberties & Oversight Board (PCLOB), *Report on the Telephone Records Program Conducted under Section 215 of the USA PATRIOT Act and on the Operations of the Foreign Intelligence Surveillance Court* (Jan. 23, 2014)
PCLOB reached negative conclusions about the NSA's bulk collection of telephone metadata conducted under Section 215 of the USA PATRIOT Act. It called for an end to the program because it did not meet the "strong showing of efficacy" required of a government program with such "serious implications for privacy and civil liberties." Short of this recommendation, the PCLB also called for immediate changes to the program, including reducing the retention period for bulk telephone records from five years to three and restricting the number of "hops" used in contact chaining from three to two.

President's Civil Liberties & Oversight Board (PCLOB), *Report on the Surveillance Program Operated Pursuant to Section 702 of the Foreign Intelligence Surveillance Act* (July 2, 2014)
PCLOB's Report on NSA bulk data collection program that drew on Internet Service Providers and the Internet's basic infrastructure and was justified under Section 702, FISA. PCLOB found the program to be legal under Section 702. While the report noted that components of the program "push the program close to the line of constitutional reasonableness," it concluded that the program was useful for gathering intelligence, reasonable under the Fourth Amendment, and authorized by Congress.

Articles and Other Sources

William C. Banks, *The Death of FISA*, 91 Minn. L. Rev. 1209 (2007)
Argues that FISA is no longer effective and that there has been a decline in effective oversight of national security surveillance by Congress and the judiciary.

Robert M. Chesney, *State Secrets and the Limits of National Security Litigation*, 75 Geo. Wash. L. Rev. 1249 (2007)
Examines the state secrets doctrine and proposes alternatives.

Laura K. Donahue, *The Shadow of State Secrets*, 159 U. Pa. L. Rev. 77 (2010)
Major empirical study of the use of the state secrets evidentiary privilege, including how private-sector companies are now relying on it.

Orin Kerr, *Updating the Foreign Intelligence Surveillance Act*, 75 U. Chi. L. Rev. 225 (2008)
Calls for a rewriting of FISA to account for changes in communications technology and Fourth Amendment doctrine that have occurred since the 1970s.

Susan Landau, *Making Sense from Snowden: What's Significant in the NSA Surveillance Revelations, IEEE Security & Privacy* (2013); and *Making Sense of Snowden, Part II: What's Significant in the NSA Revelations,* IEEE Security & Privacy (2014)

In these two articles, security researcher Susan Landau summarizes key points of NSA surveillance activities revealed by Edward Snowden's disclosures regarding the NSA. The first article discusses the leaked materials, the scope of the government's powers, and the NSA's international spying activities. The second article discusses wiretap law, the NSA's collection of communications metadata and content, and the government's ability to undermine widely used security technologies.

Mark M. Lowenthal, *Intelligence: From Secrets to Policy* (6th ed. 2014)
Classic reference work explaining the organization and workings of the U.S. intelligence community.

Jon Michaels, *Deputizing Homeland Security*, 88 Tex. L. Rev. 1435 (2010)
Identification of a dramatic rise of corporate participation in efforts to identify and counter threats of terrorism as well as the legal uncertainties and ambiguities about some of these "deputization programs."

Paul M. Schwartz, *Warrantless Wiretapping, FISA Reform, and the Lessons of Public Liberty*, 97 Cal. L. Rev. 407 (2009)
Detailed analysis of FISA Amendments Act of 2008, current status of FISA and institutional lessons from this amendment process.

Peter P. Swire, *The System of Foreign Intelligence Surveillance*, 72 Geo. Wash. L. Rev. 1306 (2004)
Thoughtful analysis of FISA and practical suggestions for reform.

Stephen I. Vladeck, *The Case Against National Security Courts*, 45 Willamette L. Rev. 505 (2009)
Discusses the pros and cons of national security courts and ultimately finds that the negative aspects predominate.

CHAPTER 6

Health Privacy

ESSENTIAL POINTS

• HIPAA lacks a private right of action.

• The HIPAA regulations permit the enactment of stronger state law provisions. Some states, such as Texas, have health privacy laws that have a broader scope than HIPAA as well as certain more stringent protections.

• The HITECH Act requires notification of a data security breach of HIPAA-covered entities when protected health information is involved.

• Many HIPAA rules apply directly to business associates of covered entities.

• State institutions must be aware of constitutional protections, including the constitutional right to information privacy.

• In certain cases, medical providers have legal duties to disclose personal data about dangerous patients or to protect public safety.

• Physicians and psychotherapists need to walk a fine line when dealing with the confidentiality of a patient who potentially poses a danger to others. If they disclose improperly, they can be liable for breach of confidentiality. If they fail to disclose or warn, they can be liable to victims if a patient attacks a reasonably identifiable future victim.

PATIENT-PHYSICIAN CONFIDENTIALITY

Ethical Rules

Current Opinions of the Judicial Council of the American Medical Association, Canon 5.05

"The physician should not reveal confidential communications or information without the express consent of the patient, unless required to do so by law."

Evidentiary Privileges

Physician-Patient Privilege: A majority of the states (more than 40) have a physician-patient privilege. The privilege protects communications and information relating to the patient's medical treatment. With the privilege, a patient can prohibit a doctor from disclosing the confidential information. States have restricted the use of the privilege in many types of criminal cases, as well as in worker compensation cases and child custody cases. Physicians are also required by statute to disclose certain data to state authorities, such as child abuse and communicable disease.

In federal proceedings, where privileges are left to the courts to recognize under Federal Rule of Evidence 501, most courts have not recognized a physician-patient privilege.

Psychotherapist-Patient Privilege: Every state has adopted a psychotherapist-patient privilege. Exceptions to the psychotherapist-patient privilege are similar to those for the physician-patient privilege.

The psychotherapist-patient privilege is also recognized under the Federal Rules of Civil Procedure. *Jaffee v. Redmond*, 518 U.S. 1 (1996).

The Breach of Confidentiality Tort

Applies to: When a physician reveals a patient's confidential information, in a majority of states the patient can bring a tort action for breach of confidentiality. A cause of action exists whenever a person (1) is under a duty of confidentiality and (2) breaches that duty.

The Source of the Duty of Confidentiality: The source of the duty of confidentiality can be found in: "(1) state physician licensing statutes, (2) evidentiary rules and privileged communication statutes which prohibit a physician from testifying in judicial proceedings, (3) common law principles of trust and (4) the Hippocratic Oath and principles of medical ethics which proscribe the revelation of patient confidences." *McCormick v. England*, 494 S.E.2d 431 (S.C. Ct. App. 1997).

Liability for Inducing a Breach of Confidentiality: Inducing a breach of physician-patient confidentiality can also make one liable under the breach of confidentiality tort: "The law is settled in Ohio and elsewhere that a third party who induces a breach of a trustee's duty of loyalty, or participates in such a breach, or knowingly accepts any benefit from such a breach, becomes directly liable to the aggrieved party." *Hammonds v. Aetna Casualty & Surety Co.,* 243 F. Supp. 793 (D. Ohio 1965).

Exception: Physicians will not be liable for disclosing confidential medical information when it is necessary to protect others from danger or when it is required by law. *Simonsen v. Swenson,* 177 N.W. 831 (Neb. 1920).

Public Disclosure of Private Facts

Many courts have found that the disclosure of medical information can give rise to a claim for public disclosure of private facts, which is one of the four privacy torts. In *Urbaniak v. Newton,* 277 Cal. Rptr. 354 (Cal. App. 1991), the court held that the disclosure of a patient's HIV status was "clearly a 'private fact' of which the disclosure may 'be offensive and objectionable to a reasonable [person] of ordinary sensibilities.'" See also *Susan S. v. Israels,* 67 Cal. Rptr. 2d 42 (Cal. App. 1997) (public disclosure action for disclosure of mental health records).

Tort Liability for Failing to Disclose Personal Data

Duty to Warn: In the famous case *Tarasoff v. Regents of University of California,* 551 P.2d 334 (Cal. 1976), the California Supreme Court declared: "We conclude that the public policy favoring protection of the confidential character of patient-psychotherapist communications must yield to the extent to which disclosure is essential to avert dangers to others. The protective privilege ends where the public peril begins."

A psychotherapist can be liable for failing to warn a victim if:

1. The doctor has a "special relationship" with the harm-causer;
2. The victim is a person who is reasonably identifiable; and
3. The harm to the victim is foreseeable and serious.

Thus, a psychotherapist's treatment of a dangerous patient can create an affirmative duty to a third party, namely, a reasonably identifiable future victim of the patient.

Through subsequent codification in California, the *Tarasoff* duty requires a psychotherapist to make "reasonable efforts to communicate the threat to the victim or victims and to a law enforcement agency." California Civil Code § 43.92.

A majority of states have a duty to warn similar to that in *Tarasoff*.

Mandatory Reporting Laws: Many states require that medical personnel or institutions report certain health information to state agencies or to others.

Research Disclosure Laws: A number of states regulate the use of medical data for research purposes.

MEDICAL INFORMATION

State Regulation

Medical Confidentiality Laws: Many states have specific statutes providing civil and criminal protection against the disclosure of medical information. Some laws restrict disclosure of medical data by particular entities: government agencies, HMOs, insurance companies, employers, pharmacists and health data clearinghouses. Other laws prohibit the disclosure by any entity of particular types of medical data, such as AIDS/HIV, alcohol or drug abuse, mental health and genetic information. See, e.g., Cal. Health & Safety Code § 199.21 (prohibiting disclosure of HIV test results); N.Y. Pub. Health L. § 17 (prohibiting the nonconsensual disclosure of medical records of minors relating to sexually transmitted diseases and abortion; even the disclosure to parents is prohibited without consent); Pa. Cons. Stat. § 1690.108 (prohibiting the disclosure of all records prepared during alcohol or drug abuse treatment).

Patient Access Laws: The vast majority of states have statutes providing patients with a right to access certain medical records. A few states grant wide access to medical records held by all types of entities. On the other end of the spectrum, some states have no right of access, and others have only a limited right to access mental health records. The remaining states fall somewhere in between, permitting access to records from certain healthcare providers but not others (e.g., from some but not all of the following entities: hospitals, HMOs, insurers and pharmacists).

Comprehensive Health Privacy Laws: Most states do not have a comprehensive law governing medical privacy, but some states do.

Texas' Medical Privacy Act, Tex. Health & Safety Code §§ 181.001 et seq. After new amendments (H.B. 300) effective in 2012, Texas now has one of the broadest and strictest medical privacy laws in the country. The law mandates broader coverage and requires stricter rules in many areas than HIPAA. The law covers any organization that (1) assembles, collects, stores or transmits protected health information (PHI); (2) comes into possession of, obtains or stores PHI; or (3) is an employee, agent or contractor of an entity that fits within the preceding two categories. Thus, many law firms and accounting firms may be covered entities.

All employees of covered entities must be trained in the applicable obligations of federal and state law at least every two years, with initial training of all employees occurring within 60 days of hiring. The statute also mandates that people have access to their electronic health data in 15 days (a shorter period than HIPAA's 30-day requirement). Notification of a health data breach must be made "as quickly as possible" to "any individual whose sensitive personal information" was affected. Thus, the law covers all affected parties and not just Texas residents. The law's fines mirror HIPAA's.

Health Insurance Portability and Accountability Act Regulations (HIPAA) 45 C.F.R. §§ 160-164 (2002)

Primary Function: Pursuant to the Health Insurance Portability and Accountability Act of 1996, the Department of Health and Human Services (HHS) promulgated regulations to regulate the privacy and security of medical information—the "Privacy Rule" and the "Security Rule."

In 2009, Congress passed the HITECH Act as part of the American Recovery and Reinvestment Act. The act extends HIPAA rules to business associates (previously regulated by contractual arrangements with covered entities) and provides for direct HHS enforcement over business associates. Among other things, the act increases the fines for HIPAA violations and requires data security breach notification. In 2013, HHS issued a regulation (the Omnibus Rule) to implement the HITECH Act changes.

Applies to: "Covered entities" include "health plans, healthcare clearinghouses and healthcare providers." 45 C.F.R. § 160.102. The regulations apply only to those who transmit health information electronically in HIPAA's standard format. Most healthcare providers who deal with insurance—physicians, hospitals, insurance companies and pharmacists—are covered. Business associates that receive PHI from covered entities (and subcontractors that receive PHI from business associates) are also directly subject to the HIPAA Security Rule and parts of the Privacy Rule.

Hybrid Entities: When an organization provides a variety of products and services, only some of which pertain to healthcare, they are known as "hybrid entities." Only the component that performs the healthcare functions must comply with HIPAA.

Protected Health Information: The data protected by HIPAA is called PHI, which consists of "individually identifiable health information."

The Right to Request Restrictions: An individual retains the right to request restrictions on the use or disclosure of health information by all covered entities. 45 C.F.R. § 164.502(c).

Notice: Covered entities must produce a notice of privacy practices.

Right of Access: Individuals have a right to access any protected health information that is used in whole or in part to make decisions about the individual.

Authorization: For all uses and disclosures beyond those for treatment, payment or healthcare operations, a patient's authorization is required. 45 C.F.R. § 164.508(a). Treatment cannot be made conditional on authorization unless the covered entity's purpose is research, determining health plan eligibility or underwriting.

Marketing: Authorization is required for data use in marketing. But, a covered entity can use PHI to market its own healthcare products, and the individual cannot opt out. 45 C.F.R. § 164.501.

Business Associates: Entities that contract with a covered entity are "business associates" and are permitted to receive PHI "if the covered entity obtains satisfactory assurance that the business associate will appropriately safeguard the information." 45 C.F.R. § 164.502. Business associates that violate HIPAA are subject to the same punishments as covered entities. The HITECH Act provides for direct HHS enforcement power over business associates. Subcontractors of business associates that receive PHI are deemed to be business associates.

Psychotherapy Notes: Authorization is required "for any use or disclosure of psychotherapy notes" even if that use or disclosure is for treatment, payment and healthcare operations. 45 C.F.R. § 164.508. According to the regulation commentary, psychotherapy notes require authorization because they "do not include information that covered entities typically need for treatment, payment or other types of healthcare operations."

Disclosure and Use Without Authorization: The regulation provides for a number of situations where health information can be used or disclosed without authorization: (1) required by law; (2) for public health activities; (3) regarding victims of abuse, neglect or domestic violence (under certain circumstances); (4) for health oversight activities; (5) for judicial and administrative proceedings; (6) for law enforcement purposes; (7) to avert a serious threat to health or safety; (8) for specialized government functions; and (9) for workers' compensation. 45 C.F.R. § 164.512.

De-Identified Health Information: HIPAA does not place restrictions on the use or disclosure of de-identified data.

De-Identifying Data Under HIPAA

There are two methods to de-identify data:

Statistician Method
Have an expert certify that the data is not individually identifiable. This expert must have the appropriate statistical and scientific knowledge for data de-identification. The expert must determine that the risk of re-identifying individuals is "very small" and must document the methods and results of the analysis that justifies this determination.

Safe Harbor Method
Remove 18 identifying data elements that HIPAA specifies and have no actual knowledge that the remaining data could be used to identify the individual. If all these identifying data elements are removed, then the data is de-identified. No expert is required. The 18 identifiers are:

1. Names

2. All geographic subdivisions smaller than a state
   • Includes street address, city, county, precinct or zip code
   • May use the first three digits of the zip code if the geographic unit formed by combining all zip codes with the same three initial digits contains more than 20,000 people and the initial three digits of the zip codes for geographic units containing 20,000 or fewer people are changed to 000)

3. All elements of dates related to an individual except the year
   • Includes birth date, admission date, discharge date, date of death and all ages over 80

4. Telephone numbers

5. Fax numbers

6. E-mail addresses

7. Social Security numbers

8. Medical record numbers

9. Health plan beneficiary numbers

10. Account numbers

11. Certificate/license numbers

12. Vehicle identifiers, such as serial numbers and license plate numbers

13. Device identifiers and serial numbers

14. URLs

15. IP addresses

16. Biometric identifiers (fingerprint, voice print)

17. Full-face photographs

18. Any other unique identifying number, characteristic or code

Disclosure to Law Enforcement Officials: PHI may be disclosed to law enforcement officials without consent or authorization if required by a court order, warrant or subpoena. Moreover, certain health information may also be disclosed "in response to a law enforcement official's request for such information for the purpose of identifying or locating a suspect, fugitive, material witness or missing person." 45 C.F.R. § 164.512(f).

Privacy Officials: Covered entities must have a designated privacy official.

Enforcement: Under the HIPAA statute, 42 U.S.C. § 1320d-6(a), a person who knowingly obtains or discloses individually identifiable health information in violation of the Privacy Rule can be fined up to $50,000 and imprisoned for up to one year. If the violation occurred via false pretenses, the fine is up to $100,000 and five years imprisonment. If the violation was done for commercial advantage, personal gain or malicious harm, then the penalties are up to a $250,000 fine and 10 years imprisonment. The maximum penalties under HIPAA are $50,000 per violation, with an annual maximum of $1.5 million. The HIPAA regulations do not grant a private cause of action. Criminal enforcement is via the Department of Justice. Civil enforcement is via the Department of Health and Human Services, Office for Civil Rights (OCR).

Preemption: HIPAA does not preempt more stringent state law. 45 C.F.R. § 160.203(b).

The Security Rule: Unlike the Privacy Rule, which applies to all PHI, the Security Rule applies only to "electronic protected health information" (e-PHI). The Security Rule requires covered entities to "protect against reasonably anticipated threats or hazards to the security and integrity of [e-PHI]." 45 C.F.R. § 164.306(a). Requires a security officer, security training and other procedures.

Data Breach Notification: The HITECH Act of 2009 establishes a data breach notification requirement. A breach consists of an unauthorized disclosure of "unsecured PHI," which is unencrypted PHI. Affected individuals must be notified "without reasonable delay" and no later than 60 days after discovery of the breach. Breaches of 500 people or more require notice to the media and to HHS.

Court Cases

United States v. Zhou, 678 F.3d 1110 (9th Cir. 2012)
The court concluded that for the purpose of a misdemeanor violation of HIPAA under 42 U.S.C. § 1320d-6(a)d, a violator need only knowingly obtain "individually identifiable health information relating to an individual." The court held there was no requirement of knowledge of violating HIPAA.

HIPAA Myths and Facts

MYTH: HIPAA regulates all medical information.

FACT: HIPAA regulates only medical information maintained by "covered entities" that use the standard HIPAA format.

MYTH: Complying with HIPAA will ensure a healthcare provider is properly protecting privacy under the law.

FACT: HIPAA is often weaker than state law protections. Since it does not preempt more stringent state laws, healthcare providers must be familiar with state statutory and common law privacy protections. Public hospitals must also comply with the U.S. Constitution and state constitutions.

MYTH: HIPAA prevents physicians from disclosing information about a person's care to relatives or from having office sign-in sheets.

FACT: HIPAA does not make such restrictions.

HIPAA Problems to Avoid

• **Removing unencrypted data:** Providence Health & Services stored unencrypted PHI in electronic storage devices and laptops that were taken outside the institution and then lost. Penalty: Providence agreed to pay the Department of Health & Human Services (HHS) a $100,000 fine plus establish a three-year corrective action plan.

• **Improperly disposing of prescription data:** CVS inadequately discarded labels from prescription bottles. Penalty: $2.25 million fine plus a corrective action plan.

• **Failing to provide adequate training:** HHS settlements with Phoenix Cardiac Surgery for $100,000 and with the Alaska Department of Health and Social Services (DHSS) for $1.7 million involved, in part, inadequate training.

• **Inadequate policies and safeguards:** HHS's settlement with the Alaska DHSS was due, in part, to these deficiencies.

• **Failure to conduct risk analysis:** HHS's settlement with Phoenix Cardiac Surgery was due, in part, to the failure to conduct risk analysis.

• **Failing to cooperate with HHS's investigation:** HHS fined Cignet Health $4.3 million for denying 41 patients access to their records and for not cooperating in the investigation. Most of the fine was for the failure to cooperate.

OCR HIPAA Enforcement Actions

HHS HIPAA RESOLUTION AGREEMENTS

CASE	HHS FACTUAL ALLEGATIONS	ALLEGED HIPAA VIOLATIONS	PENALTIES / TERMS
Parkview Health System, Inc. (June 23, 2014)	Parkview took custody of medical records pertaining to approximately 5,000 to 8,000 of a retiring physician's patients to consider purchasing the physician's practice. Parkview employees left 71 cardboard boxes of these medical records unattended in the physician's home driveway.	Parkview failed to appropriately and reasonably safeguard PHI.	$800,000 monetary settlement Corrective Action Plan (CAP): - 1 year - designate a compliance representative - develop, distribute, and update policies and procedures - provide adequate training to employees - submit final report detailing compliance - document retention of compliance records for 6 years
New York and Presbyterian Hospital (May 7, 2014)	NYP and CU participate in a joint arrangement in which CU faculty members serve as attending physicians at NYP. The two separate entities operate a shared data network and a shared network firewall that is administered by employees of both entities. The shared network links to NYP patient information systems containing ePHI. A computer sever that had access to NYP ePHI was errantly reconfigured.	NYP impermissibly disclosed the ePHI of 6,800 patients to Google and other Internet search engines NYP failed to implement processes for assessing and monitoring all IT equipment, applications, and data systems that were linked to NYP patient databases. NYP failed to implement security measures sufficient to reduce risks and vulnerabilities to ePHI. NYP failed to implement appropriate processes and procedures for authorizing access to its NYP patient databases.	$3.3 million monetary settlement CAP: - 3 years - designate a compliance representative - modify existing risk analysis process - develop and implement risk management plan - review and revise policies and procedures on information access management - develop a process to evaluate environmental or operational changes affecting security of ePHI - implement process with HHS' changes - review and revise policy and procedures on device and media controls - develop an enhanced privacy and security training program - promptly investigate and report potential violations - submit implementation and annual reports - document retention of compliance records for 6 years

CASE	HHS FACTUAL ALLEGATIONS	ALLEGED HIPAA VIOLATIONS	PENALTIES / TERMS
Columbia University (May 7, 2014)	A CU physician who developed applications for both NYP and CU attempted to deactivate a personally owned computer server on the network containing NYP patient ePHI. Because of a lack of technical safeguards, deactivation of the server resulted in ePHI being accessible on Internet search engines.	CU failed to conduct an accurate and thorough risk analysis that incorporates all IT equipment, applications, and data systems utilizing ePHI, including the server accessing the NYP-ePHI. CU failed to implement processes for assessing and monitoring IT equipment, applications, and data systems that were linked to NYP patient data bases prior to the breach incident and failed to implement security measures sufficient to reduce the risk of inappropriate disclosure to an acceptable level.	$1,500,000 monetary settlement CAP: - 3 years - designate a compliance representative - conduct thorough risk analysis of security risks incorporating all electronic equipment, data systems, and applications - develop and implement risk management plan - review and revise policies and procedures on information access management - develop a process to evaluate environmental or operational changes affecting security of ePHI - implement process with HHS' changes - review and revise policy and procedures on device and media controls - develop privacy and security training program - promptly investigate and report potential violations - submit implementation and annual reports - document retention of compliance records for 6 years
Concentra Health Services (April 21, 2014)	An unencrypted laptop was stolen out of Concentra's physical therapy center.	Concentra failed to adequately remediate and manage it identified lack of encryption or, alternatively, document why encryption was not reasonable and appropriate and implement an equivalent alternative to encryption. Concentra also did not sufficiently implement policies and procedures to prevent, detect, contain, and correct security violations under the security management process standard when it failed to adequately execute risk management measures to reduce its identified lack of encryption to a reasonable and appropriate level.	$1,725,220 monetary settlement CAP: - 6 years - designate a compliance representative - perform through risk analysis on ePHI security - submit risk analysis and risk management plan - submit evidence of implemented and planned remediation actions - provide specific timelines for planned actions - provide updated risk analysis w/ any changes/updates to IT infrastructure affecting ePHI security - promptly implement security management process including training - provide update on encryption status - submit implementation and annual reports - document retention of compliance records for 6 years

QCA Health Plan, Inc. (April 14, 2014)	An unencrypted laptop computer containing the ePHI of 148 individuals was stolen from a workforce member's car.	QCA did not implement policies and procedures to prevent, detect, contain and correct security violations, including conducting an accurate and thorough assessment of potential risks and vulnerabilities to the confidentiality, integrity, and availability of ePHI it held, and implementing security measures sufficient to reduce risks and vulnerabilities to a reasonable and appropriate level. QCA did not implement physical safeguards for all workstations that access ePHI to restrict access to authorized users. QCA impermissibly disclosed the ePHI of 148 individuals.	$250,000 monetary settlement CAP: - 2 years - designate a compliance representative - perform risk analysis and submit risk management plan addressing ePHI security - provide adequate training to employees - promptly investigate and report potential violations - submit annual reports - document retention of compliance records for 6 years
Skagit County, Washington (March 6, 2014)	Unknown parties accessed money receipts with ePHI of seven individuals after the ePHI had been inadvertently moved to a publicly accessible server maintained by Skagit County.	Skagit disclosed the ePHI of 1,581 individuals by providing access to ePHI on its public web server. Skagit failed to provide notification to individuals whose ePHI had been compromised as required by the Breach Notification Rule. Skagit failed to implement sufficient security policies and procedures to prevent, detect, contain, and correct security violations. Skagit failed to implement and maintain in written or electronic form policies and procedures to ensure compliance with the Security Rule.	$215,000 monetary settlement CAP: - 6 years - designate a compliance representative - provide breach notification to affected individuals - submit accounting of disclosures - submit hybrid entity documentation - conduct thorough assessment of potential risks to ePHI - submit risk management measures - adopt risk management measures with HHS' changes - provide adequate training to employees - submit annual reports - document retention of compliance records for 6 years

CASE	HHS FACTUAL ALLEGATIONS	ALLEGED HIPAA VIOLATIONS	PENALTIES / TERMS
Adult & Pediatric Dermatology, P.C. (December 24, 2013)	An unencrypted thumb drive that contained the ePHI relating to the performance of Mohs surgery of approximately 2,200 individuals was stolen from one of its employees' vehicles.	APDerm did not conduct an accurate and thorough analysis of the potential risks and vulnerabilities to the confidentiality of ePHI as part of its security management process. APDerm did not fully comply with the administrative requirements of the Breach Notification Rule to have written policies and procedures and train its employees regarding the requirements. APDerm impermissibly disclosed the ePHI of up to 2,200 individuals by providing an unauthorized individual access to said ePHI.	$150,000 monetary settlement CAP: - 3 years - designate a compliance representative - conduct comprehensive risk analysis of ePHI security risks - develop risk management plan - implement risk management plan with HHS' changes - promptly investigate and report potential violations - provide adequate training to employees - submit implementation reports - document retention of compliance records for 3 years
Affinity Health Plan, Inc. (August 7, 2013)	AHP returned multiple photocopiers to a leasing agent without erasing the data contained on the copier hard drives.	AHP impermissibly disclosed the protected health information of up to 344,579 individuals. AHP failed to incorporate ePHI stored in photocopiers' hard drives in its analysis of risks and vulnerabilities. AHP failed to implement its policies and procedures when returning the hard drives to its leasing agents.	$1,215,780 monetary settlement CAP: - 120 days - designate a compliance representative - use best efforts to retrieve hard drives and safeguard ePHI contained therein - conduct comprehensive risk analysis that incorporates all electronic equipment and systems that AHP owned or leased - develop, plan to mitigate identified risks - implement plan with HHS' changes - document retention of compliance records for 6 years

WellPoint Inc. (July 8, 2013)	Security weaknesses in an online application database left the ePHI of 612,402 individuals accessible to unauthorized individuals over the Internet. This data included names, dates of birth, addresses, Social Security numbers, telephone numbers and health information.	WellPoint did not implement appropriate administrative and technical safeguards as required under the HIPAA Security Rule. WellPoint did not perform adequate technical evaluation. WellPoint did not adequately implement technology to verify the identity of the person or entity seeking access to ePHI maintained in its web-based application database. WellPoint impermissibly disclosed the ePHI of 612,402 individuals by allowing access to the ePHI of such individuals maintained in the application database.	$1.7 million monetary settlement.
Shasta Regional Medical Center (June 6, 2013)	An article in the *Los Angeles Times* indicated that two of SRMC's senior leaders met with the media to discuss the medical services provided to a patient without valid written authorization.	SRMC failed to safeguard its patient from any impermissible intentional or unintentional disclosure on multiple occasions. SRMC impermissibly used patient's PHI. SRMC failed to sanction employees pursuant to its internal sanctions policy for HIPAA violations.	$275,000 monetary settlement CAP: - 1 year - designate a compliance representative - develop, distribute, and update policies and procedures - provide adequate training to employees - submit implementation and annual reports - document retention of compliance records for 6 years

CASE	HHS FACTUAL ALLEGATIONS	ALLEGED HIPAA VIOLATIONS	PENALTIES / TERMS
Idaho State University (May 13, 2013)	Firewall protections at ISU servers maintained were disabled for at least 10 months, causing a breach of the ePHI of 17,500 ISU patients.	ISU did not conduct an analysis of the risk to the confidentiality of ePHI as part of its security management process. ISU did not adequately implement security measures sufficient to reduce the risks and vulnerabilities to a reasonable and appropriate level. ISU did not adequately implement procedures to regularly review records of information system activity to determine if any ePHI was used or disclosed in an inappropriate manner.	$400,000 monetary settlement CAP: - 2 years - designate a compliance representative - provide documentation designating ISU as hybrid entity - submit risk management plan and implement approved changes - submit information system activity review and implement approved changes - submit documentation of compliance gap analysis - promptly investigate and submit report to HHS on potential violations - document retention of compliance records for 6 years
Hospice of Northern Idaho (December 17, 2012)	A laptop computer containing the ePHI of 441 individuals was stolen.	HONI did not conduct an accurate and thorough analysis of the risk to the confidentiality of ePHI on an ongoing basis as part of its security management process. HHS also found that HONI did not adequately adopt or implement security measures sufficient to ensure the confidentiality of ePHI it created, maintained, and transmitted using portable devices.	$50,000 monetary settlement CAP: - 2 years - designate a compliance representative - submit report to HHS on potential violations - document retention of compliance records for 6 years

| Massachusetts Eye and Ear Infirmary and Massachusetts Eye and Ear Associates, Inc. (September 17, 2012) | An unencrypted personal laptop containing the ePHI of MEEI patients and research subjects was stolen. | MEEI did not demonstrate that it conducted a thorough analysis of the risk to the confidentiality of ePHI on an on-going basis as part of its security management process.

MEEI's security measures were not sufficient to ensure the confidentiality of ePHI that it created, maintained, and transmitted using portable devices to a reasonable and appropriate level.

MEEI did not adequately adopt or implement policies and procedures to address security incident identification, reporting, and response.

MEEI did not adequately adopt or implement policies and procedures to restrict access to authorized users for portable devices that access ePHI to provide it with a reasonable means of knowing whether or what type of portable devices were being used to access its network.

MEEI did not adequately adopt or implement policies and procedures governing the receipt and removal of portable devices into, out of, and within its facilities.

MEEI did not adequately adopt or implement technical policies and procedures to allow access to ePHI using portable devices only to authorized persons or software programs. | $1.5 million monetary settlement

CAP:
- 3 years
- designate a compliance representative
- develop, distribute, and update policies and procedures
- provide adequate training to employees
- submit implementation and annual reports
- document retention of compliance records for 6 years |

CASE	HHS FACTUAL ALLEGATIONS	ALLEGED HIPAA VIOLATIONS	PENALTIES / TERMS
Alaska Department of Health and Social Services (June 25, 2012)	A portable electronic device (USB hard drive) potentially containing ePHI was stolen from the vehicle of a DHSS employee.	DHSS did not complete a risk analysis, implement sufficient risk management measures, complete security training for its employees, implement device and media controls, and address device and media encryption.	$1.7 million monetary settlement CAP: - 3 years - designate a compliance representative - develop, distribute, and update policies and procedures - provide adequate training to employees - submit implementation and annual reports - document retention of compliance records for 6 years
Phoenix Cardiac Surgery (April 11, 2012)	PCS was posting clinical and surgical appointments for its patients on an Internet-based calendar that was publicly accessible.	PCS did not provide and document employee training on PHI security. PCS failed to have in place appropriate and reasonable administrative and technical safeguards to protect PHI. PCS did not implement required administrative and technical security safeguards to protect ePHI. PCS also failed to obtain satisfactory assurances in business associates agreements that these entities would appropriately safeguard ePHI received from PCS.	$100,000 monetary settlement CAP: - 1 year - designate a compliance representative - develop, distribute, and update policies and procedures - provide adequate training to employees - submit implementation report - document retention of compliance records for 6 years

Entity (Date)	Facts	HIPAA Violation	Settlement / CAP
Blue Cross Blue Shield of Tennessee (March 9, 2012)	57 unencrypted computer hard drives containing PHI of over 1 million individuals had been stolen from a leased facility in Tennessee.	HIPAA Privacy and Security Rules (HHS did not allege violation of specific standards)	$1,500,000 monetary settlement CAP: - 450 days - designate a compliance representative - develop, distribute, and update policies and procedures - provide adequate training to employees - submit biannual reports - document retention of compliance records for 3 years
University of California at Los Angeles Health System (July 6, 2011)	Unauthorized UCLAHS employees repeatedly looked at the electronic protected health information of numerous other UCLAHS patients.	UCLAHS did not provide and/or document the provision of necessary and/or Security Rule training for its employees. UCLAHS also failed to apply and/or document appropriate sanctions on employees who impermissibly accessed PHI. UCLAHS failed to implement security measures sufficient to reduce the risks of impermissible access to ePHI.	$865,500 monetary settlement CAP: - 3 years - designate a compliance representative - develop, distribute, and update policies and procedures - provide adequate training to employees - submit implementation and annual reports - document retention of compliance records for 6 years
General Hospital Corp. and Massachusetts General Physicians Organization, Inc. (February 14, 2011)	An MGH employee, while commuting to work, left the documents on the subway train, which contained billing forms that the contained the names, dates of birth, medical record numbers, health insurer and policy numbers, diagnoses and provider names of 66 patients. One of the documents contained the practice's three-day schedule, which had the names and medical record numbers of 192 patients.	MGH failed to implement reasonable, appropriate safeguards to protect the privacy of PHI when removed from its premises and impermissibly disclosed PHI.	$1,000,000 monetary settlement CAP: - 3 years - designate a compliance representative - develop, distribute, and update policies and procedures - provide adequate training to employees - submit implementation and annual reports - document retention of compliance records for 6 years

CASE	HHS FACTUAL ALLEGATIONS	ALLEGED HIPAA VIOLATIONS	PENALTIES / TERMS
Cignet Health (February 4, 2011)	Cignet denied 41 patients access to their medical records. Cignet refused to respond to HHS' repeated demands to produce the records and failed to cooperate with HHS' investigations of the complaints, including failure to produce the records in response to HHS' subpoena.	The HIPAA Privacy Rule requires that a covered entity provide a patient with a copy of their medical records within 30 (and no later than 60) days of the patient's request. Cignet failed to cooperate with HHS' investigations was due to willful neglect.	$4.3 million in civil money penalties ($1.3 million for failing to provide patients with copy of medical records and $3 million for failing to cooperate with HHS' investigations).
Management Services Organization Washington Inc. (December 13, 2010)	MSO disclosed ePHI to its subsidiary information for marketing purposes.	MSO intentionally did not have in place or implement appropriate and reasonable administrative, technical, and physical safeguards to protect the privacy of the protected health information.	$35,000 monetary settlement CAP: - 2 years - designate a compliance representative - enact, distribute, and update policies and procedures - provide adequate training to employees - submit implementation and annual reports - document retention of compliance records for 6 years
Rite Aid Corp. (June 7, 2010)	Rite Aid pharmacies disposed of prescriptions and labeled pill bottles containing ePHI in dumpsters that were accessible to the public.	Rite Aid's policies and procedures establishing physical and administrative safeguards were inadequate to reasonably safeguard PHI. Rite Aid did not maintain a sanctions policy for employees who failed to comply with its policies and procedures governing PHI security. It did not have a training program to ensure that its employees knew how to properly dispose of PHI.	$1,000,000 CAP: - 3 years - designate a compliance representative - develop, distribute, and update policies and procedures - provide adequate training to employees - submit implementation and periodic reports - document retention of compliance records for 6 years

CVS Pharmacy Inc. (January 15, 2009)	CVS disposed of non-electronic PHI in open dumpsters, accessible to unauthorized persons.	$2,250,000 monetary settlement
	CVS' policies and procedures establishing physical and administrative safeguards were found inadequate to reasonably safeguard PHI.	CAP: - 3 years - designate a compliance representative - develop, distribute, and update policies and procedures - provide adequate training to employees - submit implementation and annual reports - document retention of compliance records for 6 years
	CVS did not maintain a sanctions policy for employees who failed to comply with its policies and procedures governing PHI security.	
	CVS' training program was inadequate to ensure that its employees knew how to dispose of non-electronic PHI.	
Providence Health and Services (July 16, 2008)	Unencrypted ePHI on four back-up tapes and two optical disks were left unattended overnight in employee's personal vehicle and were stolen.	$100,000 fine.
	Providence failed to implement policies and procedures to safeguard ePHI.	CAP: - 3 years - designate a compliance representative - develop, distribute, and update policies and procedures - provide adequate training to employees - submit implementation and annual reports - document retention of compliance records for 6 years
	On four other occasions, laptops containing unencrypted ePHI were left unattended and were stolen from Providence employees.	

The Common Rule
45 C.F.R. § 46.101 (2005)

Primary Function: To ensure that the rights of a human subject are protected throughout a research project.

Applies to: Most federally funded research conducted on humans. 45 C.F.R. § 46.101.

Key Protections: The key protections of the Common Rule concern individual autonomy and consent, the need for independent review of research by an institutional review board (IRB) and the minimization of physical and mental harm to research subjects. Privacy and confidentiality are considered important components of the risk of harm from any research project.

Exceptions: The Common Rule also exempts from its requirements research that involves publicly available information or information "recorded by the investigator in such a manner that subjects cannot be identified, directly or through identifiers linked to the subjects." 45 C.F.R. § 46.101(b)(4).

Preemption: The Common Rule's requirements for informed consent do not preempt any applicable federal, state or local laws that set stricter standards for legally effective informed consent.

Federal Drug and Alcohol Confidentiality Statute
42 U.S.C. § 290dd-2

Primary Purpose: To protect the confidentiality of records of drug and alcohol abuse treatment.

Applies to: Regulates "any program or activity relating to substance abuse education, prevention, training, treatment, rehabilitation or research which is conducted, regulated or directly or indirectly assisted by any department or agency of the United States." 42 U.S.C. § 290dd-2(a).

Regulations: The regulations relating to this statute are at 42 C.F.R. §§ 2.1 – 2.67.

Relationship to HIPAA: A drug and alcohol treatment program can be covered under both HIPAA and the federal drug and alcohol confidentiality rules. The confidentiality rules are more privacy-protective than HIPAA.

Confidentiality Protections: The confidentiality rules generally restrict disclosure of personal information. There are only a few exceptions: (1) written consent from the patient, (2) scientific research and evaluation of the program, provided the records are de-identified, (3) emergencies, (4) court orders, (5) data relating to a crime on the program premises or against program employees and (6) suspicion of child abuse or neglect.

Restriction from Use in Criminal Cases: With limited exceptions (e.g., crime on program premises), records of drug and alcohol abuse treatment cannot be used "to initiate or substantiate any criminal charges against a patient or to conduct any investigation of a patient." 42 U.S.C. § 290dd-2(c).

Subpoenas for Medical Information

Although the law governing subpoenas is generally permissive in allowing demands for information, courts tend to be more exacting when they face challenges to subpoenas for medical information.

Northwestern Memorial Hospital v. Ashcroft, **362 F.3d 923 (7th Cir. 2004)**
Quashing a subpoena to doctors for partial birth abortion records even though they would be de-identified. The court noted a risk of re-identification and noted that even if they could not be re-identified, the patients might still feel their privacy was invaded by the revelation of details about their abortions.

New York City Health & Hospitals Corp. v. Morgenthau,
764 N.E.2d 394 (N.Y. Ct. App. 2001)
Quashing a subpoena to obtain emergency room data from hospitals to locate a bleeding suspect who fled a crime scene. Divulging medical records pertaining to all people treated for stab wounds would violate the physician-patient privilege.

CONSTITUTIONAL PROTECTIONS

Constitutional Right to Privacy

Although the U.S. Constitution does not explicitly mention privacy, in a line of cases commonly referred to as concerning "substantive due process," the Supreme Court has held that there exists a "right to privacy" in the U.S. Constitution.

Griswold v. Connecticut, **381 U.S. 479 (1965)**
Recognizes a "right to privacy" in the Constitution based on the "penumbras" of the Bill of Rights. The right to privacy protects against a state law prohibiting the use of contraceptives in the "sacred precincts of marital bedrooms."

Eisenstadt v. Baird, 405 U.S. 438 (1972)
Strikes down a statute permitting contraceptives only to married couples. The right of privacy "is the right of the individual, married or single, to be free from unwarranted government intrusion into matters so fundamentally affecting a person as the decision whether to bear or beget a child."

Roe v. Wade, 410 U.S. 113 (1973)
The right to privacy "is broad enough to encompass a woman's decision whether or not to terminate her pregnancy."

Planned Parenthood of Southeastern Pennsylvania v. Casey, 505 U.S. 833 (1992)
Reaffirms *Roe v. Wade,* though it suggests a different standard—that no law place an "undue burden" on the right to have an abortion.

Washington v. Glucksberg, 521 U.S. 702 (1997)
Concludes that a ban on physician-assisted suicide did not run afoul of the right to privacy.

Lawrence v. Texas, 539 U.S. 558 (2003)
Overrules *Bowers v. Hardwick,* 478 U.S. 186 (1986), and concludes that the right to privacy prohibits the criminalization of homosexual sex.

Constitutional Right to Information Privacy

Whalen v. Roe, 429 U.S. 589 (1977)
The court recognizes that the constitutional right to privacy also encompasses "the individual interest in avoiding disclosure of personal matters"—which is now called the "constitutional right to information privacy."

Nixon v. Administrator of General Services, 433 U.S. 425 (1977)
Concludes that President Richard Nixon had a constitutional privacy interest in records of his private communications with his family, but not in records involving his official duties.

United States v. Westinghouse Electric Corp., 638 F.2d 570, 578 (3d Cir. 1980)
The court set forth the predominant test for determining whether there is a violation of the constitutional right to information privacy by listing seven factors that "should be considered in deciding whether an intrusion into an individual's privacy is justified": (1) "the type of record requested," (2) "the information it does or might contain," (3) "the potential for harm in any subsequent nonconsensual disclosure," (4) "the injury from disclosure to the relationship in which the record was generated," (5) "the adequacy of safeguards to prevent unauthorized disclosure," (6) "the degree of need for access" and (7)

"whether there is an express statutory mandate, articulated public policy, or other recognizable public interest militating toward access."

Fourth Amendment

The Fourth Amendment protects the privacy of medical information when government officials are seeking to obtain it.

GENETIC INFORMATION

Genetic Testing and Discrimination

State Genetic Privacy Statutes: Many states have passed statutes protecting the privacy of genetic information.

Genetic Information Nondiscrimination Act (GINA) of 2008: This federal statute prevents insurance companies and employers from using genetic tests to deny individuals health coverage or employment. GINA does not preempt stricter state laws.

Executive Order 13145 (Feb. 8, 2000): Requires all executive branch departments and agencies to refrain from genetic discrimination. Also states that the "employing department or agency shall not request, require, collect or purchase protected genetic information with respect to an employee, or information about a request for or the receipt of genetic services by such employee."

FOR FURTHER REFERENCE

Treatises

Lisa M. Boyle, *HIPAA: A Guide to Health Care Privacy and Security Law* (2013)
A 1400-page volume on HIPAA.

Patricia I. Carter, *HIPAA Compliance Handbook* (2010)
In-depth examination of the privacy and security regulations in HIPAA and enforcement mechanisms.

Khaled El Emam, *Guide to the De-Identification of Personal Health Information* (2013)
Detailed discussion about why and how to de-identify PHI.

Khaled El Emam & Luk Arbuckle, *Anonymizing Health Data: Case Studies and Methods to Get You Started* (2013)
Practical and concrete discussion of how to de-identify PHI.

Rebecca Herold & Kevin Beaver, *The Practical Guide to HIPAA Privacy and Security Compliance* (2014)
A detailed guide to HIPAA and how to develop an effective compliance program.

Stephen S. Wu, ed., *A Guide to HIPAA Security and the Law* (2007)
Focuses on liability issues and the scope of applicability of the HIPAA Security Rule.

Books

Mark A. Rothstein ed., *Genetic Secrets: Protecting Privacy and Confidentiality in the Genetic Era* (1997)
A sterling collection of interdisciplinary essays by leading scholars regarding privacy and genetic information.

Articles and Other Sources

Fred H. Cate, *Protecting Privacy in Health Research: The Limits of Individual Choice*, 98 Cal. L. Rev. 1765 (2010)
Argues that the policy and legal reliance on individual choice concerning the use of personal information health research is a flawed approach.

Lawrence O. Gostin, *Health Information Privacy*, 80 Cornell L. Rev. 451 (1995)
A classic article that identifies the key issues in the health privacy debate.

Institute of Medicine, *Beyond the HIPPA Privacy Rule: Enhancing Privacy, Improving Health Through Research* (2009)
Report of Blue Ribbon panel proposed changes to HIPPA Privacy Rule and other privacy regulations with goal of improving healthcare research while also protecting personal privacy.

Peter H. Schuck & Daniel J. Givelber, *Tarasoff v. Regents of the University of California*, Torts Stories 99 (Robert L. Rabin & Stephen D. Sugarman, eds., 2003)
Fascinating background and valuable information on the leading case about a healthcare professional's duty to warn a victim about a threat from a potential harm-causer whom the professional is treating.

Paul M. Schwartz, *Privacy and Participation: Personal Information and Public Sector Regulation in the United States*, 80 Iowa L. Rev. 553 (1995)
Examination of the constitutional right to informational privacy, including discussion of lower court opinions.

Peter A. Winn, *Criminal Prosecutions Under HIPAA*, 53 U.S. Attorneys Bulletin 21 (2005)
Advances an influential theory about prosecutions of employees and business associates of covered entities under HIPAA pursuant to 18 U.S.C. § 2(b).

Government Records

ESSENTIAL POINTS

- Federal agencies have statutory and constitutional duties both to make information available to the public and to protect the privacy of people's personal data in record systems.

- The privacy of court records is primarily governed by judicial discretion, and there is a presumption of public access.

- The privacy of other government records is primarily governed by the Freedom of Information Act and state analogues. Many of these laws have exemptions from disclosure to protect privacy.

- Under the First Amendment, once the government releases information to the public, nobody can be sanctioned for further disclosing it. But the government can make information available on the condition of agreeing to curtail how one disseminates it.

- The federal Privacy Act regulates the way that federal agencies collect, use and disclose personal data. In general, it does not apply to private-sector entities or state or local governments. The one exception to this rule concerns its limitations on the use of Social Security numbers.

- The constitutional right to information privacy requires that the government avoid making unwarranted disclosures of personal information. The government must keep data adequately secure.

FAIR INFORMATION PRACTICES (FIPs)

In 1973, the U.S. Department of Health, Education & Welfare (HEW) issued the highly influential report, *Records, Computers, and the Rights of Citizens: Report of the Secretary's Advisory Committee on Automated Personal Data Systems* (1973). The report recommended a code of "fair information practices":

- There must be no personal-data recordkeeping systems whose very existence is secret.

- There must be a way for an individual to find out what information about him is in a record and how it is used.

- There must be a way for an individual to prevent information about him that was obtained for one purpose from being used or made available for other purposes without his consent.

- There must be a way for an individual to correct or amend a record of identifiable information about him.

- Any organization creating, maintaining, using or disseminating records of identifiable personal data must assure the reliability of the data for their intended use and must take reasonable precautions to prevent misuse of the data.

These FIPs have been embodied throughout U.S. privacy statutes as well as in laws around the world.

COURT RECORDS

Common Law Right to Access Court Records
Under the common law, the U.S. Supreme Court concluded that a right exists, though not an absolute one, to access court records. *Nixon v. Warner Communications, Inc.*, 435 U.S. 589 (1978).

The privacy of court records is generally within the discretion of trial court judges. Courts also have the discretion to seal certain court proceedings or portions of court proceedings from the public.

Protective Orders

Federal Rule of Civil Procedure 26(c) provides that judges may, "for good cause shown," issue protective orders where disclosure of information gleaned in discovery might cause a party "annoyance, embarrassment, oppression or undue burden or expense."

Depositions and Interrogatories

"[P]retrial depositions and interrogatories are not public components of a civil trial. Such proceedings were not open to the public at common law, and, in general, they are conducted in private as a matter of modern practice." *Seattle Times Co. v. Rhinehart*, 467 U.S. 20 (1984).

Pseudonymous Litigation

Courts may permit parties to proceed anonymously under special circumstances. "The ultimate test for permitting a plaintiff to proceed anonymously is whether the plaintiff has a substantial privacy right that outweighs the "customary and constitutionally embedded presumption of openness in judicial proceedings." It is the exceptional case in which a plaintiff may proceed under a fictitious name. *Doe v. Frank*, 951 F.2d 320 (11th Cir. 1992).

Juror Privacy

There is a strong presumption that jurors' names be made public, but there is no absolute right of public access to jurors' identities. "[A] judge must find some unusual risk to justify keeping jurors' names confidential; it is not enough to point to possibilities that are present in every criminal prosecution." *United States v. Blagojevich*, 612 F.3d 558 (7th Cir. 2010).

The First Amendment Right to Access

The First Amendment requires that certain judicial proceedings be open to the public when: (1) the proceeding "historically has been open to the press and general public" and (2) access "plays a particularly significant role in the functioning of the judicial process and the government as a whole." *Globe Newspaper v. Superior Court*, 457 U.S. 596 (1982).

The First Amendment requires public access to criminal trials, and the government can deny access only if "the denial is necessitated by a compelling governmental interest and is narrowly tailored to serve that interest." *Globe Newspaper v. Superior Court*, 457 U.S. 596 (1982).

The First Amendment right to access extends to voir dire in criminal cases as well as to pretrial proceedings.

PUBLIC RECORDS

Freedom of Information Act (FOIA)
5 U.S.C. § 552(a) (1966)

Primary Function: To promote transparency in government by requiring federal agencies to disclose information to people who request it.

Applies to: Any person may request records from federal agencies. Congress is not a federal agency and is therefore not subject to the act. Nor is the president or his advisors.

Exemptions: FOIA contains nine enumerated exemptions to disclosure: (1) classified information; (2) internal personnel rules and practices; (3) information exempted by statute; (4) trade secrets and confidential information; (5) certain litigation materials; (6) "personnel and medical files and similar files the disclosure of which would constitute a clearly unwarranted invasion of personal privacy"; (7) law enforcement records that would interfere with litigation, invade privacy, reveal confidential sources or endanger people's safety; (8) certain information involved with the supervision of financial institutions and (9) geological and geophysical data concerning wells. 5 U.S.C. § 552(b).

The Privacy Exemptions: Two of these exemptions explicitly reference privacy concerns:

- Exemption 6 applies to "personnel and medical files and similar files." It has been interpreted broadly to apply beyond personnel and medical information to all types of data.

- Exemption 7(C) exempts law enforcement records from disclosure that "could reasonably be expected to constitute an unwarranted invasion of personal privacy."

When the FOIA otherwise mandates releases of documents, it also requires the redaction of data that would violate privacy, where possible.

Only the government agency can raise Exemptions 6 and 7(C). The individual to whom the information pertains has no right to litigate the issue if the agency does not choose to; nor does the individual have a right to be given notice that her personal information falls within a FOIA request.

Exemption 7(C) has been held to permit more categorical approaches to a decision to withhold information compared to Exemption 6, which typically requires an identification and balancing of relevant interests in disclosure and in privacy. For example, courts will draw a "bright line" and withhold information that identifies third parties in law enforcement records.

Leading Cases

U.S. Dep't of Justice v. Reporters Committee for Freedom of the Press,
489 U.S. 749 (1989)
Concludes that FBI "rap sheets" (aggregated compilations of publicly available information) about individuals are exempt under Exemption 7(C). The court notes that although the information is in the public domain, "there is a vast difference between the public records that might be found after a diligent search of courthouse files, county archives and local police stations throughout the country and a computerized summary located in a single clearinghouse of information." This understanding of privacy differs greatly from the way that most courts understand privacy. Typically, courts often conclude that once information is exposed to the public, it can no longer be private.

United States Dep't of State v. Washington Post Co., 456 U.S. 595 (1982)
Under Exemption 6, "similar files" has a "broad rather than a narrow meaning" and applies to any information that constitutes "a clearly unwarranted invasion of that person's privacy."

National Archives and Records Administration v. Favish,
541 U.S. 157 (2004)
Under FOIA Exemption 7(C), surviving family members have a privacy right "with respect to their close relative's death-scene images."

State Public Records

Common Law Right to Access Public Records
Under the common law, there is "a general right to inspect and copy public records and documents." *Nixon v. Warner Communications, Inc.,* 435 U.S. 589 (1978).

State Freedom of Information Laws
Privacy in records maintained by state agencies is protected under each state's freedom of information law. Most states have some form of exemption for privacy, often patterned after the federal Freedom of Information Act's privacy exemptions. Not all states interpret their privacy exemptions as broadly as the Supreme Court has interpreted FOIA's. Further, certain state FOIAs do not have privacy exemptions.

AL	Ala. Code § 36-12-40		NV	Nev. Rev. Stat. § 239.001
AK	Alaska Stat. § 40.25.110		NH	N.H. Rev. Stat. Ann. § 91:A-1
AZ	Ariz. Rev. Stat. § 39-121		NJ	N.J. Stat. Ann. § 47:1A-1
AR	Ark. Code Ann. § 25-19-101		NM	N.M. Stat. Ann. § 14-2-1
CA	Cal. Gov't Code § 6250		NY	N.Y. Public Officers Law § 84
CO	Colo. Rev. Stat. § 24-72-200.1		NC	N.C. Gen. Stat. § 132-1
CT	Conn. Gen. Stat. § 1-200		ND	N.D. Cent. Code § 44-04-01
DE	Del. Code Ann. tit. 29, § 10001		OH	Ohio Rev. Code § 149.43
DC	D.C. Code Ann. § 2-531		OK	Okla. Stat. tit. 51, § 24A.1
FL	Fla. Stat. § 119.01		OR	Or. Rev. Stat. § 192.410
GA	Ga. Code Ann. § 50-18-70		PA	65 Pa. Stat. Ann. § 67.101
HI	Haw. Rev. Stat. § 92F-11		RI	R.I. Gen. Laws § 38-2-1
ID	Idaho Code § 9-337		SC	S.C. Code Ann. § 30-4-10
IL	5 Ill. Comp. Stat. § 140/1		SD	S.D. Codified Laws § 1-27-1
IN	Ind. Code Ann. § 5-14-3-1		TN	Tenn. Code Ann. § 10-7-501
IA	Iowa Code § 22.1		TX	Tex. Gov't Code Ann. § 552.001
KS	Kan. Stat. Ann. § 45-215		UT	Utah Code Ann. § 63G-2-101
KY	Ky. Rev. Stat. Ann. § 61.870		VT	Vt. Stat. Ann. tit. 1, § 315
LA	La. Rev. Stat. § 44:1		VA	Va. Code Ann. § 2.2-3700
ME	Me. Rev. Stat. Ann. tit. 1, § 401		WA	Wash. Rev. Code § 42.56.001
MD	Md. Code Ann., State-Gov't § 10-611		WV	W. Va. Code § 29B-1-1
MA	Mass. Gen. Laws ch. 66, § 10		WI	Wis. Stat. § 19.31
MI	Mich. Comp. Laws § 15.231		WY	Wyo. Stat. § 16-4-201
MN	Minn. Stat. § 13.01			
MS	Miss. Code Ann. § 25-61-1			
MO	Mo. Rev. Stat. § 610.010			
MT	Mont. Code Ann. § 2-6-101			
NE	Neb. Rev. Stat. § 84-712			

Source: Reporters Committee for Freedom of the Press, Open Government Guide, *www.rcfp.org/ogg.*

The Constitution and Personal Data in Public Records

Prohibited: Establishing post-access restrictions on the disclosure or use of information that is publicly available. Once the information is made available to the public, a state cannot restrict use.

Permitted: Making a record available on *the condition* that certain information is not disclosed or used in a certain manner.

Florida Star v. B.J.F., 491 U.S. 524 (1989)

"[W]here a newspaper publishes truthful information which it has lawfully obtained, punishment may lawfully be imposed, if at all, only when narrowly tailored to a state interest of the highest order."

Los Angeles Police Department v. United Reporting Publishing Corp., 528 U.S. 32 (1999)

A state can make the disclosure of certain public records contingent upon a requester agreeing to refrain from disclosing that information for commercial or other purposes. Such a restriction does not trigger the First Amendment because it is "nothing more than a governmental denial of access to information in its possession."

Ostergren v. Cuccinelli, 615 F.3d 263 (4th Cir. 2010)

A law criminalizing the intentional communication of another person's Social Security number (SSN) violated the First Amendment because the law was not narrowly tailored to achieve its goal. The state made records publicly available without redacting SSNs, and taking measures to redact SSNs would be a narrower way of achieving the government interest in protecting the privacy of SSNs.

When Does the Constitution Limit the Government from Disclosing Personal Information?

Disclosure of personal information in public records can trigger the constitutional right to information privacy in *Whalen v. Roe,* 429 U.S. 589 (1977)—"the individual interest in avoiding disclosure of personal matters." Courts will balance the need for disclosure against the privacy interests of the individuals. See *Paul P. v. Verniero,* 170 F.3d 396 (3d Cir. 1999) (Megan's law information); *Kallstrom v. City of Columbus,* 136 F.3d 1055 (6th Cir. 1998) (personal data of police officers).

Critical Infrastructure Information Act (CIIA)
6 U.S.C. § 131 et seq. (2002)

Primary Function: This law creates new safeguards to prevent governmental disclosure of certain kinds of information by crafting a new FOIA exemption.

Applies to: "Critical infrastructure" is a term that refers to systems and assets vital to the United States. The Critical Infrastructure Information Act (CIIA) covers information about these systems and assets that is not customarily in the public domain and is given to the Department of Homeland Security and accompanied by an express statement indicating an expectation of protection from disclosure.

Exemptions from Disclosure: Under the CIIA, critical infrastructure information is exempt from disclosure under FOIA. Unlike FOIA, which permits rather than requires the withholding of information pursuant to its nine exemptions, the CIIA also requires that covered information voluntarily submitted to DHS not be disclosed under FOIA.

PRIVACY RIGHTS IN GOVERNMENT RECORDS

The Privacy Act
5 U.S.C. § 552a (1974)

Primary Function: To regulate the collection, use and disclosure of personal data by federal agencies.

Applies to: Federal agencies. Does not apply to businesses, private-sector organizations, courts or state or local governments. Although state and local agencies are not covered by the Privacy Act, the exception to this rule concerns the act's rules for use of the Social Security number.

Protects Citizens and Lawfully Admitted Aliens: The Privacy Act applies only to "a citizen of the United States or an alien lawfully admitted for permanent residence." 5 U.S.C. § 552a(a)(2). In contrast, the FOIA applies more broadly to "any person." 5 U.S.C. § 552(a)(3).

Information Protected: Applies only to a "record" contained within a "system of records." A record must be identifiable to an individual. 5 U.S.C. § 552a(a)(4). The record must be kept as part of a "system of records," which is group of records retrievable by people's names or other identifying information. 5 U.S.C. § 552a(a)(5).

The Department of Justice has observed, "The highly technical 'system of records' definition is perhaps the single most important Privacy Act concept, because (with some exceptions ...) it makes coverage under the Act dependent upon the method of retrieval of the record rather than its substantive content." DOJ, Overview of the Privacy Act, Definitions, D. Record, Comment (2010), at http://www.justice.gov/opcl/1974definitions.htm.

Limits on Disclosure: Pursuant to the Privacy Act: "No agency shall disclose any record which is contained in a system of records by any means of communication to any person, or to another agency, except pursuant to a written request by, or with prior written consent of, the individual to whom the record pertains." 5 U.S.C. § 552a(b).

Limited Data Collection and Retention: Agencies shall maintain "only such information about an individual as is relevant and necessary to accomplish a purpose of the agency required to be accomplished by statute or by executive order of the President." 5 U.S.C. § 552a(e)(1).

Notice: Agencies shall inform individuals who make a request about how their personal information will be used. Agencies must publish in the *Federal Register* notices about the systems of records they maintain. 5 U.S.C. §§ 552a(e)(3)-(4).

Data Security: Agencies must also "establish appropriate administrative, technical and physical safeguards to insure the security and confidentiality of records." 5 U.S.C. § 552a(e)(10).

Right to Access and Correct Records: Upon request, individuals can review their records and can ask that the agency correct any inaccuracies in their records. 5 U.S.C. § 552a(d).

Social Security Number (SSN) Usage: The Privacy Act prohibits "any Federal, State, or local government agency" from denying any individual "any right, benefit or privilege provided by law because" of a refusal to disclosure her SSN. Section 7 of the Privacy Act (codified at 5 U.S.C. § 552a note [Disclosure of Social Security Number]). This provision applies beyond federal agencies. It does not apply, however, to any disclosure that is required by federal statute or disclosures of an SSN that have occurred before January 1, 1975, "if such disclosure was required under statute or regulation adopted prior to such date to verify the identity of an individual."

Enforcement: Civil action and/or injunction. 5 U.S.C. § 552a(g). If the agency "acted in a manner which was intentional or willful," it shall be liable for "actual damages sustained by the individual as a result of the refusal or failure, but in no case shall a person entitled to recovery receive less than the sum of $1,000" and costs and attorney fees. 5 U.S.C. § 552a(g)(4).

Exceptions: The Privacy Act has a number of exceptions for records not covered by the requirements of the statute. These exceptions include, among other things: (1) records for law enforcement and prosecution purposes, (2) records required to be disclosed under FOIA, (3) records disclosed for any "routine use" if disclosure is "compatible" with the purpose for which the agency collected the information, (4) disclosure of records to the Census Bureau, (5) disclosure "to a person pursuant to a showing of compelling circumstances affecting the health or safety of an individual," (6) disclosure to Congress, (7) disclosure to the comptroller general, (8) disclosure pursuant to a court order and (9) disclosure to a credit reporting agency. 5 U.S.C. § 552a(b).

Establishing a Violation of the Privacy Act

To establish a violation of the Privacy Act, a plaintiff must prove:

1. The information is a "record" contained "within a system of records."
2. The agency violated its obligations under the act.
3. The violation was "willful or intentional."
4. The plaintiff suffered actual damages.

Leading Cases

Doe v. Chao, 540 U.S. 614 (2004)
The Privacy Act provides for "actual damages sustained by the individual as a result of the refusal or failure [to follow the Privacy Act], but in no case shall a person entitled to recovery receive less than the sum of $1,000." The court held that this provision means that plaintiffs must first prove actual damages to qualify for a minimum statutory award of $1,000. The court reasoned that the words "entitled to recovery" meant that only people entitled to recover actual damages could receive the liquidated sum of $1,000.

FAA v. Cooper, 132 S.Ct. 1441 (2012)
"Actual damages" under the Privacy Act does not extend to damages for mental or emotional distress but only to damages for pecuniary harm.

Pippinger v. Rubin, 129 F.3d 519 (10th Cir. 1997)
Disclosure of records do not violate an individual's rights under the "routine use" exception of 5 U.S.C. § 552a(b)(3) if such records were maintained "for the purpose of properly administering" the workplace and its systems.

United States Dep't of Defense v. Federal Labor Relations Authority, 510 U.S. 487 (1994)
The Privacy Act does not apply to information that must be disclosed under FOIA. If a FOIA privacy exemption applies to the information, however, then the Privacy Act would control and require that the government refrain from disclosing the information to third parties.

Albright v. United States, 631 F.2d 915 (D.C. Cir. 1980)
A videotape of a meeting can be a "record" under the Privacy Act if it "contains a means of identifying an individual by picture or voice."

Quinn v. Stone, 978 F.2d 126 (3d Cir. 1992)
Even publicly accessible information is protected against disclosure.

State Privacy Acts

Most states do not have a statute comparable to the federal Privacy Act. California, Massachusetts, Minnesota, New York and Wisconsin do have such statutes. These states also supplement these omnibus privacy acts for state agencies with more narrowly targeted laws. In the states without such a broad information practices law, there are often narrow laws regulating limited aspects of the state government's use of personal information.

California's Information Practice Act, Cal. Civ. Code § 1798 *et seq.* (1977)

Establishes a number of fair information practices for state agencies, including limitations on the collection of unnecessary data. Cal. Civ. Code § 1798 *et seq.*, § 1798.3-14. The act requires that agencies maintain in their records only information "relevant and necessary to accomplish a purpose of the agency required or authorized by the California Constitution or statute or mandated by the federal government." *Id.* It places general limits on secondary limits of information that agencies collect. It also provides numerous statutory exceptions that permit disclosures of such information. § 1798.24. The sharing of data with governmental agencies outside the state government, such as with federal agencies or agencies in other states, can take place in California only when a state or federal law requires that information be transferred. § 1798.24(f). Individuals have a right to inspect and amend their personal information in agency records. § 1798.32.

Massachusetts' Fair Information Practices Act, Mass. Gen. L. Ann. 66A §1 (1975)

Sets requirements for a "holder" of personal information. It defines a "holder" as "an agency which collects, uses, maintains or disseminates personal data or any person or entity which contracts or has an arrangement with an agency." Mass. Gen. L. Ann. 66A, § 1. A holder maintaining personal data must identify one individual responsible for ensuring that the law's requirements are followed. § 2(a). Holders must "maintain personal data with such accuracy, completeness, timeliness, pertinence and relevance as is necessary to assure fair determination of a data subject's qualifications, character, rights, opportunities or benefits when such determinations are made based upon such data." § 2(h). The law also requires that the data subject be notified of "a demand for data made by means of compulsory legal process." § 2(k).

Minnesota's Government Data Practices Act, Minn. Stat. Ann. 13.01 *et seq.* (1974)

Establishes statutory obligations and responsibilities for all government entities that collect, process and disseminate personal information. Minn. Stat. Ann. 13.01 *et seq.* A state agency must clearly inform the individual about its purposes when collecting personal data as well as the parties authorized by law to receive the data. § 13.04(2). The act allows agencies to share nonpublic data with one another only when such access is specifically authorized or required by state statute or federal law, by the informed consent of the data subject or pursuant to other exceptions. § 13.05(4). Additionally, individuals have a right to access their records. § 13.04(3).

New York's Personal Privacy Protection Act, 46 N.Y. Pub. Off. Law. § 94 (1983)
Fair Information Practices for each state agency "that maintains a system of records." 46 N.Y. Pub. Off. Law § 94. These begin with the requirement that an agency "maintain in its records only such personal information which is relevant and necessary to accomplish a purpose of the agency required to be accomplished by statute or executive order, or to implement a program specifically authorized by law." Such records, when used "to make any determination about any data subject," must also be maintained with "accuracy, relevance, timeliness and completeness." Detailed notice of planned use of the information and other relevant issues is to be provided to the data subject at the time of the initial request. § 94 (d). State agencies are to provide access to their records to data subjects. § 95. Finally, the act forbids release of personal information unless it falls into one of its exceptions to the general rule barring disclosure. § 96.

Wisconsin's Fair Information Practices Act, Wisc. Stat. Ann. § 19.62 *et seq.* (1991)
Sets standards for state agencies in their use of personal information. Wisc. Stat. Ann. § 19.62 *et seq.* These limitations include procedural limits on computer matching. § 19.69. This approach generally tracks that of the federal Computer Matching and Privacy Protection Act (CMPAA). Wisconsin law also forbids state government websites from collecting personally identifiable information from Internet users. § 19.68. It provides an exception, however, for acquisition of IP addresses. It also forbids the state from selling or renting "a record containing an individual's name or address of residence, unless specifically authorized by state law." § 19.71.

State Statutes Regulating Government Website Privacy Policies

AZ	Ariz. Rev. Stat. Ann. §§ 41-4151, 41-4152
AR	Ark. Code § 25-1-114
CA	Cal. Govt. Code § 11019.9
CO	Colo. Rev. Stat. §§ 24-72-501, 24-72-502
DE	Del. Code tit. 29, § 9017C et seq.
IA	Iowa Code § 22.11
IL	Ill. Rev. Stat. ch. 5, § 177/15
ME	Me. Rev. Stat. Ann. tit. 1, § 14-A § 541- 542
MD	Md. State Govt. Code Ann. §§ 10-624 (4)

MI	2003 Mich Pub. Acts, Act 161 (sec. 572 (7))
MN	Minn. Stat. § 13.15
MT	Mont. Code Ann. §§ 2-17-550 to - 553
NY	N.Y . State Tech. Law §§ 201 to 207
SC	S.C. Code Ann. §§ 30-2-10 to 30-2-50
TX	Tex. Govt. Code Ann. § 10-2054.126
UT	Utah Code Ann. §§ 63D-2-101, -102, -103, -104
VA	Va. Code §§ 2.2-3800, - 3801, -3802, -3803

Computer Matching and Privacy Protection Act (CMPPA)
5 U.S.C. § 552a(o) *et seq.* (1988)

The CMPPA amends the Privacy Act to establish procedures for federal agencies engaging in computer matching of records. The CMPPA does not restrict matching programs; instead, it requires agencies to promulgate procedures and provide notice prior to matching. Agencies desiring to implement a matching program must establish a data integrity board and obtain approval from this board. The Office of Management and Budget (OMB) oversees matching programs.

DNA Databases

DNA Identification Act
42 U.S.C. §§ 14131-14135 (1994)

The DNA Identification Act establishes rules for the FBI's index of DNA identification records, called the Combined DNA Index System (CODIS). The database consists of DNA samples from people convicted of a crime or charged with a crime, as well as samples recovered from crime scenes. The statute also sets out the information to be contained in this index and the circumstances under which the data is to be disclosed to other agencies and individuals. 43 U.S.C. § 14133(b)(1)(A)-(C). DNA records can be expunged from CODIS if the conviction that led to inclusion in the index is overturned or the arrest that resulted in inclusion results in dismissed charges or acquittal. 42 U.S.C. § 14132(d).

Leading Cases

U.S. v. Kincade, 379 F.3d 813 (9th Cir. 2004)
The government may store a parolee's DNA and subject the parolee to a blood test without violating the Fourth Amendment, which prohibits unreasonable searches and seizures.

Maryland v. King, 133 S. Ct. 1958 (2013)
Following an arrest supported by probable cause for a serious offense, the government may bring the suspect to the station to be detained in custody and also take and analyze a cheek swab of the arrestee's DNA without violating the Fourth Amendment.

Drivers Privacy Protection Act (DPPA) 18 U.S.C. §§ 2721–2725 (1994)

Primary Function: Regulates the collection, use and disclosure of motor vehicle records.

Protections: States cannot knowingly disclose personal information in motor vehicle records for a purpose not permitted by the DPPA. 18 U.S.C. § 2721(a). No person can knowingly obtain, use or disclose personal information from a motor vehicle record for purposes beyond those permitted by the statute. 18 U.S.C. § 2724(a).

DPPA: Key Points

- DPPA does not just regulate states—it regulates anyone who obtains, uses or discloses personal data from motor vehicle records.

- Even if data is properly obtained under the DPPA, the statute can be violated if data is later used or disclosed improperly.

Exclusions: DPPA defines "personal information" as data "that identifies an individual," but it specifically excludes "information on vehicular accidents, driving violations and driver's status." 18 U.S.C. § 2725(3).

Permissible Uses: DPPA-protected information can be disclosed: (1) for use by any government agency; (2) for motor vehicle safety, theft, recalls and other related matters; (3) for use by a legitimate business to verify personal data submitted by the individual or to obtain correct information to prevent fraud, pursue litigation or recover a debt; (4) in connection with litigation or other legal proceeding; (5) for use in research; (6) for use by insurers for fraud investigation or underwriting; (7) to provide notice to owners of towed or impounded vehicles; (8) for use by a licensed private investigator; (9) for use by an employer to verify information relating to a holder of a commercial driver's license; (10) for use in the operation of private toll transportation facilities; (11) with the express consent of the person to whom the information pertains; (12) for bulk distribution for surveys, marketing and solicitation with express consent of the person to whom the information pertains; (13) for use by any requester after obtaining the express consent of the person to whom the information pertains or (14) for any other use specifically authorized by state law if such use involves motor vehicle operation or public safety. 18 U.S.C. § 2721(b).

Opt In: In order to disclose a driver's personal information for marketing or other restricted uses, the driver must affirmatively indicate her consent (opt in). 18 U.S.C. § 2721(b) and (d).

Enforcement: Civil liability and criminal fines. Private right of action when a person "knowingly obtains, discloses or uses personal information from a motor vehicle record for a purpose not permitted under this chapter." 18 U.S.C. § 2724.

Leading Cases

Reno v. Condon, 528 U.S. 141 (2000)
DPPA is a valid exercise of Congress's Commerce Clause powers because personal identifying information is a thing in interstate commerce.

Kehoe v. Fidelity Federal Bank & Trust, 421 F.3d 1209 (11th Cir. 2005)
"A plaintiff need not prove a measure of actual damages to recover liquidated damages under the DPPA and certainly need not prove actual damages to recover the other types of remedies listed in § 2724(b)."

Pichler v. UNITE, 542 F.3d 380 (3d Cir. 2007)
For civil liability, a defendant does not need to know that its obtaining, use or disclosure of information is prohibited by DPPA; acting "knowingly" only requires knowledge of the obtaining, use or disclosure, not its impermissibility.

Senne v. Village of Palatine --- F.3d ----, 2012 WL 315633 (7th Cir. 2012)
Placement of personal data from DMV records such as sex, age, height, weight and home address on parking citations left on cars in public violated DPPA. The disclosure of the data on the citation did not fall under DPPA's exceptions for carrying out law enforcement agency functions or for use in connection with any legal proceedings. The disclosure of the data was more than the minimum necessary to achieve the law enforcement purpose.

Identification Records and Requirements

Leading Cases

Kolender v. Lawson, 461 U.S. 352 (1983)
A law requiring any person who "loiters or wanders . . . without apparent reason or business" to "identify himself and to account for his presence when requested by any peace officer to do so" was struck down as unconstitutionally vague.

Carey v. Nevada Gaming Control Board, 279 F.3d 873 (9th Cir. 2002)
Statutes requiring individuals detained by officials to identify themselves or face criminal sanctions were struck down as violating the Fourth Amendment because the statutes did not require probable cause or any type of suspicion on the part of the officials.

Hiibel v. Sixth Judicial District Court, 542 U.S. 177 (2004)
Upholding a Nevada statute permitting officers to stop and to request the name of an individual based on reasonable and articulable suspicion of criminal involvement. This statute did not violate the Fourth Amendment.

Social Security Numbers

Social Security Numbers

The closest thing that the United States has to a national identifier is the Social Security number (SSN). A nine-digit identifier, the SSN was created in 1936 as part of the Social Security System.

Section 7 of the Privacy Act of 1974 prohibits any governmental agency from denying any right, benefit, or privilege merely because an individual refused to disclose his or her SSN.

Several states have passed laws providing special protections against the use and disclosure of SSNs.

Leading Cases

Greidinger v. Davis, 988 F.2d 1344 (4th Cir. 1993)
Virginia statute requiring disclosure of voters' SSNs was not narrowly tailored to advance a compelling state interest.

Beacon Journal v. City of Akron, 70 Ohio St. 3d 605 (Ohio 1994)
SSNs were not considered "public records" for the purposes of Ohio's Public Records Act.

City of Kirkland v. Sheehan, 2001 WL 1751590 (Wash. Sup. Ct. 2001)
Disclosure of police officers' personal data was protected under the First Amendment, except for the disclosure of SSNs.

PRIVACY IMPACT ASSESSMENTS (PIAs)

E-Government Act
44 U.S.C. § 208 (2002)

Section 208 of the E-Government Act requires all federal agencies to conduct a Privacy Impact Assessment (PIA) whenever they develop a new technology involving the collection, use or disclosure of personal data. Under applicable OMB guidance for implementing the E-Government Act, PIAs are to identify and evaluate potential threats to individual privacy, identify appropriate risk mitigation measures and explain the rationale behind the final design choice.

CHIEF INFORMATION OFFICERS (CIOs)

Federal Information Security Management Act (FISMA)
44 U.S.C. § 3541 (2002)

Enacted as part of the E-Government Act, FISMA aims to provide a "comprehensive framework" for data security to protect federal information systems. Federal agencies must designate a chief information officer (CIO), develop an information security program and evaluate the effectiveness of information security policies and practices.

FOR FURTHER REFERENCE

Treatises

Department of Justice, *Guide to the Freedom of Information Act* (2009)
Comprehensive and highly useful guide to FOIA, posted online at http://www.justice.gov/oip/foia_guide09.htm.

Department of Justice, *Office of Privacy and Civil Liberties,*
Overview of the Privacy Act (2010)
Comprehensive and highly useful guide to the Privacy Act, posted online at http://www.justice.gov/opcl/1974privacyact-overview.htm.

Richard Pierce, *Administrative Law Treatise* (5th ed., 2010)
Leading administrative law treatise features detailed analysis of FOIA and other open government acts.

Jacob Stein et al., *Administrative Law* (2010)
The third volume of this multivolume treatise examines the FOIA and Privacy Act.

Articles and Other Sources

Kenneth A. Bamberger & Deirdre K. Mulligan, *Privacy Decisionmaking in Administrative Agencies,* 75 U. Chi. L. Rev. 75 (2008)
Explores the different paths taken for the development of PIAs by the Department of Homeland Security and the Department of State.

Anthony T. Kronman, *The Privacy Exemption to the Freedom of Information Act,* 9 J. Legal Stud. 727 (1980)
Classic article about FOIA and privacy.

Erin Murphy, License, Registration, *Cheek Swab: DNA Testing and the Divided Court,* 127 Harv. L. Rev. 161 (2013)
Criticizes *Maryland v. King* and argues that the Supreme Court broadly embraced expansive forensic DNA testing without meaningful oversight.

Priscilla Regan, *Legislating Privacy* (1995)
Background of congressional enactment of leading privacy laws, including the Privacy Act of 1974.

Daniel J. Solove, *Access and Aggregation: Public Records, Privacy, and the Constitution,* 86 Minn. L. Rev. 1137 (2002)
Examines the tension between transparency and privacy in the context of public records.

Lior Strahilevitz, *Pseudonymous Litigation,* 77 U. Chi. L. Rev. 1239 (2010)
Argues that in certain instances it will be optimal for the legal system to permit a party to litigate to final judgment using a pseudonym and only then to consider revealing the litigant's identity at the conclusion of proceedings.

Peter A. Winn, *Online Court Records: Balancing Judicial Accountability and Privacy in an Age of Electronic Information,* 79 Wash. L. Rev. 307 (2004)
Numerous new privacy issues are being raised as court records are digitized and made accessible online.

CHAPTER 8

Financial Data

ESSENTIAL POINTS

The Financial Services Industry

- The category of the applicable regulation of financial information will turn on the legal category in which the data falls or the industry that processes the information. For example, the Fair Credit Reporting Act applies to "any consumer reporting agency" that furnishes a "consumer report." The Gramm-Leach-Bliley Act applies to all financial institutions.

- Tort regulations, such as breach of confidentiality and negligence, can set common law standards for the processing and storage of personal information.

- A special federal statute, Internal Code § 6103, regulates access to federal tax return information. This law provides for numerous exceptions to the general rule of tax return confidentiality.

- Many important regulations for financial information occur at the state level.

- As in other areas of information privacy, California has its own regulations in place for financial information. Its SB1 requires opt-in sharing for financial institutions sharing data with nonaffiliated companies. Vermont also has issued a similar rule.

Fair Credit Reporting Act (FCRA)
15 U.S.C. § 1681 (1970)

Primary Function: To regulate the consumer reporting industry and provide privacy rights in consumer reports.

Scope: FCRA applies to "any consumer reporting agency" that furnishes a "consumer report." 15 U.S.C. § 1681b.

Key Definitions: The key definitions under FCRA are what constitutes a "consumer report" and what constitutes a "consumer reporting agency" (CRA):

1. *Consumer Report:* A "consumer report" is any communication by a consumer reporting agency relating to a consumer's creditworthiness, reputation and character that is for the purpose of determining eligibility for credit, insurance, employment or other authorized purposes under § 1681b (see permissible uses of credit reports below). 15 U.S.C. § 1681a(d).

2. *Consumer Reporting Agency:* A "consumer reporting agency" is any person who regularly assembles or evaluates consumer credit information for the purpose of furnishing consumer reports to third parties. 15 U.S.C. § 1681b(f).

FCRA Applicability Is Determined by the Purpose of Original Collection: Courts have held that "even if a report is used or expected to be used for a non-consumer purpose, it may still fall within the definition of a consumer report if it contains information that was originally collected by a consumer reporting agency with the expectation that it would be used for a consumer purpose." *Ippolito v. WNS, Inc.,* 864 F.2d 440 (7th Cir. 1988); *Bakker v. McKinnon,* 152 F.3d 1007 (8th Cir. 1998).

Permissible Uses of Consumer Reports: A consumer reporting agency can furnish a consumer report only for certain uses. These uses also define FCRA's applicability—if any entity collects information for these purposes in order to provide it to others, then it becomes a consumer reporting agency. Permissible purposes include: (1) in response to a court order or grand jury subpoena; (2) to the person to whom the report pertains; (3) to a "person which [the agency] has reason to believe" intends to use the information in connection with (a) the extension of credit to a consumer, (b) employment purposes, (c) insurance underwriting, (d) licensing or the conferral of government benefits, (e) assessment of credit risks associated with an existing credit obligation or (f) a "legitimate business need" when engaging in "a business transaction involving the consumer"; (4) to establish a person's capacity to pay child support; (5) to an agency administering a state plan for use to set initial or modified child support award; or (6) to the FDIC or National Credit Union Administration. 15 U.S.C. § 1681b(a).

Employment Purposes: When an employer or potential employer seeks a consumer report for employment purposes, she must first disclose in writing to the consumer that a consumer report may be obtained, and the consumer must authorize in writing that the report can be obtained. The person seeking the report from a consumer reporting agency must certify that she obtained the consent of the individual and that she will not use the information in violation of any equal employment opportunity law or regulation. 15 U.S.C. § 1681b(b). If the person who obtained the report takes adverse action based in any way on the report, she must provide the consumer with a copy of the report and a description of the consumer's rights under the FCRA. § 1681b(b).

Government Access: Pursuant to the FCRA, "a consumer reporting agency may furnish identifying information respecting any customer, limited to his name, address, former addresses, places of employment or former places of employment, to a governmental agency." 15 U.S.C. § 1681f.

The Consumer Financial Protection Bureau

The Dodd-Frank Act of 2010 assigned a new federal agency, the Consumer Financial Protection Bureau (CFPB), primary federal authority for enforcement and rule making regarding the FCRA. The CFPB is an independent agency located within the Federal Reserve. It is also funded by the Federal Reserve.

The Dodd-Frank Act also creates a Consumer Financial Civil Penalty Fund to receive civil penalties obtained by the CFPB for violations of consumer financial protection statutes. The fund is to be used to pay victims of these violations and to support financial literacy and consumer education programs.

The Dodd-Frank Act gives the CFPB broad rule-making authority to "administer and carry out the purposes and objectives of" FCRA and "to prevent evasions thereof." Dodd-Frank Act, § 1022(b)(1). It also has broad powers of supervision and examination of financial institutions in the market for consumer financial products or services. Finally, the CFPB has enforcement powers over FCRA and a number of other consumer protection laws, including the Electronic Funds Transfer Act, the Fair Debt Collection Practices Act and certain sections of the Gramm-Leach-Bliley Act.

Under the Dodd-Frank Act, however, the FTC retains rule-making authority regarding the Disposal Rule, the Red Flags Rule and the Gramm-Leach-Bliley Act's Safeguards Rule. The FTC also retains power to carry out certain kinds of investigations and shares power with the CFPB to enforce consumer protection laws with regard to nonbank financial institutions.

Memorandum of Understanding (MOU) Between the Consumer Financial Protection Bureau and the Federal Trade Commission (2012)
MOU jointly issued by FTC and CFPB in light of the grant of FCRA enforcement power to CFPB in the Dodd-Frank Act. The agencies have agreed to meet regularly to coordinate enforcement actions, inform the other agency before initiating enforcement actions to avoid duplicative enforcement efforts, consult on rulemaking and guidance initiatives, cooperate on consumer education efforts and to share consumer complaints.

Limitations on Information Contained in Consumer Reports: Consumer reporting agencies are excluded from providing certain information in consumer reports. 15 U.S.C. § 1681c(b).

CREDIT REPORTING LIMITS		
	WHEN DISCLOSURE IS PROHIBITED	**WHEN DISCLOSURE IS ALWAYS ALLOWED**
Bankruptcy Proceedings	> 10 years old	Credit transaction > $150,000
Suits and Judgments	> 7 years old	Life Insurance Policy > $150,000
Paid Tax Liens	> 7 years old	Employment Salary > $75,000
Criminal Records	> 7 years old	

Investigative Consumer Reports: An "investigative consumer report" is "a consumer report or portion thereof in which information on a consumer's character, general reputation, personal characteristics or mode of living is obtained through personal interviews with neighbors, friends or associates." 15 U.S.C. § 1681a(f). Consumers must be notified about the preparation of these reports. If the report contains any adverse information about a person gleaned from interviews with neighbors, friends or associates, the agency must take reasonable steps to corroborate that information "from an additional source that has independent and direct knowledge of the information" or ensure that "the person interviewed is the best possible source of the information." 15 U.S.C. § 1681d(d).

Accuracy: "Whenever a consumer reporting agency prepares a consumer report, it shall follow reasonable procedures to assure maximum possible accuracy of the information concerning the individual about whom the report relates." § 1681e(b).

Disclosures to the Consumer: The FCRA requires that consumer reporting agencies, upon request of the consumer, disclose, among other things, "[a]ll the information in the consumer's file at the time of the request, except … any information concerning credit scores or any other risk scores or predictors relating to the consumer" as well as the sources of the information and a list of each person who procured a consumer report. 15 U.S.C. § 1681g.

Procedures in Case of Disputed Accuracy: Consumers can dispute the completeness or accuracy of information in their file. The agency must reinvestigate free of charge. 15 U.S.C. § 1681i(a)(1). Errors must be fixed promptly. "If the reinvestigation does not resolve the dispute, the consumer may file a brief statement setting forth the nature of the dispute." 15 U.S.C. § 1681i(b). In any subsequent consumer report, the agency must clearly note that the information in question is disputed by the consumer and provide the consumer's statement. 15 U.S.C. § 1681i(c).

Requirements on Users of Consumer Reports: If a user of a consumer report takes any adverse action on a consumer based in any way on the report, the user shall provide notice of the adverse action to the consumer, information for the consumer to contact the consumer reporting agency that prepared the report and notice of the consumer's right to obtain a free copy of the report and to dispute its accuracy. 15 U.S.C. § 1681m(a).

Civil Liability: A person who "willfully fails to comply with any requirement" of the FCRA is liable to the consumer for actual damages or damages between $100 and $1,000, as well as punitive damages and attorneys' fees and costs. 15 U.S.C. § 1681n. Negligent failure to comply with any requirement of the FCRA results in liability to the consumer for actual damages as well as attorneys' fees and costs. § 1681n. The FTC also has the power to enforce the FCRA.

One-Call Fraud Alerts: When a consumer alerts one consumer reporting agency of potential fraud, that agency must notify the other consumer reporting agencies. 15 U.S.C. § 1681c-1.

Business Transaction Data: Victims of identity theft can require creditors to disclose information about the fraudulent transactions carried out in the victim's name. 15 U.S.C. § 1681g(e)(1).

Block of Identity Theft Information: FCRA allows identity theft victims to block the reporting of information related to the identity theft. 15 U.S.C. § 1681c-2.

Free Consumer Reports: Consumer reporting agencies must provide a free consumer report once a year at the request of a consumer. Consumers can obtain their reports at http://annualcreditreport.com.

Statute of Limitations: FCRA's statute of limitation extends to two years after the date when the plaintiff discovers the violation or five years after the date of the violation, whichever occurs earlier.

Enforcement: FCRA creates liability for willfully or negligently failing to comply with its requirements:

1. *Willful Violations:* People can recover actual damages or statutory damages between $100 and $1,000 for willful violations, plus punitive damages and attorneys' fees and costs. 15 U.S.C. § 1681n. "Willful" means that one intentionally commits an act "in conscious disregard for the rights of others." In *Safeco Insurance Co. v. Burr,* 551 U.S. 47 (2007), the Supreme Court held that acting in "reckless disregard" of a consumer's rights under FCRA was sufficient to establish willfulness.

2. *Negligent Violations:* People can recover actual damages as a result of negligent violations plus attorneys' fees and costs. 15 U.S.C. § 1681o.

Qualified Immunity: FCRA provides for civil liability for willful and negligent noncompliance. 15 U.S.C. §§ 1681n-1681o. Beyond these provisions in FCRA, "no consumer may bring any action or proceeding in the nature of defamation, invasion of privacy or negligence with respect to the reporting of information against any consumer reporting agency, or any user of information, or any person who furnishes information to a consumer reporting agency, based on information disclosed pursuant to [FCRA]." The only exception to this immunity is for "false information furnished with malice or willful intent to injure such consumer." § 1681h(e).

Preemption: After amendment through the Fair and Accurate Credit Transactions Act of 2003 (FACTA), FCRA has complicated measures in place for preemption. Sometimes it preempts state laws for certain kinds of subject matters. 15 USC § 1681t(b). At other times, FCRA preempts only for certain required conduct. § 1681t(b)5. This kind of preemption restricts the assignment of federal power only to the behavior mandated. For example, FACTA requires consumer reporting agencies to place fraud alerts on consumer credit files under certain circumstances. Beyond this conduct preemption, however, it allows states to engage in further regulation regarding the larger subject area, which is identity theft.

FCRA: Keys to Compliance

1. FCRA applies only to a "consumer reporting agency" that furnishes a " consumer report." Many uses of financial information fall outside its jurisdictional scope.

2. Important restrictions are placed on certain kinds of information by FCRA simply because of the age of the underlying information.

3. Once a consumer report contains certain kinds of information relating to the consumer's character and gained through interviews, the credit reporting agency must meet additional safeguards.

4. The overall touchstone of FCRA is to follow "reasonable procedures to assure maximum possible accuracy of the information" about the concerned individual.

Leading Cases

Dun & Bradstreet, Inc. v. Greenmoss Builders, Inc., 472 U.S. 749 (1985)
A consumer reporting agency reporting on an individual is engaging in "speech on matters of purely private concern" and its report receives lesser First Amendment protection than other forms of speech. All forms of damages (compensatory, presumed and punitive) are available without showing "actual malice."

Sarver v. Experian Information Solutions, 390 F.3d 969 (7th Cir. 2004)
Seventh Circuit finds that FCRA does not require each credit reporting agency to examine each credit report for "anomalous information" in order for its procedures to be considered reasonable. Such an examination is not needed in the "absence of notice of prevalent unreliable information from a reporting lender."

Dennis v. BEH-1, LLC, 520 F.3d 1066 (9th Cir. 2007) (amended opinion)
Ninth Circuit finds that a credit reporting agency can be liable under FCRA when it overlooks or misinterprets documents in a court file. After the plaintiff notified the credit reporting agency of the error in its report, the credit reporting agency failed to follow reasonable procedures by incorrectly interpreting a registry entry in a court's file and a legal document of which it had received a copy. The Ninth Circuit stated, "This case illustrates how important it is for Experian, a company that traffics in the reputation of ordinary people, to train its employees to understand the legal significance of the documents they rely upon."

Sloane v. Equifax Information Services, LLC, 510 F.3d 495 (4th Cir. 2007)
Equifax failed to correct errors in Sloane's credit report 21 months after she had reported them. The Fourth Circuit upholds the verdict that Equifax violated FCRA by negligently failing to, among other things, "follow reasonable procedures to assure maximum accuracy on her credit report" and "failing to conduct a reasonable investigation to determine whether disputed information in her credit report was inaccurate."

FTC FCRA Enforcement Actions

FTC v. Teletrack, Inc. (2011)
Teletrack sold credit reports to various lenders and created a database of information gleaned from this business. It then sold the database to marketers. The FTC charged that Teletrack violated FCRA because marketing was not a "permissible purpose" under FCRA. The settlement included a $1.8 million penalty.

FTC v. Spokeo (2012)
Spokeo, a data broker, settled with the FTC for marketing consumer profiles to employers without complying with FCRA. FCRA's scope is based on the way data is used. It limits the use of data even in the context of determinations of eligibility for employment. FCRA's applicability turns on the way the data is marketed and the amount used by entities that typically use data to evaluate employment eligibility. The FTC did not accept as valid Spokeo's disclaimer that it was not a consumer reporting agency. Spokeo agreed to pay $800,000 to settle the FTC charges.

FTC v. HireRight Solutions, Inc. (2012)
HireRight, an employment background screening company, is subject to FCRA because its reports are "consumer reports." HireRight did not follow many FCRA requirements. In its settlement with the FTC, it agreed to pay a $2.6 million penalty.

TeleCheck Services, Inc. (FTC 2014)
TeleCheck is a leading check authorization service company. It provides recommendations to merchants as to whether or not to accept checks from consumers. In its complaint, the FTC argued that the check authorization recommendations of TeleCheck were consumer reports under the FCRA. Although its practices were regulated by this statute, TeleCheck violated FCRA by failing to follow its procedures for disputed information, including reinvestigations of the information and providing FCRA-required notice to consumers. It was also alleged to have failed to follow reasonable procedures to assure the maximum possible accuracy of the information that it provided to merchants. TeleCheck agreed to a $3.5 million penalty, the second largest obtained by the FTC in an FRCA case. TeleCheck also agreed to follow all FCRA requirements, including those for reinvestigations of disputes and notice to consumers.

Certegy Check Services, Inc. (FTC 2013)

According to the FTC's complaint, Certegy, a leading check authorization service company, was also a consumer reporting agent (CRA) under the FCRA. Moreover, the FTC alleged that Certegy was also a "nationwide specialty consumer reporting agency" with additional responsibilities under the FCRA section 603(x). Certegy violated the Fair Credit Reporting Act by failing: (1) to follow proper reasonable procedures to assure maximum possible accuracy of consumers' report information; (2) to reinvestigate disputed information; and (3) to provide consumers with an annual file disclosure as required by law. Certegy agreed to a $3.5 million civil penalty and to follow required procedures for tracking the handling of customer disputes and correcting inaccuracies in a credit report.

Filiquarian Publishing, LLC, Choice Level, LLC, and Joshua Linsk (FTC 2013)

This settlement was the first FCRA case involving mobile apps. Filiquarian, Choice Level, and CEO Linsk (respondents) were responsible for a mobile app that compiled and sold criminal record reports from specific states. It advertised its service as allowing individuals to conduct a "quick criminal background check for convictions" in specific states. It also had provided a disclaimer in its "terms and conditions" stating that its products were not to be considered "screening products" for employment, credit, and certain other purposes. Its disclaimer also stated that the company was not compliant with FCRA and that any person using its product for FCRA purposes would assume sole responsibility for compliance with this statute and any other applicable laws. Despite this disclaimer, the FTC alleged that Filiquarian was a consumer reporting agency and had violated the law by failing to comply with required FCRA procedures. Its disclaimers could not be used to avoid FCRA liability because the company had advertised that its reports could be used by customers for employment purposes and could expect such use of its reports. Under the terms of the settlement, the respondents agreed to follow the FCRA and only to furnish reports to persons who have a "permissible purpose" under the statute and "maintain reasonable procedures to assure the maximum possible accuracy" of information.

THE USE AND DISCLOSURE OF FINANCIAL INFORMATION

Gramm-Leach-Bliley Act (GLBA)
15 U.S.C. §§ 6801–6809 (1999)

Primary Function: To facilitate data sharing among financial institutions and their affiliates while protecting customer privacy.

Applies to: All financial institutions.

Key Definition—Nonpublic Personal Information: The privacy provisions of the GLBA apply only to "nonpublic personal information" that consists of "personally identifiable financial information." 15 U.S.C. § 6809(4).

Sharing of Information with Affiliated Companies: Financial institutions can share nonpublic personal information with affiliates. Customers must be provided notice via a general privacy policy. No right to opt out. 15 U.S.C. § 6802(a).

Sharing of Information with Third Parties: Financial institutions can share nonpublic personal information with nonaffiliated companies only if they first provide individuals with the ability to opt out of the disclosure. 15 U.S.C. § 6802(b). The financial institution must have a contract with the third party requiring it to maintain the confidentiality of the information. These provisions do not apply to disclosures to consumer reporting agencies.

Limits on Disclosure: Financial institutions cannot disclose (other than to consumer reporting agencies) account numbers or credit card numbers for use in direct marketing. 15 U.S.C. § 6802(d).

Privacy Notices: The GLBA requires that financial institutions inform customers of their privacy policies. 15 U.S.C. § 6803(a).

Security: Financial institutions "shall develop, implement and maintain a comprehensive information security program." 16 C.F.R. § 314.3(a), 67 Fed. Reg. 36484 (2002).

Preemption: The GLBA does not preempt state laws that provide greater privacy protection. 15 U.S.C. § 6807(b).

The Safeguards Rule: As part of its role implementing GLBA, the FTC issued the Safeguards Rule. 16 CFR Part 314, 67 Fed. Reg. 36484 (2002). This regulation requires financial institutions that fall under the FTC's jurisdiction to establish administrative, technical and physical information safeguards. These companies must develop a comprehensive written information security program, and one that appropriately responds to the company's size and complexity, the nature and scope of its activities and the sensitivity of the customer data that it handles. The Safeguards Rule also requires designation of an employee or employees to coordinate the company's information security program, which can encourage introduction of a chief privacy officer position at organizations that do not yet have one. 16 C.F.R. § 314 (2002).

Consumer Financial Protection Bureau (CFPB) and FTC: The Dodd-Frank Act, which created the CFPB, also assigned that agency broad enforcement powers over a series of "enumerated consumer laws," including the GLBA. It preserved a continuing FTC role, however, for GLBA's provisions concerning a financial institution's use and protection of nonpublic consumer information. 15 U.S.C. §§ 6802-6809. The CFPB also has authority to make determinations as to whether or not a state law is preempted.

Consumer Financial Protection Bureau (CFPB), Amendment to the Annual Privacy Notice Requirement Under Gramm-Leach-Bliley (Regulation P), 12 CFR Part 1016 (2014)

The CFPB amended Regulation P to allow certain financial institutions that meet its new requirements to post privacy policies on their website rather than engage in an annual mailing of such privacy policies to their customers. Financial institutions must still mail annual notices, however, to any customer who requests them by telephone. To be eligible for this alternative method of providing notice, the financial institution must (1) not have information sharing practices that trigger opt-out rights under GLBA; (2) not have included in its annual privacy notice the notice and opt-out rights of FCRA section 603; (3) not share information with an affiliate and previously provided notice and opt-out rights pursuant to FCR section 624 in the annual notice; (4) have information in the privacy notice that has not changed since the last notice was sent; and (5) utilize the model form provided in Regulation P. This CFPB Rule is not applicable to an entity that is subject to the GLBA regulations of the FTC, the Securities and Exchange Commission, or the Commodities Futures Trading Commission.

Torts and Financial Privacy

Breach of Confidentiality Tort

A bank can be liable to a customer when it has a duty to maintain the confidentiality of the customer's information and it breaches that duty. For example, in *Peterson v. Idaho First Nat'l Bank,* 367 P.2d 284 (Idaho 1961), the court held that a bank could be sued for breach of confidentiality for disclosing customer information because "it is an implied term of the contract between the banker and his customer that the banker will not divulge to third persons, without the consent of the customer, express or implied, either the state of the customer's account or any of his transactions with the bank, or any information relating to the customer acquired through the keeping of his account."

Several other jurisdictions have held likewise. See, e.g., *Barnett Bank of West Florida v. Hooper,* 498 So. 2d 923 (Fla. 1986); *Indiana Nat'l Bank v. Chapman,* 482 N.E.2d 474 (Ind. App. 1985); *Suburban Trust Co. v. Waller,* 408 A.2d 758 (Md. App. 1979); *Richfield Bank & Trust Co. v. Sjogren,* 244 N.W.2d 648 (Minn. 1976); *McGuire v. Shubert,* 722 A.2d 1087 (Pa. Super. 1998).

Negligence

The tort of negligence requires that a plaintiff prove, among other elements, a duty of care that the defendant owed to the plaintiff, and conduct by the defendant that falls below the applicable standard of care, i.e., that breaches that duty. In general, the defendant's required duty of conduct is that of "reasonable care" under the circumstances. In *Wolfe v. MBNA America Bank*, 485 F. Supp. 2d 874 (W.D. Tenn. 2007), the district court found that the defendant bank had "a duty to verify the authenticity and accuracy of a credit account application before issuing a credit card." This duty did not involve an obligation to prevent all identity theft, but rather one "to implement reasonable and cost-effective verification methods that can prevent criminals, in some instances, from obtaining a credit card with a stolen identity."

A different result was reached in *Huggins v. Citibank, N.A.*, 585 S.E.2d 275 (W.C. 2003), where the South Carolina Supreme Court found no duty between a credit card–issuing bank and a victim of identity theft. The Huggins court placed significant weight on the lack of an established prior relationship between the bank and the plaintiff, who was not a customer of the defendant bank.

State Financial Statutes

Vermont's Privacy of Consumer Financial and Health Information Regulation, 21-010-16 Vt. Code R. (2001)

Requires opt in for financial institutions sharing data with nonaffiliated companies.

California's Financial Information Privacy Act (SB1), Cal. Fin. Code §§ 4050–4060 (2003)

Requires opt in for financial institutions sharing data with nonaffiliated companies. Permits financial institutions to offer incentives or discounts for people to opt in.

California's SB1 and FCRA Preemption

Financial institutions challenged SB1, arguing that it was preempted by FCRA. In *American Bankers Association v. Gould,* 412 F.3d 1081 (9th Cir. 2005), the court concluded that "SB1 is preempted [by FCRA] to the extent that it applies to information shared between affiliates concerning consumers' credit worthiness, credit standing, credit capacity, character, general reputation, personal characteristics or mode of living that is used, expected to be used or collected for the purpose of establishing eligibility for 'credit or insurance,' employment or other authorized purpose."

In a later opinion, *American Bankers Association v. Lockyer,* 541 F.3d 1214 (9th Cir. 2008), the Ninth Circuit held that SB1 had valid non-preempted applications pertaining to the sharing of non-consumer report information by affiliates. SB1 remains valid when narrowed to exclude the regulation of consumer report information from its reach.

TAX PRIVACY

Internal Revenue Code
26 U.S.C. §§ 6103, 7216 (1976)

Primary Function: To protect confidentiality of tax information.

Confidentiality: Prior to the Tax Reform Act of 1976, federal tax returns were considered "public records," but ones available only upon order of the president and rules and regulations prescribed by the secretary of the treasury. The Tax Reform Act changed this previous default of publicity for tax information to one of confidentiality that could be altered only through statutory disclosure permissions. Only an explicit legal authorization can trump the general mandate of confidentiality of tax return information.

Permissible Disclosures: There are many legal authorizations for disclosure of tax information, such as: (1) to Congress if the head of a congressional committee makes a written request to the IRS, 26 U.S.C. § 6103(f)(1-3); (2) to the president and executive branch employees if the president issues a written request "signed by him personally," 26 U.S.C. § 6103(g); (3) to the Department of Treasury and Department of Justice for purposes of tax administration, such as for use in judicial or administrative tax proceedings; (4) pursuant to an ex parte order from a federal district judge or magistrate to federal officials who are preparing for a proceeding pertaining to "the enforcement of a specifically designated federal criminal statute (not involving tax administration) to which the United States … may be a party," 26 U.S.C. § 6103(i); (5) to inform appropriate officials for investigations of terrorist activities; (6) to various parties in an emergency situation; and (7) to child support enforcement agencies in the states.

Restrictions on Tax Preparers: The Internal Revenue Code, 26 U.S.C. § 7216, prohibits anyone preparing tax returns from knowingly or recklessly disclosing any data furnished for the preparation of the return or using such data for any purpose beyond preparing the return. Violations are punished as a misdemeanor, with a fine of up to $1,000 and up to one year of imprisonment, along with paying the costs of prosecution.

IDENTITY THEFT

Identity Theft Assumption and Deterrence Act
18 U.S.C. § 1028 (1998)

The act makes it a federal crime to "knowingly transfer or use, without lawful authority, a means of identification of another person with the intent to commit, or to aid or abet, any unlawful activity that constitutes a violation of federal law, or that constitutes a felony under any applicable state or local law."

State Identity Theft Statutes

The vast majority of states have statutes concerning identity theft, often focusing primarily on criminalizing it. See, e.g., Ariz. Rev. Stat. Ann. § 13-2008(D); Cal. Penal Code § 530.5(a); Fla. Stat. Ann. § 817.568. Many states punish identity theft based on the dollar value of the things the thief wrongfully took.

California has enacted numerous innovative provisions to combat identity theft. These include:

Cal. Civil Code § 1748.95
Victims can obtain the fraudulent applications that the identity thief made as well as a record of the thief's transactions in the victim's name.

Cal. Civ. Code § 1788.18
Assists victims in stopping debt collectors from continuing to try to collect debts that the thief created.

Cal. Civ. Code § 1785.15.3(b
Requires consumer credit reporting agencies to furnish identity theft victims, upon request, with up to 12 free copies of their credit files during a consecutive 12-month period.

Wolfe v. MBNA America Bank, 485 F. Supp. 2d 874 (W.D. Tenn. 2007)
The plaintiff sued a bank that issued a credit card in his name to an identity thief. The court held that the duty to verify the information contained in a credit card application required only "reasonable and cost-effective verification methods that can prevent criminals, in some instances, from obtaining a credit card with a stolen identity." That issue is one for the trier of fact.

Huggins v. Citibank, N.A., 585 S.E.2d 275 (S.C. 2003)
The relationship between credit card issuers and potential victims of identity theft was far too attenuated to rise to the level of duty between them. There can be no negligence in tort without a duty running from the defendant to the plaintiff.

GOVERNMENT ACCESS TO FINANCIAL INFORMATION
See Chapter 7

FOR FURTHER REFERENCE

Treatises

L. Richard Fischer, *The Law of Financial Privacy* (2004)

IRS, *Disclosure and Privacy Law Reference Guide* (2007)
Analysis of the chief disclosure laws that affect the IRS, including the applicable aspects of the Internal Revenue Code, FOIA and the Privacy Act. This guide also considers litigation privileges and disclosures for nontax criminal purposes.

Articles and Other Sources

Congressional Research Service, *The Dodd-Frank Wall Street Reform and Consumer Protection Act: Title X, The Consumer Financial Protection Bureau* (July 21, 2010)
Discusses the power of the Consumer Financial Protection Bureau to enforce a variety of consumer protection statutes.

Elizabeth D. De Armond, *Frothy Chaos: Modern Data Warehousing and Old-Fashioned Defamation,* 41 Val. U. L. Rev. 1061 (2007)
A critique of FCRA preemption and duties to consumers under FCRA.

Evan Hendricks, *Credit Scores and Credit Reports: How the System Really Works, What You Can Do* (2004)
An accessible introduction to how the credit reporting system functions.

Chris Jay Hoofnagle, *Identity Theft: Making the Known Unknowns Known*, 21 Harv. J. L. & Tech. 97 (2007)
Argues for a reporting requirement on financial institutions about identity theft incidents.

M. Maureen Murphy, *Privacy Protection for Customer Financial Information (Congressional Research Service*, January 12, 2012)
Analyzes the Dodd-Frank Act's changes to the administration and enforcement of FCRA, GLBA and other statutes.

Paul M. Schwartz, *The Future of Tax Privacy*, 61 National Tax J. 883 (2008)
Explores the history of tax privacy, current rules and likely impact of issues such as data security on the future development of existing statutory regulation.

Paul M. Schwartz & Edward Janger, *The Gramm-Leach-Bliley Act, Information Privacy, and the Limits of Default Rules*, 86 Minn. L. Rev. 1219 (2002)
Criticism of GLBA's privacy safeguards as failing both to reflect majority preferences and to provide consumers with adequate information.

Daniel J. Solove, *Identity Theft, Privacy, and the Architecture of Vulnerability*, 54 Hastings L.J. 1227 (2003)
Argues that identity theft can be better prevented by regulating the way financial institutions handle personal data.

Peter Swire, *The Surprising Virtues of the New Financial Privacy Law*, 86 Minn. L. Rev. 1263 (2002)
Praises GLBA's privacy protections as addressing legitimate industry concerns about excessive costs and legal barricades to needed information.

CHAPTER 9

Consumer Data

ESSENTIAL POINTS

- A series of targeted, sectoral information privacy laws governs the use of business records in different settings.

- The federal laws regulating business data and consumer privacy offer different kinds of protections. These safeguards vary in some of the following ways: (1) opt-out rules versus opt-in rules, (2) preemption of state law and (3) the existence of a private right of action for violations.

- The FTC has played an important role in policing the privacy practices of companies.

- Numerous federal statutes provide for liquidated damages in the case of privacy violations.

- Damages are often difficult for plaintiffs to establish when businesses misuse or improperly disclose personal data.

- With a few exceptions, courts generally sustain privacy regulations under the First Amendment when the law requires opt-in rules or when it enables consumers to restrict the marketing solicitations they receive.

- In the few cases decided thus far, courts have rejected breach of contract claims when companies violate their privacy policies. These holdings have been based primarily on two rationales: (1) privacy policies are notices, not contracts, and (2) the plaintiffs failed to establish damages.

PERSONALLY IDENTIFIABLE INFORMATION

Personally identifiable information (PII) is one of the most central concepts in privacy regulation. It defines the scope and boundaries of a large range of privacy statutes and regulations. Numerous federal statutes turn on this distinction. Similarly, many state statutes also rely on PII as a jurisdictional trigger. These laws all share the same basic assumption—that in the absence of PII, there is no privacy harm. Thus, privacy regulation focuses on the collection, use and disclosure of PII, and leaves non-PII unregulated.

Approaches to Defining PII

In the United States, there are three predominant approaches to defining PII in various laws and regulations:

1. **The Tautological Approach.** Defines PII as any information that identifies a person. Example: VPPA

2. **The Nonpublic Approach.** Defines PII as any nonpublic personal information or as non-aggregate data. Examples: GLBA, Cable Act

3. **The Specific-Types Approach.** Defines PII by listing specific types of data that constitutes PII. Examples: COPPA, many state data security breach notification laws

Source: Paul M. Schwartz & Daniel J. Solove, The PII Problem: Privacy and a New Concept of Personally Identifiable Information, *86 N.Y.U. L. Rev. 1814 (2011)*

Leading Cases

Pineda v. Williams-Sonoma Stores, **246 P.3d 612 (Cal. 2011)**
California's Song-Beverly Act prohibits merchants who accept credit cards from collecting a cardholder's "personal identification information" when transacting business with her. More specifically, it prohibits retailers from requesting or requiring "as a condition to accepting the credit card" that a cardholder provide "any personal identification information upon the credit card transaction form or otherwise." Cal. Civ. Code § 1747.08(a)(1).

The critical language in the act defines PII as "information concerning the cardholder, other than information set forth on the credit card, and including, but not limited to, the cardholder's address and telephone number." In *Pineda*, the California Supreme Court analyzed the statutory language and legislative history of the act and found that both demonstrated a legislative intent to include a zip code as part of the "cardholder's address." In other words, that statutory category included "not only a complete address, but also its components."

Apple, Inc. v. Krescent, 292 P.3d 883 (Cal. 2013)

Online digital media retailer did not violate provision of the Song-Beverly Credit Card Act prohibiting merchants from requesting and recording "personal identification information" concerning the cardholder. The California Supreme Court found that the overall statutory scheme of the Song-Beverly Act indicated a legislative desire to balance privacy protection and fraud protection. For electronically downloadable products, online merchants faced limitations on their anti-fraud activities that brick-and-mortar retailers did not face for their own anti-fraud activities. The California Court was unwilling to assume that the Legislature that enacted Song-Beverly in 1990 would have extended its prohibitions to electronically downloadable products.

Injury and Standing

Standing

An overarching issue in privacy cases is whether the privacy violation caused any harm. Plaintiffs must typically allege a cognizable injury in order to have a viable cause of action. In federal courts, in order to have standing, the plaintiff must show that:

1. it has suffered an 'injury in fact' that is (a) concrete and particularized and (b) actual or imminent, not conjectural or hypothetical;

2. the injury is fairly traceable to the challenged action of the defendant; and

3. it is likely, as opposed to merely speculative, that the injury will be redressed by a favorable decision.

Leading Cases

Friends of the Earth, Inc. v. Laidlaw Envtl. Sys. (TOC), Inc., 528 U.S. 167 (2000)

If a plaintiff cannot establish standing, then a plaintiff's lawsuit cannot proceed forward in federal court.

Clapper v. Amnesty International, 133 S. Ct. 1138 (2013)
Although this is a case involving a constitutional challenge to the Foreign Intelligence Surveillance Act (FISA), it has relevance for standing in consumer privacy cases. The U.S. Supreme Court held that plaintiffs failed to allege a legally cognizable injury when they challenged a provision of FISA that permits the government to engage in surveillance of their communications. The plaintiffs claimed that there was an "objectively reasonable likelihood" that their communications would be monitored, and as a result, they had to take "costly and burdensome measures to protect the confidentiality of their international communications." The Supreme Court concluded that the plaintiffs were speculating and that "allegations of possible future injury are not sufficient" to establish an injury. According to the Court, "fears of hypothetical future harm" cannot justify the countermeasures the plaintiffs took. "Enterprising" litigants could establish an injury "simply by making an expenditure based on a nonparanoid fear."

In Re Google, Inc. Cookie Placement Consumer Privacy Litigation,
988 F. Supp. 2d 434 (D. Del. 2013)
Plaintiffs alleged that Google "'tricked' their Apple Safari and/or Internet Explorer browsers into accepting cookies, which then allowed defendants to display targeted advertising." The court held that the plaintiffs couldn't prove a harm because they couldn't demonstrate that Google interfered with their ability to "monetize" their personal data.

TORT LAW

The privacy torts have thus far *not* provided a good fit for addressing complaints about improper collection, use or disclosure of personal data by businesses. The breach of confidentiality tort has not been used in this manner. Negligence has sometimes been recognized as a viable cause of action to protect consumer privacy, but significant precedent does not exist in this area.

Leading Cases

Dwyer v. American Express Co., 652 N.E.2d 1351 (Ill. App. 1995)
American Express sold cardholder information to marketers. Cardholders did not have an action for intrusion upon seclusion because they had voluntarily exposed their information to American Express. They lacked a cause of action for appropriation of name or likeness because "an individual name has value only when it is associated with one of defendants' lists."

Shibley v. Time, Inc. 341 N.E.2d 337 (Ohio Ct. App. 1975)
Plaintiff sued the publishers of magazines for selling subscription lists to direct-mail advertising businesses. There was no liability for public disclosure of private facts because the sale of the lists did not "cause mental suffering, shame or humiliation to a person of ordinary sensibilities." The appropriation tort was not available because the defendant had not used the plaintiff's name or likeness to endorse a product.

Remsburg v. Docusearch, Inc., 816 A.2d 1001 (N.H. 2003)
A database company released the victim's address and other personal information to a man who hunted her down and murdered her. The court held that if a private investigator or information broker discloses information to a client and creates a foreseeable risk of criminal misconduct against the third person whose information was disclosed, there is a duty to exercise reasonable care not to subject the third person to an unreasonable risk of harm. Due to the risks posed by stalking and identity theft, the threat of criminal misconduct was sufficiently foreseeable that an investigator had a duty to exercise reasonable care in disclosing a third person's personal information. Few other courts have found such a duty.

Fraley v. Facebook, 830 F.Supp.2d 785 (N.D. Cal. 2011)
This case concerned a Facebook feature called "Sponsored Stories." Plaintiffs alleged a "coherent theory of how they were economically injured by the misappropriation of their names, photographs, and likenesses for use in paid commercial endorsements targeted not at themselves, but at *other* consumers, without their consent." Their "personalized endorsement" of products and services to their friends "has a concrete, provable value." In a subsequent order, Judge Richard Seeborg rejected a proposed settlement of the case. C 11-1726 RS (N.D. Cal.; Aug. 17, 2012). In his order, Judge Seeborg requested more information about the scope of the injunctive relief to which Facebook agreed. In August 2013, the court approved a $20 million settlement with Facebook. Court held that the plaintiffs successfully stated a claim for misappropriation under Cal. Civ. Code §3344.

CONTRACT AND PROMISSORY ESTOPPEL

Contract and promissory estoppel appear highly relevant as causes of action to remedy the improper collection, use or disclosure of personal data, because many companies have privacy policies that make promises about privacy that consumers rely upon. In the few cases decided thus far, however, courts have not been receptive to these theories.

Breach of Contract

To establish a breach of contract claim, a plaintiff must prove:

1. The existence of a contract
2. Breach of the contract
3. Damages that flow from the breach

Promissory Estoppel

Under the doctrine of promissory estoppel, a "promise which the promisor should reasonably expect to induce action or forbearance on the part of the promisee or a third person and which does induce such action or forbearance is binding if injustice can be avoided only by enforcement of the promise. The remedy granted for breach may be limited as justice requires." Restatement (Second) of Contracts § 90.

Are Privacy Policies Contracts?

Thus far, only a few courts have addressed this question, and they have uniformly held that privacy policies are not contracts. These courts view privacy policies as mere notices of a company's practices. Cases have also failed because plaintiffs have not established contractual damages. Examples:

Dyer v. Northwest Airlines Corp., 334 F. Supp. 2d 1196 (D.N.D. 2004)
Breach of contract claim against Northwest Airlines for disclosing passenger records to the government in violation of its privacy policy. The court held that "broad statements of company policy do not generally give rise to contract claims." The court also noted that the plaintiffs failed to allege they had read or relied upon the privacy policy or that they suffered any "contractual damages arising out of the alleged breach."

In re Jet Blue Airways Corp. Privacy Litigation, 379 F. Supp. 2d 299 (E.D.N.Y. 2005)
Plaintiffs sued Jet Blue Airlines for breach of contract for sharing passenger records with the government. The court granted Jet Blue's motion to dismiss because plaintiffs failed to prove damages. It stated: "There is … no support for the proposition that an individual passenger's personal information has or had any compensable value in the economy at large."

Liability for Third-Party Apps?

In re iPhone Application Litigation, 844 F.Supp.2d 1040 (N.D. Cal. June 12, 2012)
The court denied Apple's motion to dismiss two state law claims against it based on a class action against Apple for the practices of third-party apps. Despite Apple's Privacy Policy and Terms of Use, which disclaimed liability from third-party conduct, the court concluded that Apple's promise to protect consumer privacy encompasses data it provides to third parties. This general promise overrode the disclaimer of liability. The court recognized that increased security risks and lessened device resources (storage, battery life and bandwidth) from third-party apps could constitute concrete injuries.

FTC ENFORCEMENT OF SECTION 5 OF THE FTC ACT

FTC Act: Since 1998, the FTC has been bringing enforcement actions against companies for privacy and data security practices that the FTC deems to be in violation of Section 5 of the Federal Trade Commission Act (FTC Act), 15 U.S.C. § 45. The FTC Act prohibits "unfair or deceptive acts or practices in or affecting commerce. In some instances, the actions of a company can be both deceptive and unfair.

Deception: A deceptive act or practice is a material "representation, omission or practice that is likely to mislead the consumer acting reasonably in the circumstances, to the consumer's detriment." Letter from James C. Miller III, Chairman, FTC, to Hon. John D. Dingell, Chairman, House Comm. on Energy & Commerce (Oct. 14, 1983).

Unfairness: The FTC Act classifies a trade practice as unfair if it "causes or is likely to cause substantial injury to consumers which is not reasonably avoidable by consumers themselves and is not outweighed by countervailing benefits to consumers or competition." 15 U.S.C. § 45(n).

The Types of Cases Brought: Early FTC actions involved charging companies that violated the promises made in their privacy policy with engaging in a deceptive practice. In the ensuing years, the FTC has found violations of the FTC Act beyond broken promises in privacy policies. Most cases brought by the FTC have settled.

Enforcement: The FTC can obtain injunctive remedies. The FTC Act does not provide for private causes of action; only the FTC can enforce it. The FTC does not have the ability to issue fines for violations of Section 5, but the FTC can issue fines up to $16,000 for each violation when companies violate a consent decree previously entered into for a violation of Section 5.

FTC Jurisdiction: Section 5 gives the FTC a broad authority to regulate most companies. However, several types of financial institutions, airlines, telecommunications carriers and other types of entities are exempt from Section 5. In addition to its Section 5 authority, the FTC has regulatory authority from a number of statutes.

Statutes Granting Enforcement Authority to the FTC

• Federal Trade Commission Act (FTC Act)
• Children's Online Privacy Protection Act (COPPA)
• Gramm-Leach-Bliley Act (GLBA)
• Telemarketing and Consumer Fraud Abuse Prevention Act (TCFAPA)
• Fair Credit Reporting Act (FCRA)

Leading Cases

In re Liberty Financial Cos. (1999)
Website for children and teen investors falsely promised that personal data collected in a survey would be kept anonymous, but it was kept in an identifiable form. Liberty Financial settled with the FTC, agreeing to refrain from making future misrepresentations, to post a privacy notice on its website and to obtain parental consent prior to gathering personal data from children.

In re Toysmart.com, LLC (2000)
An Internet toy retailer went bankrupt and planned to sell its customer database to pay back creditors. This action violated its privacy policy, which stated that customer data "is never shared with a third party." The FTC charged this behavior was a deceptive practice. Toysmart and the FTC settled, agreeing that the bankruptcy court had to approve the buyer and that the buyer would be limited in how it could use the information.

In re ReverseAuction.com, Inc. (2000)
ReverseAuction.com improperly obtained personal information from eBay customers and used it to e-mail them to promote its own auction website. Their e-mail falsely stated to the recipients that their eBay user

IDs would expire soon. The FTC charged that ReverseAuction's practice was both unfair and deceptive. ReverseAuction settled, agreeing to be barred from making future misrepresentations and to notify the customers and correct the falsehood.

In re Gateway Learning Corp. (2004)

When Gateway Learning Corp. collected personal information from its consumers, its privacy policy stated that it would not sell, rent or loan personal information to third parties unless people consented. Subsequently, Gateway altered its privacy policy to allow the renting of personal information to third parties without informing customers or obtaining their consent. The FTC alleged this practice was unfair, and Gateway settled, agreeing to avoid making deceptive claims or retroactively changing its privacy policy without consumer consent. Gateway agreed to pay $4,608, the amount it earned from renting the information.

In re Vision I Properties (2005)

Vision I Properties licensed shopping cart software and provided related services to small online retail merchants. The company's software created customizable shopping cart pages for client merchants' websites. The resulting pages resided on websites managed by Vision I Properties, but resembled the other pages on its client merchants' websites. Vision I Properties violated the privacy promises of some of these client merchants as stated in their websites; it rented consumers' personal information collected through its shopping cart software. This personal information was then used by third parties to send direct mail and make telemarketing calls to consumers. For the FTC, it was reasonable for consumers to rely on merchants' privacy policies. Moreover, Vision I Properties did not adequately inform merchants of its information sharing. Vision I settled, agreeing to cease selling the data, to provide better notice and to disgorge $9,101 of profits.

In re Sears Holdings Management Corp. (2009)

Sears invited website users to "participate in exciting, engaging and on-going interactions—always on your terms and always by your choice." Customers were paid to participate and had to download software that would track their Internet browsing. A long user license agreement informed users of the extensiveness of the tracking. The FTC alleged Sears engaged in a deceptive practice by failing to adequately disclose the extent of the tracking. The settlement requires Sears to destroy all data collected and to clearly disclose the scope of the tracking before the software is installed and apart from the user license agreement.

In re Facebook, Inc. (2011)

The FTC charged that Facebook's changes to its privacy policy in December 2009 resulted in data about its users being exposed to the public. The FTC alleged both deception (failing to properly notify people) and unfairness (making a retroactive material change to its privacy policies without consumer consent). The FTC also alleged that Facebook had not adhered to the Safe Harbor principles regarding notice and choice. The settlement requires Facebook to develop and maintain a "comprehensive privacy program."

In re Google, Inc. (2011)

Google Buzz violated the FTC Act and Safe Harbor by suggesting that Gmail users could choose whether to join Buzz, but then enrolling some people who had not wanted to join Buzz in certain Buzz features. The FTC required Google to institute a "comprehensive privacy program." This was the first case involving a Safe Harbor violation and the requirement that a company develop a comprehensive privacy program.

In re Google, Inc. (2012)

Google agreed to pay a $22.5 million fine to the FTC based on the charge that, in violation of its promises, it placed a tracking cookie on the computers of Safari users. This practice violated the October 2011 settlement with the FTC that Google not misrepresent the extent to which it provided users control over their data.

In the Matter of MySpace, LLC (2012)

"Constructive sharing"—sharing non-PII with third parties that can be used by third parties to access PII—without indicating it to users is a "deceptive act or practice" under the FTC Act as well as a violation of Safe Harbor. If non-PII is shared with third parties, and that non-PII can be used by the third parties to obtain PII, then a business is not accurate in stating that it does not share PII with third parties. Consistent with other recent cases, the FTC required MySpace to implement a comprehensive privacy program.

In re Epic Marketplace (FTC 2012)

A behavioral advertising company, Epic engaged in "history sniffing." This practice involves a company accessing a user's browsing history to determine whether the user had previously visited a webpage. Epic then used this information within interest segments, including such sensitive categories as "Incontinence," "Arthritis," and "Pregnancy—Fertility Getting Pregnant." Once placed in such categories, the consumer would receive targeted ads based on this classification. The FTC settlement prohibited Epic from engaging in history sniffing and from misrepresenting its practices. It was also required to delete any information collected using history sniffing.

In re DesignerWare, LLC and other Software and Rent-to-Own Companies (FTC 2013)

The FTC brought this action against seven rent-to-own companies (and a software company and others) for spying on consumers from computers they were renting. Without knowledge of the customers, software on the computer (called "Detective Mode") took screenshots of confidential and personal information, logged customers' computer keystrokes, and in certain cases, took webcam pictures of people in their own homes. The FTC settlement includes 20 years of auditing and a prohibition on the use of GPS information without consumer consent and notice. Information improperly gathered from consumers cannot be used by the companies to collect on accounts.

In re Aaron's (FTC 2013)

A follow-up to the *DesignerWare* and related settlements. Although Aaron's own stores did not license or use the contested DesignerWare product, Aaron's knew that some of its franchisee's had done so. It also knew, according to the FTC's complaint, that "Detective Mode captured confidential and personal information from consumer computer users without notice to those users." Under the terms of the FTC settlement, Aaron's will be prohibited from utilizing "monitoring technology to gather data or information from or about a consumer from any computer rented to a consumer." The order also prohibits it from "[r]eceiving, storing, or communicating" data gathered from a computer rented to a consumer using monitoring technology.

In re Goldenshares Technologies, LLC (FTC 2014)

A company offered "Brightest Flashlight Free," a popular Android mobile application. Users had downloaded it tens of millions of time. The flashlight app transmitted user geolocation data and persistent device identifiers from Android mobile devices to third parties, including advertising networks. The FTC alleged that Brightest Flashlight's Privacy Policy did not adequately disclose this fact. Although the EULA presented a choice to "Accept" or "Refuse" the terms of the Agreement, the app was already collecting and sending information to third parties before a consumer was presented with this choice. The settlement required improved notice and also for "just-in-time" notice and affirmative consent when geolocation data is collected.

Triggers for FTC Complaints

The following practices represent the types of privacy practices that will trigger FTC complaints:

- *Inadequate Security.* Promising security but failing to provide adequate security. No data security breach needs to occur and no data needs to be lost. See *In the Matter of Microsoft Corp.* (2002); *In re Guess.com, Inc.* (2003).

- *Security Gaffes and Failure to Train.* Suffering a data security breach due to negligence or failure to properly train employees about adequate security practices. *FTC v. Eli Lilly* (2002).

- *Broken Promises.* Failing to adhere to promises made in a privacy policy. *In re Liberty Financial Cos.* (1999). Selling customer data at a bankruptcy proceeding when a privacy policy states that data will not be shared with third parties. *In re Toysmart.com, LLC* (2000).

- *Retroactive Privacy Policy Changes.* Altering a privacy policy to allow more disclosure of personal information without acquiring people's consent to the change. *In re Gateway Learning Corp.* (2004).

- *Deceptive Data Collection.* Collecting data about people deceptively, even if they are not visiting or using the company's website. *FTC v. ReverseAuction.com, Inc.* (2000).

- *Inadequate Disclosure of Extent of Data Gathering.* Failing to clearly and conspicuously inform users about the extensiveness of Internet browsing tracking by software. *In re Sears Holdings Management Corp.* (2009).

FTC Consent Decrees

FTC consent decrees often contain at least some of the following elements:

- prohibition on the activities in violation of the FTC Act

- steps to remediate the problematic activities, such as software patches or notice to consumers

- deletion of wrongfully-obtained consumer data

- modifications to privacy policies

- establishment of a comprehensive privacy program, including risk assessment, appointment of a person to coordinate the program, and employee training, among other things

- biennial assessment reports by independent auditors

- recordkeeping to facilitate FTC enforcement of the order

- obligation to alert the FTC of any material changes in the company that might affect compliance obligations (such as mergers or bankruptcy filings)

- a twenty year compliance period

FEDERAL STATUTES: ENTERTAINMENT RECORDS

Cable Communications Policy Act (CCPA)
47 U.S.C. § 551 (1984)

Primary Function: To protect the privacy of cable subscribers.

Applies to: Cable operators and service providers. 47 U.S.C. § 551(a)(1).

Notice and Access: Requires cable service providers to notify subscribers of the nature and uses of personal information collected. Subscribers must have access to their personal data held by cable operators.

Limitations on Data Collection: Cable operators "shall not use the cable system to collect personally identifiable information concerning any subscriber without the prior written or electronic consent of the subscriber concerned." 47 U.S.C. § 551(b)(1).

Opt In: Cable operators cannot disclose personally identifiable information about any subscriber without the subscriber's consent. 47 U.S.C. § 551(c)(1).

Opt Out: Cable operators may disclose subscriber names and addresses if "the cable operator has provided the subscriber the opportunity to prohibit or limit such disclosure." 47 U.S.C. § 551(c)(2).

Exceptions: Disclosure permitted when necessary for a "legitimate business activity" or pursuant to a court order if the subscriber is notified. 47 U.S.C. § 551 (c)(2).

Data Destruction: Cable operators must destroy personal data if the information is no longer necessary for the purpose for which it was collected. 47 U.S.C. § 551(e).

Government Access to Cable Information: The government can obtain cable subscriber data pursuant to a court order justified by "clear and convincing evidence" the subscriber is "reasonably suspected of engaging in criminal activity and that the information sought would be material evidence in the case." The subscriber must be notified and allowed to challenge the order. 47 U.S.C. § 551(h).

Enforcement: Private cause of action and actual damages, with a minimum of $1,000 or $100 for each day of the violation, whichever is higher. Punitive damages and attorneys' fees. 47 U.S.C. § 551(f).

Leading Case

Kilmas v. Comcast Cable, 465 F.3d 271 (6th Cir. 2006)
The Sixth Circuit held that the Cable Act did not apply to a cable company's alleged collection of IP-URL linkage information. The plain language of the Cable Act precluded application of its privacy protections to the cable company's offering of broadband Internet service. As the Sixth Circuit observed, "[B]roadband Internet service delivered via cable is not 'cable services' in the sense of the Cable Act."

Video Privacy Protection Act (VPPA)
18 U.S.C. § 2710 (1988

Primary Function: To protect the privacy of video watching.

Applies to: Covers any "videotape service provider"—"any person engaged in the business, in or affecting interstate or foreign commerce, of rental, sale or delivery of prerecorded video cassette tapes or similar audio visual materials." 18 U.S.C. § 2710(a)(4). It covers DVDs and online delivery of videos.

Opt In: Videotape service providers cannot knowingly disclose personal information without the individual's written consent. 18 U.S.C. § 2710(2)(B).

Opt Out: Videotape service providers can disclose the names and addresses of consumers if the consumer has been given the right to opt out, and the disclosure does not identify information about the videos the consumer rents. 18 U.S.C. § 2710(b)(2)(D). "[T]he subject matter of such materials may be disclosed if the disclosure is for the exclusive use of marketing goods and services directly to the consumer." 18 U.S.C. § 2710(b)(2)(D)(ii).

Destruction of Records: Records of personal information must be destroyed as soon as practicable. 18 U.S.C. § 2710(e).

Exceptions: VPPA contains several exceptions, such as permitting videotape providers to disclose "to any person if the disclosure is incident to the ordinary course of business of the videotape service provider." 18 U.S.C. § 2710(b)(2)(E).

Government Access: Permits disclosure to a law enforcement agency pursuant to a warrant, court order or subpoena. 18 U.S.C. § 2710(b)(2)(C).

Preemption: VPPA does not block states from enacting statutes that are more protective of privacy. 18 U.S.C. § 2710(f).

Enforcement: Private cause of action when a videotape service provider "knowingly discloses ... personally identifiable information concerning any consumer of such provider." 18 U.S.C. § 2710(b)(1). Actual damages and liquidated damages in the amount of $2,500. Punitive damages, attorneys' fees, equitable and injunctive relief. 18 U.S.C. § 2710(c). The VPPA also includes a statutory exclusionary rule that prevents the admission into evidence of any information obtained in violation of the statute. 18 U.S.C. § 2710(d).

Leading Case

In re Hulu Privacy Litigation, 2014 WL 1724344 (N.D. Cal. 2014)
Class action brought by viewers of Hulu's on-line video content alleged that Hulu wrongfully disclosed to third parties their video viewing selections and other data linked to their unique identifiers. The court held that the classification of information as PII under VPPA does not require disclosure of a person's actual name—all that is required is "identification of a specific person tied to a specific transaction." Anonymized IDs alone are not PII "but context could render it not anonymous and the equivalent of the identification of a specific person." Certain disclosures made by Hulu were thus not PII but other disclosures, such as sending cookies that could "show the Hulu user's identity on Facebook" would constitute the disclosure of PII. To be liable under VPPA, Hulu would have to know that it was "transmitting both an identifier and the person's video watching information," and facts remained in dispute about intent, and thus Hulu's motion to dismiss was denied.

In re Hulu Privacy Litigation, C 11-03764 LB, 2012 WL 3282960 (N.D. Cal. Aug. 10, 2012)
Hulu, an online provider of streaming video, was a "video tape service provider" under VPPA because the definition of a "video tape service provider" regulates "any person, engaged in the business ... of rental, sale, or delivery of prerecorded video cassette tapes or similar audio visual materials." The term "similar" is deliberately broad and "designed to include new technologies for pre-recorded video content."

Sterk v. Redbox Automated Retail, LLC, 672 F.3d 535, 537 (7th Cir.2012)
Damages are not available under VPPA for simply failing to destroy old
records. There must be a subsequent disclosure for there to be an injury
and damages.

FEDERAL STATUTES: MARKETING

Telecommunications Act
47 U.S.C. § 222 (1996)

Primary Function: The Telecommunications Act requires a telecommunications
carrier "to protect the confidentiality of proprietary information of, and relating
to … customers."

CPNI: The act establishes the important legal category of "customer proprietary
network information" (CPNI). It places certain kinds of restrictions on the use,
disclosure of and access to CPNI. In a nutshell, a telecommunications carrier
does not need customer approval to use and disclose CPNI to provide or market
offerings among the categories of service to which the customer already
subscribes from the carrier. Unless it meets certain exceptions provided in the
regulations, a carrier must obtain opt-in consent from a customer before
sharing CPNI with joint venture partners and independent contractors for
marketing purposes.

In *U.S. West, Inc. v. Federal Communications Commission*, 182 F.3d 1224 (10th
Cir. 1999), U.S. West had objected to FCC regulations, enacted pursuant to the
Telecommunications Act, which required an opt-in rule for use of a customer's
CPNI for marketing purposes. The Tenth Circuit found that this aspect of the
CPNI regulations violated the First Amendment. The FCC had failed to demon-
strate a real harm to customer privacy that the regulation prevented and also failed
to adequately consider a less restrictive alternative, namely an opt-out strategy.

The FCC responded to the *U.S. West* decision at length in its 2007 CPNI
Order and rejected its holdings. Specifically, the FCC declared that the Tenth
Circuit in that case based its decision "on a different record than the one
compiled here" and in particular on premises that were no longer valid. First,
there was now ample evidence of disclosure of CPNI and the adverse effects it
could have on customers. Second, there was now substantial evidence that an
opt-out strategy would not adequately protect customer privacy "because most
customers either do not read or do not understand carriers' opt-out notices."
FCC Report and Order, 07-22 (April 2, 2007), at ¶ 44. The FCC also stated that
requiring opt-in consent from customers before sharing CPNI with joint
venture partners and independent contractors for marketing purposes would
pass First Amendment scrutiny. Id. at 45.

Telephone Consumer Protection Act (TCPA)
47 U.S.C. § 227 (1991)

Primary Function: Permits people to stop unwanted telemarketing calls.

Key Provisions: Authorizes the federal Do Not Call Registry, where people can sign up their numbers if they do not wish to receive telemarketing calls. Does not apply to charitable or political calls. 47 U.S.C. § 227(c)(3). Prohibits marketers from calling residences and using prerecorded messages without the consent of the called party. 47 U.S.C. § 227(b)(1)(B). The TCPA prohibits the use of a fax, computer or other device to send an unsolicited advertisement to a fax machine.

Enforcement: Permits individuals to sue a telemarketer in small claims court for an actual loss of up to $500 (whichever is greater) for each call received after requesting to be placed on its Do Not Call list. States may initiate actions against telemarketers "engaging in a pattern or practice of telephone calls or other transmissions to residents of that state" in violation of the TCPA. 47 U.S.C. § 227(f)(1). If a telemarketer has acted "willfully or knowingly," then damages are trebled.

Leading Cases

Gager v. Dell, 727 F.3d 265 (3rd Cir. 2013)
Consumer brought action against creditor, alleging that creditor violated the TCPA by calling her through an automated telephone dialing system after prior express consent to be contacted had been revoked. The Third Circuit held that a contractual relationship between consumer and creditor does not exempt the creditor from TCPA requirements and that the creditor violated the TCPA.

Chesbro v. Best Buy Stores, --- F.3d ----, 2012 WL 4902839 (9th Cir. 2012)
The TCPA generally prohibits robocalls to residential phone lines without prior consent. Calls that do not adversely affect privacy and do not transmit unsolicited ads are exempt. Yet, FCC regulations under TCPA do not exempt from regulation "dual-purpose" robocalls, which inquire about customer satisfaction plus market goods or services. As a result, the TCPA regulates "dual-purpose" robocalls. Although Best Buy made robocalls to follow up on customer purchases, the calls concerned a rewards program for points to be redeemed for other Best Buy purchases. The court deemed them "dual-purpose" calls subject to TCPA because the reward points were designed to entice customers to Best Buy stores to make future purchases.

Controlling the Assault of Non-Solicited Pornography and Marketing (CAN-SPAM) Act
15 U.S.C. §§ 7701 et seq. (2003)

Primary Function: To regulate commercial e-mail.

Applies to: Commercial e-mail—a "message the primary purpose of which is the commercial advertisement or promotion of a commercial product or service."

Restrictions: Prohibits the knowing sending of commercial messages with the intent to deceive or mislead recipients.

Opt Out: The CAN-SPAM Act also requires that a valid opt-out option be made available to e-mail recipients. To make opt out possible, the act requires senders of commercial e-mail to contain a return address "clearly and conspicuously displayed." 15 U.S.C. § 7704(a)(3).

Enforcement: No private right of action. Enforced by the FTC and other agencies. Violations are deemed an "unfair and deceptive act or practice." 15 U.S.C. § 7706(a). State attorneys general can bring actions for damages suffered by the state's residents as well as injunctive and equitable relief. Criminal penalties against predatory and abusive commercial e-mail. 15 U.S.C. § 7703.

Preemption: Preempts state regulation that "expressly regulates the use of electronic mail to send commercial messages, except to the extent that any such statute, regulation or rule prohibits falsity or deception in any portion [of the e-mail message]." 15 U.S.C. § 7707(b).

State Anti-Spam Laws: At least 20 states have anti-spam statutes.

International Approaches: Most other countries favor an opt-in approach as a legal response to commercial unsolicited emails and may provide for strong administrative penalties as well as a private right of action. The EU E-Privacy Directive requires prior consent. In German law, prior express consent requires a process termed "double opt-in," meaning a consumer has to agree to receive commercial emails by checking a box and then again opt-in in by clicking on a link contained in the first email received after enrollment. Canada's Anti-Spam Law (CASL) requires opt in consent, and provides for high monetary penalties as well as a private right of action. For more on CASL, see Chapter 13.

FEDERAL STATUTES: INTERNET USE AND ELECTRONIC COMMUNICATIONS

Children's Online Privacy Protection Act (COPPA)
15 U.S.C. §§ 6501-6506 (1998)

Primary Function: Regulates the collection and use of children's information by Internet websites by requiring parental consent.

Applies to: Applies only to websites that collect personal information from children under age 13. 15 U.S.C. § 6502(1). More specifically, it applies to:

1. "[A]n operator of a website or online service directed to children." 15 U.S.C. § 6502(a)(1).

2. "[A]ny operator that has actual knowledge that it is collecting personal information from a child." 15 U.S.C. § 6502(a)(1).

Personal Information: FTC amendments to the COPPA rule in 2013 expanded the definition of "personal information" to clearly include persistent identifiers, such as IP addresses and mobile device IDs, that recognize users over time and across different online services. As a result, behavioral advertising on child-directed online services now requires parental notice and consent.

Notice: Children's websites must post privacy policies describing "what information is collected from children by the operator, how the operator uses such information and the operator's disclosure practices for such information." 15 U.S.C. § 6502(b)(1)(A)(i).

Opt In: Children's websites must "obtain verifiable parental consent for the collection, use or disclosure of personal information from children." 15 U.S.C. § 6502(b)(1)(A)(ii). Websites cannot condition child's participation in a game or receipt of a prize on the disclosure of more personal information than is necessary to participate in that activity. 15 U.S.C. § 6502(b)(1)(C).

Third-Party Ad Networks, Plug-Ins and Apps: Pursuant to the FTC's amended COPPA rule in 2013, both websites and mobile apps will be held strictly liable for collection by third-party ad networks and plug-in providers absent parental notice and consent. Additionally, third-party social plug-ins and ad networks must comply with COPPA themselves if they have actual knowledge that they are collecting personal information from children under the age of 13.

Enforcement: Violations of COPPA are "treated as a violation of a rule defining an unfair or deceptive act or practice" under the FTCA. The FTC enforces the law and can impose fines. There is no private cause of action for violations of COPPA. States can bring civil actions for violations of COPPA in the interests of their citizens to obtain injunctions and damages. 15 U.S.C. § 6504.

Preemption: COPPA preempts state law. 15 U.S.C. § 6502(d).

Safe Harbor: If an operator follows self-regulatory guidelines issued by marketing or online industry groups that are approved by the FTC, then the COPPA requirements will be deemed satisfied. 15 U.S.C. § 6503.

FTC COPPA Enforcement Actions

In re Bigmailbox.com., Inc. et al. (2001)
Website targeted to young girls collected names, addresses and other information, despite stating in its privacy policy that such data would not be collected without verifiable parental consent. Settlement with FTC for $35,000.

In re The Ohio Art Company (the "Etch-A-Sketch Case") (2002)
The Ohio Art Company collected information from children for a contest to win an Etch-A-Sketch. To obtain parental permission, the company asked children to "get your parent or guardian's permission first." This was inadequate. Moreover, the company collected more information than reasonably necessary. Settlement with FTC for $35,000.

In re Mrs. Fields Famous Brands, Inc. (2003)
The company collected information from 84,000 children for a birthday club without obtaining parental consent. Settlement with FTC for $100,000.

In re Hershey Foods Corp. (2003)
Hershey offered an online parental consent form but did not ensure parents filled it out. The company still collected personal data even if the form was not completed. This was an inadequate way of obtaining parental consent. Settlement with FTC for $85,000.

In re Bonzi Software, Inc. (2004)
Software company had users provide their birth date when registering software. Although the site was not directed to children, Bonzi had actual knowledge children were using its software. Bonzi thus had to comply with COPPA, and it did not. Settlement with FTC for $75,000.

In re UMG (2004)
UMG notified parents *after* collecting children's data. Notice had to be given beforehand. Settlement with FTC for $85,000.

In re Xanga.com, Inc. (2006)

Social network website allowed children under 13 years old to create profiles. Had actual knowledge children were under this age but failed to obtain parental consent. Settlement with FTC for $1 million.

In re Imbee.com (2008)

Social network website directed at children 8 to 14 years old allowed them to create profiles and upload information. Profiles could not be viewed by others until parents completed the registration process. This ran afoul of COPPA because the website maintained the information prior to receiving parental consent. Settlement with FTC for $130,000.

In re Sony BMG Entertainment (2008)

Sony had actual knowledge that some of its user fan pages were created by children. Falsely stated in its privacy policy that children were not allowed to participate. Settlement with FTC for $1 million.

In re Iconix Brand Group (2009)

Knowingly collected information from children without obtaining parental consent. Settlement with FTC for $250,000.

FTC v. W-3 Innovations, LLC (2011)

In the FTC's first mobile app case, it settled with W-3 Innovations LLC for a violation of COPPA. The app collected children's personal data and allowed children to post personal data on public message boards. The company did not provide a notice or require parental consent. It also failed to provide a privacy policy.

FTC v. Playdom, Inc. (2011)

Playdom, an operator of online "virtual worlds," violated COPPA by collecting children's ages and e-mail addresses during registration. Children could publish personal data publicly on profile pages, and Playdom failed to provide proper notice or obtain parental consent. Additionally, the company violated the FTC Act because its privacy policy falsely stated that the company prohibited children under age 13 from posting personal data on the Internet. As part of its settlement, Playdom agreed to pay $3 million, which is the largest civil penalty ever assessed for a violation of the FTC's COPPA rule

FTC v. RockYou, Inc. (2012)

these slide shows, users had to enter an e-mail address and password as well as birth date. Although it collected data from children under 13, the company did not comply with COPPA. This settlement action also alleged that flaws in RockYou's game site had exposed 32 e-mail addresses and passwords to hackers.

United States v. Path, Inc. (FTC 2013)

Social networking app involved users uploading personal data to a journal that they could share with friends in the Path network. The app collected birth date information during user registration, including about 3000 children under the age of 13. Parental consent was not obtained. The settlement requires Path to pay an $800,000 penalty, to establish a comprehensive privacy program, and be audited every other year for the next 20 years.

In re Apple Inc. (FTC 2014)

Apple failed to notify parents that by entering a password they were approving 15 minutes of unlimited purchases their children could make when using apps. FTC settlement required Apple to obtain express informed consent before billing them, and consumers who consent to future charges must be allowed to withdraw consent at any time. Apple must provide refunds to consumers, for a minimum total of $32.5 million.

Note: The settlements with the FTC also involved other requirements, typically agreeing not to violate COPPA in the future and extensive compliance monitoring that can go on for as long as two decades.

Complying with COPPA

According to the FTC's website, a company's compliance with COPPA requires the following:

1. Post a clear and comprehensive privacy policy on the company's website describing its information practices for children's personal information;

2. Provide direct notice to parents and obtain verifiable parental consent, with limited exceptions, before collecting personal information from children;

3. Give parents the choice of consenting to the operator's collection and internal use of a child's information, but prohibiting the operator from disclosing that information to third parties;

4. Provide parents access to their child's personal information to review and/or have the information deleted;

5. Give parents the opportunity to prevent further use or online collection of a child's personal information;

6. Maintain the confidentiality, security and integrity of information they collect from children.

Source: FTC, COPPA FAQs, http://www.ftc.gov/privacy/coppafaqs.shtm (Oct. 2008)

How to Determine if a Website (or a portion of it) Is Directed at Children

In its regulations, 16 C.F.R. § 312.2, the FTC provides several factors that it will consider:

- Subject matter
- Visual and audio content
- Age of models
- Language or other characteristics of the site
- Empirical evidence regarding audience composition
- Evidence regarding the intended audience
- Whether a site uses animated characters
- Whether the site has child-oriented activities and incentives

Electronic Communications Privacy Act (ECPA)
18 U.S.C. §§ 2510-3127 (1986)

In several cases, plaintiffs have attempted to use the Electronic Communications Privacy Act (ECPA) to prevent certain kinds of information collection, use and disclosure by commercial entities. ECPA consists of three acts: (1) the Wiretap Act, 18 U.S.C. §§ 2510–2522, which regulates the interception of communications; (2) the Stored Communications Act (SCA), 18 U.S.C. §§ 2701–2711, which regulates communications in storage and ISP subscriber records; and (3) the Pen Register Act, 18 U.S.C. §§ 3121–3127, which regulates the use of pen register and trap and trace devices.

The attempts to use ECPA to regulate commercial entities using personal information primarily seek to use the Wiretap Act or the SCA. In most cases, ECPA does not apply because of user consent. See *In re Pharmatrak, Inc. Privacy Litigation,* 392 F.3d 9 (1st Cir. 2003); *In re Doubleclick Inc. Privacy Litigation,* 154 F. Supp. 2d 497 (S.D.N.Y. 2001); *Dyer v. Northwest Airlines Corp.,* 334 F. Supp. 2d 1196 (D.N.D. 2004).

Computer Fraud and Abuse Act (CFAA)
18 U.S.C. § 1030 (1984)

Primary Function: To prevent unauthorized access to computers.

Applies to: Any "protected computer" (used in interstate commerce or communications). Due to this broad definition, the act generally will apply to any computer connected to the Internet.

Criminal Penalties: The CFAA creates seven crimes. Among these offenses, it imposes criminal penalties when a person or entity "intentionally accesses a computer without authorization or exceeds authorized access, and thereby obtains ... information from any protected computer." 18 U.S.C. § 1030(a)(2)(c). It prohibits knowingly transmitting "a program, information, code or command" or "intentionally access[ing] a protected computer without authorization" that causes damage to a protected computer. 18 U.S.C. § 1030(5)(A)(i). Punishments range from fines to imprisonment for up to 20 years depending on the provision violated.

Damage: Some of the provisions of CFAA require causing "damage," which means "any impairment to the integrity or availability of data, a program, a system or information." 18 U.S.C. § 1030(e). In many provisions in the CFAA, the damage must exceed $5,000 in a one-year period.

Civil Remedies: "Any person who suffers damage or loss by reason of a violation of this section may maintain a civil action against the violator to obtain compensatory damages or injunctive relief or other equitable relief." 18 U.S.C. § 1030(g). "Damage" must cause a "loss aggregating at least $5,000 in value during any one-year period to one or more individuals." 18 U.S.C. § 1030(e).

Exceeding Authorized Access: Many provisions in the CFAA can be violated not just by unauthorized access, but also when one "exceeds authorized access." To "exceed authorized access" means "to access a computer with authorization and to use such access to obtain or alter information in the computer that the accesser is not entitled so to obtain and alter." 18 U.S.C. § 1030(e)(6).

Leading Cases

United States v. Drew, 259 F.R.D. 449 (C.D. Ca. 2009)
A woman who created a fake MySpace profile to harass a young girl (ultimately resulting in her suicide) was charged with exceeding authorization because MySpace's terms of service prohibited creating fictitious profiles. The court held that such an interpretation of the CFAA would transform it "into an overwhelmingly overbroad enactment that would convert a multitude of otherwise innocent Internet users into misdemeanant criminals."

LVRC Holdings, Inc. v. Brekka, 581 F.3d 1127 (9th Cir. 2009)
An employee who e-mailed files to himself from a workplace computer right before he was to leave the office did not access the computer without authorization since he originally had permission to use the computer. Although some courts have reached contrary conclusions (see Citrin

below), this decision reflects the majority view among courts that have examined this issue.

Airport Centers, LLC v. Citrin, **440 F.3d 418 (7th Cir. 2006)**
An employee accesses a computer without authorization in violation of the CFAA when he accesses it in breach of a duty of loyalty to the company. This court represents the minority view.

Is the CFAA Too Broad and Vague?

The CFAA was originally an anti-hacking statute, but its definitions of accessing a computer without authorization or exceeding authorization can be quite broad and vague under some interpretations. Under the theory expressed by the government in *United States v. Drew*, 259 F.R.D. 449 (C.D. Ca. 2009), every time people violate a website's terms of service, they may be committing a federal crime.

FEDERAL STATUTES: OVERVIEW

SCOPE OF FEDERAL STATUTE COVERAGE	
REGULATED	**NOT REGULATED***
Federal agency records (Privacy Act)	State agency records
State DMV records (DPPA)	Property records
Cable TV records (CCPA)	Library records
Video rental records (VPPA)	Supermarket purchase records
Medical records (HIPAA)	Bookstore records
Bank records (RFPA, GLB)	Department store records
Consumer reporting agency records (FCRA)	Internet websites (adult Web surfers)
Internet websites (kid Web surfers) (COPPA)	
ISP records (ECPA)	

* By not regulated, we mean not covered by a specific federal statute. Records may still be regulated by the FTC to the extent that a company makes promises in its privacy policy.

FEDERAL STATUTES AND PRIVATE RIGHTS OF ACTION

STATUTES *WITH* PRIVATE RIGHTS OF ACTION	STATUTES *WITHOUT* PRIVATE RIGHTS OF ACTION
Cable Communications Policy Act (CCPA) 47 U.S.C. § 551(f)	Children's Online Privacy Protection Act (COPPA) 15 U.S.C. §§ 6501-6505
CAN-SPAM Act 15 U.S.C. § 7706(g) (allows actions by ISPs, but not individuals)	Family Education Rights and Privacy Act (FERPA) 20 U.S.C. § 1232g
Drivers Privacy Protection Act (DPPA) 18 U.S.C. § 2724	Federal Trade Commission Act (FTC Act) 15 U.S.C. §§ 41, 45, 46, 571, 57b, 57b-1
Employee Polygraph Protection Act (EPPA) 29 U.S.C. § 2005(c)	Gramm-Leach-Bliley Act (GLBA) 15 U.S.C. §§ 6801-6809, 6821-6827
Fair Credit Reporting Act (FCRA) 15 U.S.C. § 1681n (willful violations) 15 U.S.C. § 1671o (negligent violations)	Health Insurance Portability and Accountability Act (HIPAA) 45 C.F.R. 164
Foreign Intelligence Surveillance Act (FISA) 18 U.S.C. § 1810 (improper disclosure/use of electronic surveillance) 18 U.S.C. § 1828 (improper physical search or disclosure/use)	Pen Register Act 18 U.S.C. §§ 3121- 3123
Privacy Act 5 U.S.C. § 552a(g)(1)	
Privacy Protection Act (PPA) 42 U.S.C. § 2000aa-6(a)	
Right to Financial Privacy Act (RFPA) 12 U.S.C. § 3417	
Stored Communications Act (SCA) 18 U.S.C. § 2707 (against others) 18 U.S.C. § 2712 (against U.S.)	
Telephone Consumer Protection Act (TCPA) 47 U.S.C. § 227(c)(5)	
Video Privacy Protection Act (VPPA) 18 U.S.C. § 2710(c)	
Wiretap Act 18 U.S.C. § 2520	

STATUTES *WITH* LIQUIDATED DAMAGES
No Proof of Actual Damages Required

Cable Communications Policy Act (CCPA)
47 U.S.C. § 551(f)
"actual damages but not less than liquidated damages computed at the rate of $100 a day for each day of violation or $1,000, whichever is higher."

CAN-SPAM Act
15 U.S.C. § 7706(g) (ISPs only)
Multiply the number of violations times $100 or $25 depending upon the nature of the violation.

Drivers Privacy Protection Act (DPPA)
18 U.S.C. § 2724
"actual damages, but not less than liquidated damages in the amount of $2,500"

Fair Credit Reporting Act (FCRA)
15 U.S.C. § 1681n (willful violations)
"any actual damages sustained by the consumer as a result of the failure or damages of not less than $100 and not more than $1,000"

15 U.S.C. § 1671o (negligent violations)
only actual damages allowed; no liquidated damages

Foreign Intelligence Surveillance Act (FISA)
50 U.S.C. § 1810 (improper disclosure/use of electronic surveillance)
"actual damages, but not less than liquidated damages of $1,000 or $100 per day for each day of violation, whichever is greater"

18 U.S.C. § 1828 (improper physical search or disclosure/use)
"actual damages, but not less than liquidated damages of $1,000 or $100 per day for each day of violation, whichever is greater"

Privacy Protection Act (PPA)
42 U.S.C. § 2000aa-6(f)
"actual damages but not less than liquidated damages of $1,000"

Right to Financial Privacy Act (RFPA)
12 U.S.C. § 3417
"(1) $100 without regard to the volume of records involved; (2) any actual damages sustained by the customer as a result of the disclosure."

Stored Communications Act (SCA)
18 U.S.C. § 2707 (against others)
"actual damages but not less than liquidated damages of $1,000"

CONSUMER

18 U.S.C. § 2712 (against U.S.)
"actual damages, but not less than $10,000, whichever amount is greater"

Telephone Consumer Protection Act (TCPA)
47 U.S.C. § 227(c)(5)
"recover for actual monetary loss from such a violation, or to receive up to $500 in damages for each such violation, whichever is greater"

Video Privacy Protection Act (VPPA)
18 U.S.C. § 2710(c)
"actual damages but not less than liquidated damages in an amount of $2,500"

Wiretap Act
18 U.S.C. § 2520
"the court may assess as damages whichever is the greater of (A) the sum of the actual damages suffered by the plaintiff and any profits made by the violator as a result of the violation; or (B) statutory damages of whichever is the greater of $100 a day for each day of violation or $10,000"

STATUTES *WITH* LIQUIDATED DAMAGES
Proof of Actual Damages Required

Privacy Act
5 U.S.C. § 552a
"actual damages sustained by the individual as a result of the refusal or failure, but in no case shall a person entitled to recovery receive less than the sum of $1,000."

Doe v. Chao, 540 U.S. 614 (2004), concluded that the phrase "entitled to recover" required that plaintiffs be entitled to recover actual damages before receiving liquidated damages.

Stored Communications Act (SCA)
18 U.S.C. § 2707 (against others)
"The court may assess as damages in a civil action under this section the sum of the actual damages suffered by the plaintiff and any profits made by the violator as a result of the violation, but in no case shall a person entitled to recover receive less than the sum of $1,000."

STATUTES *WITHOUT* LIQUIDATED DAMAGES

Employee Polygraph Protection Act (EPPA)
29 U.S.C. § 2005(c)

STATUTES *WITH* CRIMINAL PENALTIES	STATUTES *WITHOUT* CRIMINAL PENALTIES
CAN-SPAM Act 15 U.S.C. §§ 7703-7704 (for certain fraudulent e-mail practices)	Cable Communications Policy Act (CCPA) 47 U.S.C. § 521, 551-552
Computer Fraud and Abuse Act (CFAA) 18 U.S.C. § 1030(c)	Children's Online Privacy Protection Act (COPPA) 15 U.S.C. §§ 6501-6505
Drivers Privacy Protection Act (DPPA) 18 U.S.C. § 2723	Employee Polygraph Protection Act (EPPA) 29 U.S.C. §§ 2001-2009
Fair Credit Reporting Act (FCRA) 15 U.S.C. § 1681q (for knowingly obtaining consumer data under false pretenses)	Family Education Rights and Privacy Act (FERPA) 20 U.S.C. § 1232g
Foreign Intelligence Surveillance Act (FISA) 50 U.S.C. § 1809 (improper use and disclosure of electronic surveillance) 50 U.S.C. § 1827 (improper physical search or disclosure/use)	Privacy Protection Act (PPA) 42 U.S.C. FERPA 20 U.S.C. § 2000aa
Gramm-Leach-Bliley Act (GLBA) 15 U.S.C. § 6823 (only for obtaining customer information by false pretenses)	Right to Financial Privacy Act (RFPA) 12 U.S.C. §§ 3401-3422
Health Insurance Portability and Accountability Act (HIPAA) 42 U.S.C. § 1320d-6(a)	Video Privacy Protection Act (VPPA) 18 U.S.C. § 2710
Pen Register Act 18 U.S.C. § 3123(d)	
Privacy Act 5 U.S.C. § 552a(i)	
Stored Communications Act (SCA) 18 U.S.C. § 2701(b)	
Telephone Consumer Protection Act (TCPA) 47 U.S.C. § 227	
Wiretap Act 18 U.S.C. § 2511(4)	

9

CONSUMER

FEDERAL STATUTES: ENFORCEMENT

STATUTE	Private Cause of Action	Liqui-dated Damages	Atty Fees & Costs	Punitive Damages	Equitable Remedies	Gov't Agency Enforce-ment*	State AG Enforce-ment	Criminal Penalties
Cable Communications Policy Act (CCPA)	Yes	Yes	Yes	Yes	No	No	No	No
CAN-SPAM Act	Yes (ISPs only)	Yes	Yes	Yes	Yes	FTC and other agencies	Yes	Yes
Children's Online Privacy Protection Act (COPPA)	No	N/A	N/A	N/A	N/A	FTC	Yes	Yes
Computer Fraud and Abuse Act (CFAA)	Yes	No	No	No	Yes	DOJ	No	Yes
Drivers Privacy Protection Act (DPPA)	Yes	Yes	Yes	Yes	Yes	No	No	Yes
Employee Polygraph Protection Act (EPPA)	Yes	No	Yes	No	No	Labor Dept.	No	No
Fair Credit Reporting Act (FCRA)	Yes	Yes	Yes	Yes Willful Violations	No	FTC and other agencies	Yes	Yes
Family Education Rights and Privacy Act (FERPA)	No	No	N/A	N/A	N/A	Dep't of Education	No	No
Federal Trade Commission Act (FTCA)	No	No	N/A	N/A	N/A	FTC	No	Yes
Foreign Intelligence Surveillance Act (FISA)	Yes	Yes	Yes	Yes	No	No	No	Yes
Gramm-Leach-Bliley Act (GLBA)	No	N/A	N/A	N/A	N/A	FTC and other agencies	No	Yes
Health Insurance Portability and Account-ability Act (HIPAA)	No	N/A	N/A	N/A	N/A	HHS	Yes	Yes
Pen Register Act	No	N/A	N/A	N/A	N/A	No	No	Yes
Privacy Act	Yes	Yes	Yes	No	Yes	No	No	Yes
Privacy Protection Act (PPA)	Yes	Yes	Yes	No	No	No	No	No
Right to Financial Privacy Act (RFPA)	Yes	Yes	Yes	Yes	Yes	No	No	No
Stored Communications Act (SCA)	Yes	Yes	Yes	Yes	Yes	No	No	Yes
Telephone Consumer Protection Act (TCPA)	Yes	Yes	Yes	Yes**	No	FCC	Yes	Yes
Video Privacy Protection Act (VPPA)	Yes	Yes	Yes	Yes*	Yes	No	No	No
Wiretap Act	Yes	Yes	Yes	Yes	Yes	No	No	Yes

*The DOJ enforces statutes with criminal violations. ** Treble damages for willful or knowing violations.

FEDERAL STATUTES AND PREEMPTION

NAME OF FEDERAL STATUE	DOES THE STATUTE CONTAIN A PREEMPTION CLAUSE?	SUMMARY OF PREEMPTION CLAUSE	TEXT OF PREEMPTION CLAUSE
CAN-SPAM Act 15 U.S.C. § 7707	YES	Pre-empts any state law that "prohibits falsity or deception in any portion of a commercial electronic mail message or information attached thereto." Does not pre-empt state law that is not specific to e-mail or other state laws to the extent that they relate to computer crime or fraud. Does not pre-empt COPPA or any federal criminal law. Does not impact the FTC's ability to bring enforcement actions under the FTC act. Does not have any "effect on policies of providers of Internet access service."	(a) Federal law (1) Nothing in this chapter shall be construed to impair the enforcement of section 223 or 231 of Title 47, chapter 71 (relating to obscenity) or 110 (relating to sexual exploitation of children) of Title 18, or any other Federal criminal statute. (2) Nothing in this chapter shall be construed to affect in any way the Commission's authority to bring enforcement actions under FTC Act for materially false or deceptive representations or unfair practices in commercial electronic mail messages. (b) State law (1) In general This chapter supersedes any statute, regulation, or rule of a State or political subdivision of a State that expressly regulates the use of electronic mail to send commercial messages, except to the extent that any such statute, regulation, or rule prohibits falsity or deception in any portion of a commercial electronic mail message or information attached thereto. (2) State law not specific to electronic mail This chapter shall not be construed to preempt the applicability of-- (A) State laws that are not specific to electronic mail, including State trespass, contract, or tort law; or (B) other State laws to the extent that those laws relate to acts of fraud or computer crime. (c) No effect on policies of providers of Internet access service Nothing in this chapter shall be construed to have any effect on the lawfulness or unlawfulness, under any other provision of law, of the adoption, implementation, or enforcement by a provider of Internet access service of a policy of declining to transmit, route, relay, handle, or store certain types of electronic mail messages. d) Inconsistent State law No State or local government may impose any liability for commercial activities or actions by operators in interstate or foreign commerce in connection with an activity or action described in this chapter that is inconsistent with the treatment of those activities or actions under this section.
Children's Online Privacy Protection Act (COPPA) 15 U.S.C. § 6502(d)	YES	State and local governments cannot impose liability for the operators of websites or online services that direct their services towards children or know that children are using their services.	

NAME OF FEDERAL STATUE	DOES THE STATUTE CONTAIN A PREEMPTION CLAUSE?	SUMMARY OF PREEMPTION CLAUSE	TEXT OF PREEMPTION CLAUSE
Fair Credit Reporting Act (FCRA) 15 U.S.C. § 1681t	YES	Only preempts state laws that relate to the collection, distribution, or use of consumer information to the extent that they are inconsistent with the statute, and only to the extent of the inconsistency. Subject to numerous exceptions.	(a) In general Except as provided in subsections (b) and (c) of this section, this subchapter does not annul, alter, affect, or exempt any person subject to the provisions of this subchapter from complying with the laws of any State with respect to the collection, distribution, or use of any information on consumers, or for the prevention or mitigation of identity theft, except to the extent that those laws are inconsistent with any provision of this subchapter, and then only to the extent of the inconsistency. (b) General exceptions No requirement or prohibition may be imposed under the laws of any State-- (1) with respect to any subject matter regulated under-- (A) subsection (c) or (e) of section 1681b of this title, relating to the prescreening of consumer reports; (B) section 1681i of this title, relating to the time by which a consumer reporting agency must take any action, including the provision of notification to a consumer or other person, in any procedure related to the disputed accuracy of information in a consumer's file, except that this subparagraph shall not apply to any State law in effect on September 30, 1996; (C) subsections (a) and (b) of section 1681m of this title, relating to the duties of a person who takes any adverse action with respect to a consumer; (D) section 1681m(d) of this title, relating to the duties of persons who use a consumer report of a consumer in connection with any credit or insurance transaction that is not initiated by the consumer and that consists of a firm offer of credit or insurance; (E) section 1681c of this title, relating to information contained in consumer reports, except that this subparagraph shall not apply to any State law in effect on September 30, 1996; (F) section 1681s-2 of this title, relating to the responsibilities of persons who furnish information to consumer reporting agencies, except that this paragraph shall not apply-- (i) with respect to section 54A(a) of chapter 93 of the Massachusetts Annotated Laws (as in effect on September 30, 1996); or (ii) with respect to section 1785.25(a) of the California Civil Code (as in effect on September 30, 1996); (G) section 1681g(e) of this title, relating to information available to victims under section 1681g(e) of this title; (H) section 1681s-3 of this title, relating to the exchange and use of information to make a solicitation for marketing purposes; or (I) section 1681m(h) of this title, relating to the duties of users of consumer reports to provide notice with respect to terms in certain credit transactions; (2) with respect to the exchange of information among persons affiliated by common ownership or common corporate control, except that this paragraph shall not apply with respect to subsection (a) or (c)(1) of section 2480e of title 9, Vermont Statutes Annotated (as in effect on September 30, 1996); (3) with respect to the disclosures required to be made under subsection (c), (d), (e), or (g) of section 1681g of this title, or subsection (f) of section 1681g of this title relating to the disclosure of credit scores for credit granting purposes, except that this paragraph-- (A) shall not apply with respect to sections 1785.10, 1785.16, and 1785.20.2 of the California Civil Code (as in effect on December 4, 2003) and section 1785.15 through section 1785.15.2 of such Code (as in effect on such date); or (B) shall not apply with respect to sections 5-3-106(2) and 212-14.3-104.3 of the Colorado Revised Statutes (as in effect on December 4, 2003); and

(C) shall not be construed as limiting, annulling, affecting, or superseding any provision of the laws of any State regulating the use in an insurance activity, or regulating disclosures concerning such use, of a credit-based insurance score of a consumer by any person engaged in the business of insurance;

(4) with respect to the frequency of any disclosure under section 1681j(a) of this title, except that this paragraph shall not apply--

(A) with respect to section 12-14.3-105(1)(d) of the Colorado Revised Statutes (as in effect on December 4, 2003);

(B) with respect to section 10-1-393(29)(C) of the Georgia Code (as in effect on December 4, 2003);

(C) with respect to section 1316.2 of title 10 of the Maine Revised Statutes (as in effect on December 4, 2003);

(D) with respect to sections 14-1209(a)(1) and 14-1209(b)(1)(i) of the Commercial Law Article of the Code of Maryland (as in effect on December 4, 2003);

(E) with respect to section 59(d) and section 59(e) of chapter 93 of the General Laws of Massachusetts (as in effect December 4, 2003);

(F) with respect to section 56:11-37.10(a)(1) of the New Jersey Revised Statutes (as in effect on December 4, 2003); or

(G) with respect to section 2480c(a)(1) of title 9 of the Vermont Statutes Annotated (as in effect on December 4, 2003); or

(5) with respect to the conduct required by the specific provisions of--

(A) section 1681c(g) of this title;

(B) section 1681c-1 of this title;

(C) section 1681c-2 of this title;

(D) section 1681g(a)(1)(A) of this title;

(E) section 1681j(a) of this title;

(F) subsections (e), (f), and (g) of section 1681m of this title;

(G) section 1681s(f) of this title;

(H) section 1681s-2a(6) of this title; or

(I) section 1681w of this title.

(c) "Firm offer of credit or insurance" defined

Notwithstanding any definition of the term "firm offer of credit or insurance" (or any equivalent term) under the laws of any State, the definition of that term contained in section 1681a(l) of this title shall be construed to apply in the enforcement and interpretation of the laws of any State governing consumer reports.

(d) Limitations

Subsections (b) and (c) of this section do not affect any settlement, agreement, or consent judgment between any State Attorney General and any consumer reporting agency in effect on September 30, 1996.

Exclusive nature of remedy

The remedy provided by subsection (a)(1) of this section against the United States, a State, or any other governmental unit is exclusive of any other civil action or proceeding for conduct constituting a violation of this chapter, against the officer or employee whose violation gave rise to the claim, or against the estate of such officer or employee.

Privacy Protection Act (PPA) 42 U.S.C. § 2000aa-6(d)	YES	If a citizen has a cause of action against the United States under this staute, pursuit of that cause of action comes at the exclusion of all other potential claims.
Cable Communications Policy Act (CCPA) 47 U.S.C. §§ 521, 551-552	NO	No preemption clause.

NAME OF FEDERAL STATUE	DOES THE STATUTE CONTAIN A PREEMPTION CLAUSE?	SUMMARY OF PREEMPTION CLAUSE	TEXT OF PREEMPTION CLAUSE
Employee Polygraph Protection Act (EPPA) 29 U.S.C. §§ 2001–2009	NO	No preemption clause.	
Gramm–Leach–Bliley Act (GLBA) 15 U.S.C. §§ 6801-6809, 6821-6827	NO	No preemption clause.	
Health Insurance Portability and Accountability Act (HIPPA) 45 C.F.R. 164	NO	No preemption clause.	
Pen Register Act 18 U.S.C. §§ 3121-3123	NO	No preemption clause.	
Stored Communications Act (SCA) 18 U.S.C. §§ 2701-2712	NO	No preemption clause.	
Telephone Consumer Protection Act (TCPA) 47 U.S.C. § 227	NO	No preemption clause.	
Wiretap Act 18 U.S.C. §§ 2510-2522	NO	No preemption clause.	

OPT-IN RIGHTS	OPT-OUT RIGHTS
Cable Communications Policy Act (CCPA) 47 U.S.C. § 551(c)(1) (for PII except names and addresses)	Cable Communications Policy Act (CCPA) 47 U.S.C. § 551(c)(2) (names and addresses)
Children's Online Privacy Protection Act (COPPA) 15 U.S.C. § 6502(b)	CAN-SPAM Act 15 U.S.C. § 7704(a)(3)
Drivers Privacy Protection Act (DPPA) 18 U.S.C. § 2721(b) and (d)	Gramm-Leach-Bliley Act (GLBA) 15 U.S.C. § 6802(b) (for disclosures to nonaffiliates)
Fair Credit Reporting Act (FCRA) 15 U.S.C. § 1681b (for uses beyond permissible uses)	
Family Education Rights and Privacy Act (FERPA) 20 U.S.C. § 1232g(b)(1) (all PII except "directory information")	Family Education Rights and Privacy Act (FERPA) 20 U.S.C. § 1232g(b)(1) ("directory information"—name, address, telephone listing, date and place of birth, activities, degrees, awards, etc.)
Health Insurance Portability and Accountability Act (HIPAA) 45 C.F.R. § 164.508(a) (all uses and disclosures beyond those for treatment, payment, or healthcare operations)	Telephone Consumer Protection Act (TCPA) 47 U.S.C. § 227
Privacy Act 5 U.S.C. § 552a(b) (for disclosures)	
Video Privacy Protection Act (VPPA) 18 U.S.C. § 2710(2)(B) (all PII, especially video titles, except names/addresses)	Video Privacy Protection Act (VPPA) 18 U.S.C. § 2710(2)(D) (names/addresses and subject matter of videos for marketing)

STATE STATUTES

Deceptive Trade Practices

The FTCA is enforced exclusively by the FTC, but every state has some form of deceptive trade practices act of its own. Many of these statutes not only enable a state attorney general to bring actions but also provide a private cause of action to consumers. Several of these laws have provisions for statutory minimum damages, punitive damages and attorneys' fees. In interpreting these laws, many state courts have been heavily influenced by FTCA jurisprudence.

Radio Frequency Identification (RFID)

Many states have laws restricting the use of RFID devices. Several of these laws pertain to the government's use of RFID in driver's licenses, but some of the statutes restrict private-sector uses as well.

State Statutes Regulating Private-Sector Use of RFID

CA	Cal. Civil Code § 52.7 (S.B. 31), Cal. Civil Code §§ 1798.79, 1798.795
NV	Nev. Rev. Stat. §§ 205.461- 205.4675 (SB 125)
NH	N.H. Rev. Stat. § 236.130
ND	N.D. Cent. Code § 12.1-15-06
OK	Okla. Stat. tit. 1 § 1-1430
RI	R.I. Gen. Laws §§ 42-153-1 to 42-153-4
WA	Rev. Code Wash §§ 9A.58.020, 19.300.010 et seq.
WI	Wis. Stat. § 146.25 (2008)

Illustrative statutes include:

California, Cal. Civil Code §§ 1798.79 and 52.7
Prohibits establishing a connection with an RFID tag to access stored information without explicit consent from the tag's owner. SB 31 (2008), Civ. Code § 1798.79. California law also forbids forced implantation of RFID tags. SB 362 (2008), Cal. Civil Code § 52.7.

Nevada, Nev. Rev. Stat. §§ 205.461- 205.4675 (SB 125)
Prohibits capturing, storing or reading information from a person's "RFID document" for the purposes of knowingly or intentionally committing identity theft or any unlawful act without that person's prior knowledge and consent. The statute defines an RFID document as a document containing data issued to an individual for the primary purpose of establishing identity.

New Hampshire, N.H. Rev. Stat. § 236.130
Forbids use of surveillance devices, including an RFID device, to identify ownership of a vehicle or identity of a vehicle's occupants.

North Dakota, N.D. Cent. Code § 12.1-15-06
Prohibits required implantation of an RFID device.

Rhode Island, R.I. Gen. Laws §§ 42-153-1 to 42-153-4

Prohibits use of RFID for tracking the movement or identity of any schoolchildren on school grounds or while being transported to or from school grounds or school functions.

Washington, Rev. Code Wash. §§ 9A.58.020, 19.300.010 et seq.

Washington law generally prohibits the scanning of an RFID tag by anyone except the business or agency that issued the tag. The statute also provides for numerous exceptions, such as when the scanning is part of a sales transaction that the tag holder initiates or the reading of the tag occurs as part of good-faith security research, experimentation or scientific research. Rev. Code Wash. § 19.300.010 et seq.

Washington also has a criminal prohibition on reading RFID tags to capture information about a person without her knowledge and consent for the purpose of committing fraud, identity theft or other illegal activity. Rev. Code Wash. § 9A.58.020.

"Eraser" or "Right to Be Forgotten" Laws

California, Calif. Bus. & Prof. Code §§ 22580-22582 / SB 568 (effective Jan. 1, 2015)

California's Privacy Rights for California Minors in the Digital World Act, also called the "eraser" bill, permits minors to remove, or to request and obtain removal of, content or information posted on an Internet Web site, online service, online application, or mobile application. It also prohibits an operator of a Web site or online service directed to minors from marketing or advertising to minors specified products or services that minors are legally prohibited from buying. The law also will prohibit marketing or advertising certain products based on personal information specific to a minor or knowingly using, disclosing, compiling, or allowing a third party to do so.

Spyware

Several states have anti-spyware laws.

State Spyware Statutes

AK Alaska Stat. §§ 45.45.792, .794, .798; § 45.50.471(51)
AZ Ariz. Rev. Stat. Ann. §§ 44-7301 to 44-7304
AR Ark. Code §§ 4-11-101, -102, -103, -104, -105, § 19-6-301, § 19-6-804
CA Cal. Bus. & Prof. Code D. 8 §§ 22947 to 22947.6
GA Ga. Code §§ 16-9-152 to -157
IL 720 ILCS 5/16D-5.5
IN Ind. Code § 24-4.8-1 et seq.
IA Iowa Code §§ 715.1 to 715.8
LA La. Rev. Stat. Ann. §§ 51:2006 to 51:2014
NV Nev. Rev. Stat. § 205.4737
NH N.H. Rev. Stat. Ann. §§ 359-H:1 to 359-H:6
RI R.I. Gen. Laws §§ 11-52.2-2, -3, -4, -5, -6, -7
TX Tex. Business & Commerce Code Ann. §§ 324.001 to 324.102
UT Utah Code Ann. §§ 13-40-101 to 13-40-401
VA Virginia Va. Code 18.2-152.4
WA Wash. Rev. Code §§ 19.270.101 to 19.270.900
WY Wyoming Wyo. Stat. § 6-3-506, 40-25-101 (2014 H.B. 178, Act 48)
PR Puerto Rico 10 L.P.R.A. §§ 2181, 2182, 2183, 2184, 2185

Source: National Conference of State Legislatures, State Spyware Laws,
www.ncsl.org/default.aspx?tabid=13452

Illustrative statutes include:

California, Cal. Bus. & Prof. Code D. 8 §§ 22947 to 22947.6
California law prohibits an unauthorized user from willfully loading software onto the computer of a California resident and using the software to carry out a number of forbidden activities. These activities include modification of certain settings related to the computer's access to or use of the Internet; collection through intentionally deceptive means of certain types of PII; and preventing, through intentionally deceptive means, an authorized user's reasonable efforts to block the installation of or disabling of software. The law also forbids the taking control of the computer by e-mails or viruses, using the computer to engage in denial-of-service attacks; or allowing multiple, sequential stand-alone advertisements to be opened on the computer in a fashion that blocks a reasonable user from closing the advertisements.

Iowa, Iowa Code §§ 715.1 to 715.8
Prohibits a person who is "not an owner or operator of a computer" from transmitting computer software to a computer "knowingly or with conscious avoidance of actual knowledge," and to use such software for a number of acts, including: (1) modifying through intentionally deceptive means the settings of a computer, (2) collecting through intentionally deceptive means personally

identifiable information through a keystroke-logging function and (3) preventing through intentionally deceptive means an owner's or an operator's reasonable efforts to block the installation of, or to disable, computer software by causing computer software that the owner or operator has properly removed or disabled to automatically reinstall or reactivate on the computer.

Texas, Tex. Business & Commerce Code Ann. §§ 324.001 to 324.102

Prohibits a series of conduct or activities, including collection or culling of personally identifiable information, unauthorized access to or modifications of computer settings, unauthorized interference with installation or disabling of computer software and unauthorized creation of, access to or use of zombies or botnets.

Washington, Wash. Rev. Code §§ 19.270.101 to 19.270.900

Prohibits the transmission of software to the owner's or operator's computer or software for (1) modifying through intentionally deceptive means the settings of a computer, (2) collecting through intentionally deceptive means personally identifiable information through a keystroke-logging function that records and certain other actions and (3) preventing through intentionally deceptive means an owner's or an operator's reasonable efforts to block the installation of, or to disable, computer software by causing computer software that the owner or operator has properly removed or disabled to automatically reinstall or reactivate on the computer.

Transparency

California's "Shine the Light" Law, Cal. Civ. Code § 1798.83 (2003)

This statute permits consumers to obtain from businesses information about the personal data that the businesses disclosed to third parties for direct marketing purposes. People can find out this data as well as the "names and addresses of all of the third parties that received personal information from the business." § 1798.83(1). The law applies to businesses with 20 or more employees. § 1798(c)(1). It does not apply to financial institutions. Companies with privacy policies that allow people to opt out of sharing their data with third parties are exempt. § 1798(c)(2).

FIRST AMENDMENT

Privacy regulation of the collection, use and disclosure of personal data can come into conflict with the First Amendment.

First Amendment Protection of Commercial Speech: Although commercial speech is constitutionally protected, it has a lower value than regular categories of speech and therefore is entitled to a lesser protection. *Ohralik v. Ohio State Bar Ass'n*, 436 U.S. 447 (1978).

Defining Commercial Speech: The court has defined commercial speech as speech that "proposes a commercial transaction," *Virginia State Board*, 425 U.S. 748 (1976), and as "expression related solely to the economic interests of the speaker and its audience." *Central Hudson Gas & Electric Corp. v. Public Service Comm'n of New York*, 447 U.S. 557 (1980). The court later held that neither of these is a requirement to define commercial speech; both are factors to be considered in determining whether speech is commercial. *Bolger v. Youngs Drug Products Corp.*, 463 U.S. 60 (1983).

The Central Hudson Test: In *Central Hudson*, 447 U.S. 557 (1980), the court established a four-part test for analyzing the constitutionality of restrictions on commercial speech:
1. Is the speech about lawful activity and not misleading?
2. Is the government interest substantial?
3. Does the regulation directly advance the government interest?
4. Is the regulation "no more extensive than is necessary" to achieve the government interest?

Leading Cases

Rowan v. United States Post Office Department, 397 U.S. 728 (1970)
The Postal Revenue and Federal Salary Act, 39 U.S.C. § 4009 (1967), allowed people to request that a mailer stop all future mailings. Not a First Amendment violation because the government was not censoring—the individual makes the choice not to receive the mail. "Nothing in the Constitution compels us to listen to or view any unwanted communication."

Mainstream Marketing Services, Inc. v. FTC, 358 F.3d 1228 (10th Cir. 2004)
The Do Not Call Registry did not violate the First Amendment because it satisfied the *Central Hudson* test. Protecting people's privacy and right not to receive unwanted phone calls in their homes was a substantial government interest. Although the registry does not allow people to block all unwanted calls since it exempts political and charitable calls, it will still be effective and stop many unwanted calls. Thus, it directly advances the government's interest.

U.S. West, Inc. v. FCC, 182 F.3d 1224 (10th Cir. 1999)
FCC order limiting the disclosure and use of customer proprietary network information (CPNI) violated *Central Hudson* because privacy did not rise to a substantial interest. Disclosure and use of CPNI merely caused a "general level of discomfort" and not "undue embarrassment or ridicule."

An opt out would have been a less restrictive alternative to the FCC's opt-in requirement. The FCC later rejected this holding in its 2007 CPNI Order (see page 184).

Trans Union Corp. v. FTC, 245 F.3d 809 (D.C. Cir. 2001) (Trans Union I)

The FTC ordered Trans Union to stop selling its targeted marketing lists, claiming the sale violated FCRA. The court concluded privacy was a substantial interest and that although an opt out was a less restrictive alternative, the First Amendment does not require the least restrictive means (only in cases involving strict scrutiny). See also *Trans Union v. FTC*, 295 F.3d 42 (D.C. Cir. 2002) *(Trans Union II)*.

Sorrell v. IMS Health Inc., 131 S. Ct. 2653 (2011)

The U.S. Supreme Court struck down Vermont's Prescription Confidentiality Law as a violation of the First Amendment right to free speech. The Vermont law restricted the sale and marketing use of information that would identify prescribers without their consent. The Court reasoned that the Vermont law "enacts content- and speaker-based restrictions on the sale, disclosure, and use of prescriber-identifying information." According to the Court, the statute made content-based restrictions because it singled out marketing, and the statute made speaker-based restrictions because it focused exclusively on pharmaceutical manufacturers. The Supreme Court stated: "The law on its face burdens disfavored speech by disfavored speakers."

FOR FURTHER REFERENCE

Books

Michelle Finneran Dennedy, Jonathan Fox, & Thomas R. Finneran, *The Privacy Engineer's Manifesto* (2014)
A detailed and concrete discussion about Privacy by Design and how to implement privacy in the development of technology.

Frank Pasquale, *The Black Box Society: The Secret Algorithms That Control Money and Information* (2014)
Argues that the detailed profiles that companies are creating about people have profound implications for their reputations and opportunities as well as for society. The algorithms used to make automated decisions based on personal data re often hidden, and they should be more transparent. The law should also ensure that important decisions be made fairly and in a non-discriminatory manner.

Neil Richards, *Intellectual Privacy: Rethinking Civil Liberties in the Digital Age* (2015)
Argues that surveillance—by both the government and private-sector entities—threatens freedom of speech, belief, and intellectual exploration.

H. Jeff Smith, *Managing Privacy: Information Technology and Corporate America* (1994)
Although dated, this book remains an insightful examination of how various institutions and businesses formulate and implement their privacy policies.

Daniel J. Solove, *The Digital Person: Technology and Privacy in the Information Age* (2004)
Examines the growing collection and use of personal data and proposes how it should be regulated.

Articles and Other Sources

Danielle Keats Citron, *Reservoirs of Danger: The Evolution of Public and Private Law at the Dawn of the Information Age,* 80 S. Cal. L. Rev. 241 (2007)
A provocative argument for strict liability for harms created by the creation and use of computer databases of personal information.

Julie E. Cohen, *Examined Lives: Informational Privacy and the Subject as Object,* 52 Stan. L. Rev. 1373 (2000)
A discussion of the commercialization of personal data, the nature of privacy harms and whether the sale of personal data constitutes speech.

Chris Jay Hoofnagle & Jan Whittington, *The Price of 'Free': Accounting for the Cost of the Internet's Most Popular Price,* 61 UCLA L. Rev. 606 (2014)
Suggesting that the FTC should help consumers realize the true nature of online services by clarifying that the consumer's personal information is the basis of a bargain and will be used for secondary purposes.

Jerry Kang, *Information Privacy in Cyberspace Transactions,* 50 Stan. L. Rev. 1193 (1998)
An early and classic article about how to balance privacy and efficient consumer transactions.

Orin S. Kerr, *Cybercrime's Scope: Interpreting "Access" and "Authorization" in Computer Misuse Statutes,* 78 N.Y.U. L. Rev. 1596 (2003)
The leading article about the Computer Fraud and Abuse Act and its state statutory analogues.

Joel R. Reidenberg, *Lex Informatica: The Formulation of Information Policy Rules Through Technology,* 76 Tex. L. Rev. 553 (1998)
Classic article about how technology embedded in design and code can protect privacy.

Joel R. Reidenberg, *Privacy Wrongs in Search of Remedies,* 54 Hastings L.J. 877 (2003)
A critique of the FTC as the primary enforcer of privacy.

Neil M. Richards, *Reconciling Data Privacy and the First Amendment,* 52 UCLA L. Rev. 1149 (2005)
A thoughtful argument that the sale and use of computer databases does not constitute "speech" under the First Amendment.

Ira S. Rubinstein & Nathaniel Good, *Privacy by Design: A Counterfactual Analysis of Google and Facebook Privacy Incidents,* 28 Berkeley Tech. L. J. 1333 (2013)
Carrying out the first comprehensive analysis of engineering and usability principles specifically relevant to privacy. Based on a review of the technical literature, it proposes a small number of relevant principles and illustrates them by reference to ten recent privacy incidents involving Google and Facebook.

Paul M. Schwartz, *Privacy and Preemption,* 118 Yale L.J. 902 (2009)
Develops a proposal for an optimal dual federal-state system for information privacy law and the role of preemption rules in this system.
Paul M. Schwartz & Daniel J. Solove, *The PII Problem: Privacy and a New Concept of Personally Identifiable Information,* 86 N.Y.U. L. Rev. 1814 (2011)
Rethinks the concept of PII and discusses how the difficulties in de-identifying data can be addressed.

Daniel J. Solove & Woodrow Hartzog, *The FTC and the New Common Law of Privacy,* 114 Colum. L. Rev. 583 (2014)
Argues that "the FTC's privacy jurisprudence is functionally equivalent to a body of common law." Companies look to these agreements as a quasi-common law for determining best practices, and the structures of these FTC agreements amount to a common law equivalent—and one that is amenable to study.

Jeff Sovern, *Opting In, Opting Out, or No Options at All: The Fight for Control of Personal Information,* 74 Wash. L. Rev. 1033 (1999)
A thorough examination of the pros and cons of both opt-in and opt-out systems.

Jeff Sovern, *Protecting Privacy with Deceptive Trade Practices Legislation,* 69 Fordham L. Rev. 1305 (2001)
Discusses state deceptive trade practice acts.

Daniel J. Solove, *Privacy Self-Management and the Consent Dilemma,* 126 Harv. L. Rev. 1879 (2013)
Current approaches to privacy in law and policy rely on "privacy self-management"—providing people with notice about how their data is being collected and used, and then allowing people a choice about whether or not to consent to such collection and use. Privacy self-management, however, cannot succeed alone because a range of cognitive and structural problems make it nearly impossible for people to weigh the costs and benefits of various uses of their personal data.

Michael E. Staten & Fred H. Cate, *The Impact of Opt-in Privacy Rules on Retail Markets: A Case Study of MBNA,* 52 Duke L.J. 745 (2003)
A practical illustration of how information privacy regulation affects business practices.

Peter P. Swire, *Trustwrap: The Importance of Legal Rules to Electronic Commerce and Internet Privacy,* 54 Hastings L.J. 847 (2003)
A pragmatic argument about how privacy regulation can enhance rather than impede business interests.

CHAPTER 10

Data Security

ESSENTIAL POINTS

- The vast majority of states have enacted data breach notification statutes. These laws can contain important differences, which make multistate notifications complex undertakings.

- The FTC has brought approximately 55 enforcement actions concerning poor security practices.

DATA BREACH NOTIFICATION STATUTES

Rise of the State Statutes

California's Data Security Breach Notification Statute, S.B. 1386 (2002)
This was the first data breach notification law in the United States. Following the well-publicized data security breach at ChoicePoint, which was made public pursuant to this statute, many other states enacted similar data breach notification laws. At present, 47 states have enacted data security breach statutes.

The various statutes can differ in sometimes dramatic, and sometimes subtle, ways. These distinctions complicate the task of carrying out a multistate notification of a data breach. There has also been a discussion of the merits of enacting a federal data breach notification law, but no such bill has been enacted thus far.

State Data Security Breach Notification Statutes

The vast majority of states have data security breach notification statutes. These statutes vary primarily based on the following elements:

1. *Trigger for Notice:* The statutes differ according to when they mandate a notification. Some of the laws require a reasonable belief that information has either been accessed or acquired. These standards are on the pro-notification side of the continuum, as they require notice when a third party merely has had access to the information. A showing that this third party actually acquired the information—that is, gained control of it—is not necessary under these laws. A large number of states have a narrower trigger for notification by requiring a finding of a risk of misuse or harm to the affected party before mandating disclosure.

2. *Exceptions to Notification:* The most prevalent of the notification exceptions is one based on a finding by the breached entity that there is no reasonable likelihood of harm flowing from the breach. Sometimes such an exception also requires a consultation with law enforcement officials. Other states provide an exception built around a finding that there is no reasonable likelihood of misuse of the breached data.

3. *Parties to Whom Disclosure Is Required:* All states require disclosure to the affected individual and almost all to the owner or licensee of the data. State statutes also frequently require disclosure to credit reporting agencies but generally do so only if 1,000 or more persons are affected by the breach. Some laws also require disclosures to the state attorney general, other state agencies and information brokers.

4. *Enforcement:* Only a minority of state statutes provide a private right of action. In states with such a statutory right, private parties can sue for violations of the state breach notification laws. In the other states, only a state official, typically the state attorney general, can enforce the law. Currently, 32 of the 47 state breach notification statutes lack a private right of action.

State Data Security Breach Notification Laws
(Key to chart on page 215)

Trigger for Notification	Exceptions to Notice	Party to Whom Disclosure Is Required
• Acquisition (AQ)	• Alternative notification: Victim of breach is resident of another state that has its own breach notification law (AN)	• Affected individuals (I)
• Access (AC)		• Owner or licensee of data (O)
• Misuse (M)	• No reasonable likelihood of harm (NH)	• Credit reporting agencies if 1,000+ persons affected (CRA)
• Risk of misuse (RM)	• No reasonable likelihood of misuse (NM)	
• Risk of harm (RH)	• No breach occurred (NB)	• Information brokers (IB)
• Risk of identity theft or fraud (RID)	• Required consultation with law enforcement (RC)	• Attorney general (AG)
• Substantial risk of identity theft or fraud (SRID)		• Other state agencies (OA)

STATE DATA SECURITY BREACH NOTIFICATION LAWS

STATE STATUTE	TRIGGER FOR NOTICE	EXCEPTIONS TO NOTICE	PARTY TO WHOM NOTICE IS REQUIRED	PRIVATE RIGHT OF ACTION?
AK Alaska Stat. § 45.48.010 et seq.	AQ or AC	NH	I, CRA	No
AZ Arz. Rev. Stat. § 44-7501	AQ or AC + RH	NB	I, O	No
AR Ark. Code Ann. § 4-110-101 et seq.	AQ	NH	I, O	No
CA Cal. Civ. Code §§ 1798.29, 1798.80 et seq.	AQ		I, O	Yes
CO Colo. Rev. Stat. §§ 6-1-716	AQ	NM + notice to state AG	I, O, CRA	No
CT Conn. Gen. Stat. §§ 36a-701b	AC or AQ	NH + RC	I, O	No
DE Del. Code Ann. tit. 6, § 12B-101 et. seq.	AQ	NM + Notice to State AG	I, O	No
DC D.C. Code § 28-3851 et seq.	AQ	NM + notice to state AG	I, O, CRA	Yes
FL Fla. Stat. § 817.5681	AC	NH + RC	I, CRA, AG*	No
GA Ga. Code Ann. § 10-1-910, -911, -912; § 46-5-214	AQ		I, CRA, IB	No
HI Haw. Rev. Stat. Ann. § 487N-1 et seq.	M or RM	NH or NM	I, O, CRA, OA	No
ID Idaho Code Ann. § 28-51-104	M or RM	NM	I, O, AG	No
IL 815 Ill. Comp. Stat. 530/10, 530/12	AQ		I, O, CRA (if data collector is a state agency)	Yes
IN Ind. Code §§ 4-1-11-1 , § 24-4.9	AQ + M or RID		I, O, CRA, AG	No
IA Iowa Code § 715C.2	AQ	NH + RC	I, O	No
KS Kan. Stat. Ann. § 50-7a01	AC or AQ + RID	NM	I, O, CRA	No
KY KRS § 365.732	AQ or RHAQ		I, O, CRA	No
LA La. Rev. Stat. Ann. §§ 51:3071 et seq. La. Admin. Code tit. 16, § 701	AQ	NH + RC	I, O, AG	Yes
ME Me. Rev. Stat. Ann. tit. 10, § 1347 et seq.	M or RM	NM	I, O, CRA, AG	No
MD Md. Code Com. Law § 14-3501 et seq.MA	AQ	NM	I, O, CRA, AG	No
MA Mass. Gen. Laws ch. 93H, §§ 1-6 201 Mass. Code Regs. 17.04, 17.04	AQ + SRID or M		I, O, AG, OA	No
MI Mich. Comp. Laws §§ 445.63, 445.72	AC + AQ	NH	I, CRA (unless subject to Gramm-Leach-Bliley Act)	No
MN Minn. Stat. §§ 13.055, 325E.61	AQ		I, O, CRA (500 + only)	No

* If more than 500 people affected, must make records available to AG for investigations

State	Statute				
MS	Miss. Code Ann. § 75-24-29	AQ	NH	I, O	No
MO	Mo. Rev. Stat. § 407.1500	AC + AQ		I, O, AG, CRA	No
MT	Mont. Code Ann. § 30-14-1701 Mont. Code Ann. § 2-6-504	AQ		I, O	No
NE	Neb. Rev. Stat. § 87-801 et seq.	AQ + M or RM	NM	I, O	No
NV	Nev. Rev. Stat. §§ 603A.010–603A.920	AQ		I, O, CRA	Yes
NH	N.H Rev. Stat. Ann. § 359-C:21	AQ + M or RM or determination of use cannot be madet be made	NM	I, O, CRA (unless subject to Gramm-Leach-Bliley Act), AG, OA	Yes
NJ	N.J. Stat. Ann. § 56:8-163	AC	NM	I, O, CRA, OA	Yes
NY	N.Y. State Tech. Law § 57-A:208 N.Y. Gen. Bus. §§ 899aa	AQ		I, O, AG, OA,CRA (5000+ only)	No
NC	N.C. Gen. Stat. §§ 75-61, 75-64, 75-65	AC+AQ+M or RM	NM	I, O, AG, CRA	Yes
ND	N.D. Cent. Code § 51-30-01 et seq	AQ		I, O	Yes
OH	Ohio Rev. Code Ann. §§ 1349.19, 1349.191, 1349.192, 1347.12	AC + AQ + M or RM	NH	I, O, CRA	No
OK	Okla. Stat. Ann. tit. 24, § 161 Okla. Stat. Ann. tit. 74, § 3113.1	AQ or AC + RID		I, O	No
OR	Or. Rev. Stat. §§ 646A.600 et seq.	AQ	NH	I, O, CRA	No
PA	73 P.S. § 2301 et seq.	AC + AQ + RH	NH	I, O, CRA	No
RI	R.I. Gen. Laws § 11-49.2-1 et seq.	AQ, SRID	NH	I, O	Yes
SC	S.C. Code Ann. § 39-1-90	AQ + RH	NH	I, O, OA (1000+ only), CRA	Yes
TN	Tenn. Code Ann. § 47-18-2107	AQ		I, O, CRA	Yes
TX	Tex. Bus. & Com. Code Ann. §§ 521.002, 521.053	AQ	AN	I, O, CRA (10,000+ persons)	No
UT	Utah Code Ann. § 13-44-101 et seq.	AQ + M	NM	I, O	No
VT	Vt. Stat. Ann. tit. 9, § 2430, 2435	AC or AQ	NM + informs state AG or other state agency	I, O, CRA, AG (1000+ only)	No
VA	Va. Code Ann. §§ 18.2-186.6, 32.1 127.1:05	AC + AQ + RID		I, O, AG (1000+ only)	Yes
WA	Wash. Rev. Code §§ 19.215.010, 42.56.590	AQ	NH	I, O	Yes
WV	W. Va. Code § 46A-2A-102 et seq.	AC + AQ + RID		I, O, CRA	No
WI	Wis. Stat. § 134.98	AQ + RID	NH	I, O, CRA	No. (But breach of law is evidence of negligence or breach of duty)
WY	Wyo. Stat. Ann. § 40-12-501 et seq.	AQ + RM	NH, NM	I, O	No

Some examples of leading state breach notification laws:

California, Cal. Civ. Code §§ 1798.29, 1798.82, 1798.84

The law's trigger for notification is a reasonable belief of the acquisition of personal information. This statute does not provide for exceptions to such notice. It requires that the affected individual and the owner or licensee of the data be informed. Finally, the statute provides for a private right of action to "any customer injured by a violation of this title." It also provides an additional penalty for willful, intentional and reckless violations of the statute's requirement of reasonable security procedures and practices. A 2013 Amendment to the breach notification law expanded the definition of "personal information" to include "a user name or email address, in combination with a password or security question and answer that would permit access to an online account.

Iowa, Iowa Code § 715C.1

This state provides an acquisition trigger for notification. It exempts from disclosure obligations a breach when "no reasonable likelihood of financial harm to consumers" exists, and there has been either "an appropriate investigation" or "consultation with the relevant federal, state or local agencies responsible for law enforcement." When a breach notification is required, the notice is to be provided to affected individuals and the "owner or licensor." There is no private right of action under the act; only the attorney general may enforce it.

Massachusetts, Mass. Gen. Laws ch. 93H, § 1, 201 Mass. Code. Regs. 17.03, 17.04

This statute requires notification when there is an acquisition of breached data plus "a substantial risk of identity theft or fraud against a resident of the commonwealth." The Massachusetts statute does not provide for exceptions to such notice. It requires notification of affected state residents, the attorney general, director of consumer affairs and business regulations, other state agencies and consumer reporting agencies. There is no private right of action provided by the statute; only the attorney general may bring an action under it for a failure to "maintain a comprehensive information security program."

New York, N.Y. State Tech. Law § 57-A:208, N.Y. Gen. Bus. §§ 399-h, 899-aa

This state requires notification upon the acquisition of breached data. It does not provide for exceptions to such notice. This notification is to be provided to affected individuals, the owner or licensee of the information, the attorney general, Consumer Protection Board, State Office of Cyber Security and Critical Infrastructure Coordination and consumer reporting agencies if more than 5,000 persons must be notified of the breach.

ELEMENT OF PII (WHEN ASSOCIATED WITH FIRST NAME/INITIAL AND LAST NAME)	STATES INCORPORATING THE ELEMENT
Social Security number (SSN)	47 States and DC
Driver's license number or state identification card number (DL)	47 States and DC
Financial account number, credit card number, debit card number in combination with any required security code, access code, or password (FIN)	47 States and DC
Medical information (MED)	AR, CA, MO, TX
Health insurance information (HEALTH)	CA, CT, FL, MO, MT, TX
Passport number (PPN)	CT, MT, NC, OR
Alien registration number (ALIEN)	CT
Password, access code, PIN (PW)	AK, DC, GA, ME, MT, NY, NC, SC, VT
Unique electronic identification number (UEIN)	IA, MO, NE, NC, TX
Individual taxpayer identification number (TAX)	MD, MT, NC, ND
Tribal identification number (TRIBAL)	MT, WY
Mother's maiden name (MAIDEN)	NY, NC, ND, TX
Date of birth (DOB)	ND, TX
Digital or electronic signature (SIG)	NC, ND
Telecommunication access device (TELE)	TX
Biometric data (BIOMETRIC)	IA, NE, NC, TX, WI
DNA profile (DNA)	WI
OTHER PROVISIONS:	
Extends protection to elements even if not connected to a person's name if the information would still be sufficient for identity theft	GA, ME, OR
Social Security number is PII absent connection to name	IN, MT
Exemption for last 4 digits of SSN, driver's license number, or state/federal identification number as non-PII	NV
Includes signature, home address and telephone number along with name as first identifying element	MT
No mention of name as necessary element for PII	NY, CT, TX (lists names as an identifying element)

PII DEFNITIONS IN STATE DATA SECURITY BREACH NOTIFICATION LAWS (STATE BY STATE)

STATE STATUTE	PII ELEMENTS
AK Alaska Stat. § 45.48.010 et seq.	SSN, DL, FIN, PW
AZ Arz. Rev. Stat. § 44-7501	SSN, DL, FIN
AR Ark. Code Ann. § 4-110-101 et seq.	SSN, DL, FIN, MED
CA Cal. Civ. Code §§ 1798.29, 1798.80 et seq.	SSN, DL, FIN, MED, HEALTH
CO Colo. Rev. Stat. §§ 6-1-716	SSN, DL, FIN
CT Conn. Gen. Stat. §§ 36a-701b	SSN, DL, FIN, HEALTH, PPN, ALIEN, No mention of name as necessary element for PII
DE Del. Code Ann. tit. 6, § 12B-101 et. seq.	SSN, DL, FIN

ELEMENT OF PII (WHEN ASSOCIATED WITH FIRST NAME/INITIAL AND LAST NAME)	STATES INCORPORATING THE ELEMENT
DC D.C. Code § 28-3851 et seq.	SSN, DL, FIN, PW
FL Fla. Stat. § 817.5681	SSN, DL, FIN, PW, HEALTH
GA Ga. Code Ann. § 10-1-910, -911, -912; § 46-5-214	SSN, DL, FIN, PW, Extends protection to elements even if not connected to a person's name if the information would still be sufficient for identity theft
HI Haw. Rev. Stat. Ann. § 487N-1 et seq.	SSN, DL, FIN
ID I.C. § 28-51-104 to 107	SSN, DL, FIN
IL 815 Ill. Comp. Stat. 530/1, 530/25	SSN, DL, FIN
IN Ind. Code §§ 4-1-11-1 et seq., § 24-4.9 et seq.	SSN, DL, FIN, Social Security number is PII absent connection to name
IA Iowa Code §§ 715C.1, 715C.2	SSN, DL, FIN, UEIN, BIOMETRIC
KS Kan Stat. Ann. § 50-7a01 et seq.	SSN, DL, FIN
KY KRS § 365.732	SSN, DL, FIN
LA La. Rev. Stat. Ann. §§ 51:3071 et seq. La. Admin. Code tit. 16, § 701	SSN, DL, FIN
ME Me. Rev. Stat. Ann. tit. 10, § 1347 et seq.	SSN, DL, FIN, PW, Extends protection to elements even if not connected to a person's name if the information would still be sufficient for identity theft
MD Md. Code Com. Law § 14-3501 et seq.	SSN, DL, FIN, UEIN, TAX
MA Mass. Gen. Laws ch. 93H, §§ 1-6 201 Mass. Code Regs. 17.04, 17.04	SSN, DL, FIN
MI Mich. Comp. Laws §§ 445.63, 445.72	SSN, DL, FIN
MN Minn. Stat. §§ 325E.61, 325E.64	SSN, DL, FIN
MS Code Ann. § 75-24-29	SSN, DL, FIN
MO Mo. Rev. Stat. § 407.1500	SSN, DL, FIN, MED, HEALTH
MT Mont. Code Ann. § 30-24-1701 Mont. Code Ann. § 2-6-504	SSN, DL, FIN, HEALTH, PPN, PW, TAX, TRIBAL, Social Security number is PII absent connection to name; includes signature, home address, and telephone number along with name as first identifying element
NE Neb. Rev. Stat. § 87-801 et. seq.	SSN, DL, FIN, UEIN, BIOMETRIC
NV Nev. Rev. Stat. §§603A.010-603A.920	SSN, DL, FIN, Exemption for last 4 digits of SSN, driver's license number, or state/federal identification number as non-PII
NH N.H Rev. Stat. Ann. § 359-C:21	SSN, DL, FIN
NJ N.J. Stat. Ann. § 56:8-163	SSN, DL, FIN
NY N.Y. State Tech. Law § 57-A:208 N.Y. Gen. Bus. §§ 899aa	SSN, DL, FIN, PW, MAIDEN, No mention of name as necessary element for PII
NC N.C. Gen. Stat. §§ 75-61, 75-64, 75-65	SSN, DL, FIN, PPN, PW, UEIN, TAX, MAIDEN, SIG, BIOMETRIC
ND N.D. Cent. Code § 51-30-01 et seq.	SSN, DL, FIN, TAX, MAIDEN, DOB, SIG
OH Ohio Rev. Code Ann. §§ 1347.12, 1349.19, 1349. 191, 1349.192	SSN, DL, FIN
OK Okla. Stat. Ann. tit. 24, § 161 Okla. Stat. Ann. tit. 74, § 3113.1	SSN, DL, FIN
OR Or. Rev. Stat. §§ 646A.600 et seq.	SSN, DL, FIN, PPN, Extends protection to elements even if not connected to a person's name if the information would still be sufficient for identity theft

ELEMENT OF PII (WHEN ASSOCIATED WITH FIRST NAME/INITIAL AND LAST NAME)	STATES INCORPORATING THE ELEMENT
PA 73 P.S. § 2301 et seq.	SSN, DL, FIN
RI R.I. Gen. Laws § 11-49.2-1 et seq.	SSN, DL, FIN
SC S.C. Code Ann. § 39-1-90	SSN, DL, FIN, PW
TN Tenn. Code Ann. § 47-18-2107	SSN, DL, FIN
TX Tex. Bus. & Com. Code Ann. §§ 521.002, 521.053	SSN, DL, FIN, MED, HEALTH, UEIN, MAIDEN, DOB, TELE, BIOMETRIC, No mention of name as necessary element for PII (lists name as an identifying element)
UT Utah Code Ann. § 13-44-101 et seq.	SSN, DL, FIN
VT Vt. Stat. Ann. tit. 9, § 2430, 2435	SSN, DL, FIN, PW
VA Va. Code Ann. §§ 18.2-186.6, 32.1, 127.1:05	SSN, DL, FIN
WA Wash. Rev. Code §§ 19.255.010, 42.56.590	SSN, DL, FIN
WV W. Va. Code § 46A-2A-102 et seq.	SSN, DL, FIN
WI Wis. Stat. § 134.98	SSN, DL, FIN, BIOMETRIC, DNA
WY Wyo. Stat. Ann. § 40-12-501 et seq.	SSN, DL, FIN, TRIBAL

State Credit Freeze Statutes

Numerous states have security freeze statutes. These laws require consumer credit reporting agencies to place a security freeze on the consumer's credit report upon request by the consumer. Once such a freeze is placed on a credit report, credit reporting agencies cannot generally release the frozen report to a third party in the absence of the consumer's express authorization. States with such laws include Arizona, California, Connecticut, Florida, Indiana, Iowa, New York, Oregon, Texas, Washington and Wisconsin.

FTC ENFORCEMENT UNDER SECTION 5 OF THE FTC ACT

In a number of cases, the FTC has brought actions against companies that failed to adequately protect the security of personal information. Many of these cases involved data security breaches or improper disclosures and leaks, but some cases involved the mere failure to provide adequate security without any breach or leak occurring.

Leading Cases

FTC v. Wyndham Worldwide Corp., 2014 WL 1349019 (D.N.J. 2014)
District court upheld FTC's authority to bring cases against companies with inadequate data protection practices. Prior FTC Act actions constitute sufficient notice to companies as to what adequate and inadequate data protection practices are. FTC's allegation that Wyndham's inadequate data security practices led to theft of personal data was sufficient consumer harm to grant standing under FTC Act.

Resnick v. AvMed, Inc., 693 F.3d 1317 (11th Cir. 2012)

Class action against healthcare company that had two unencrypted laptops stolen with customers' personal information on them. The 11th Circuit granted standing where named plaintiffs alleged sufficient injury-in-fact by demonstrating they had their identities stolen after the data breach, paid for identity-theft protection services, and had never had their identities stolen prior to the breach.

PATCO Construction Co. v. People's United Bank,
684 F.3d 197 (1st Cir. 2012)

Under Article 4A of the Uniform Commercial Code, a bank is generally held not liable for losses if it followed commercially responsible security procedures to verify the transaction. The defendant bank had not used commercially reasonable security procedures in light of its "collective failures, taken as a whole" measured against security knowledge at the time of the transaction. As an example, it failed to implement additional procedures despite its knowledge of ongoing fraud involving keylogging malware.

Leading FTC Data Security Enforcement Actions

In re Eli Lilly (2002)

Eli Lilly, a pharmaceutical company, sent e-mail reminders to Prozac users with all subscribers listed in the "to" line of the message. The FTC alleged that the company's privacy policy promising confidentiality was deceptive because the company failed to establish adequate security protections for its consumers' data. The January 2002 settlement between Eli Lilly and the FTC required the company to establish a new security program.

In re Microsoft Corp. (2002)

The FTC charged that Microsoft had made unfair and deceptive representations that NET Passport, an online authentication service, was "protected by powerful online security technology and a strict privacy policy." Microsoft settled with the FTC and agreed to create a comprehensive information security program and to conduct an annual audit to assess its security practices for a period of 20 years.

In re Guess.com, Inc. (2003)

Guess, a clothing company, had promised that all personal information "including ... credit card information and sign-in password, are stored in an unreadable, encrypted format at all times." This assertion of company policy was false, and the FTC initiated an action even before data was leaked or improperly accessed. The case was eventually settled.

In re ChoicePoint (2006)

The FTC found that ChoicePoint violated the FCRA by furnishing credit histories to subscribers without a permissible purpose and violated the FTC Act by making false and misleading statements about its privacy practices. ChoicePoint agreed to pay $10 million in civil penalties and $5 million into a consumer redress fund. ChoicePoint also promised changes to its business and improvements to its security practices. One requirement that the FTC settlement placed on ChoicePoint was to verify the identity of businesses that apply to receive consumer reports by auditing subscribers' use of consumer reports and by making site visits to certain customers.

In re Reed Elsevier, Inc. and Seisint (2008)

The FTC alleged that Seisint, a wholly owned subsidy of Reed Elsevier, failed to provide "reasonable and appropriate security to prevent authorized access" to sensitive consumer information. The allegations included a failure by Seisint to establish reasonable policies and procedures to govern the creation and authentication of user credentials for authorized customers. Seisint settled with the FTC, agreeing to establish a comprehensive information security program and permit audits of its program for a period of 20 years.

In the Matter of Twitter, Inc. (2011)

The FTC charged that Twitter was deceptive in promising to protect the security of user's private tweets to approved followers. Hackers broke in (1) by gaining administrative control to Twitter because the password was weak (all lowercase) and (2) by obtaining access to passwords stored in an employee's personal e-mail account. The FTC charged Twitter with failing to require employees to use hard-to-guess passwords, to disable administrative passwords after several unsuccessful login attempts, to force periodic changes to administrative passwords and to implement other security controls.

In the Matter of Ceridian Corp., 2011 WL 2487159 (FTC 2011)

FTC entered into 20-year consent decree with provider of online payroll software for small businesses following complaint under FTC Act for inadequate data security practices. FTC complaint followed successful SQL injection attack by hackers that yielded personal information associated with over 27,000 customers of Ceridian's Powerpay software. Ceridian had indefinitely stored customers' personal information as unencrypted plaintext and failed to implement low-cost defenses against SQL injection attacks.

In the Matter of EPN, Inc. (2012)

The debt collection company's chief operating officer installed P2P file-sharing software on the system, exposing sensitive personal data to any computer connected to the P2P network. The FTC charged that the company engaged in an "unfair act or practice" because it failed to have an appropriate security plan, to adequately train employees, or to scan its networks to identify P2P applications.

In re Snapchat (FTC 2014)

Failure to secure "Find Friends" feature resulted in a breach permitting attackers to compile a database of 4.6 million Snapchat usernames and phone numbers. Snapchat failed to verify user phone numbers during registration, resulting in users sending "snaps" to strangers who registered phone numbers belonging to them.

In the Matter of TRENDnet, Inc. (FTC 2014)

FTC entered into 20-year consent decree with manufacturer of webcams marketed as secure, but the feed from which could be accessed over the Internet without properly secured login credentials. TRENDnet allegedly ignored numerous notifications from third parties that its devices were not secure, stored user login credentials as unsecured text, and generally did not implement adequate security practices. This case is notable as the first FTC enforcement action related to the "Internet of Things."

In the Matter of Credit Karma (2014)
In the Matter of Fandago (2014)

Credit Karma provided a website and mobile app that allowed consumers to monitor and evaluate their credit and financial status. Its mobile app was alleged to have failed to validate SSL certificates, which left it vulnerable to "man-in-the-middle attacks." This spoofing technique took place on a public Wi-Fi network in which an attacker presents an invalid certificate to the app. Moreover, until the staff of the FTC contacted Credit Kara, it did not perform an adequate security review of the Credit Karma mobile app and did not provide adequate oversight of its service providers' security practices. Fandango provided a website and mobile app that allowed consumers to purchase movie tickets and view showtimes. Like Credit Karma, it allegedly failed to validate SSL certificates, which also left it vulnerable to "man-in-the-middle attacks." Moreover, Fandago failed to have a "clearly publicized and effective channel for receiving security vulnerability reports" and misrepresented the security that it provided to consumers. Under the terms of the respective settlements with the two companies, the FTC required the companies to establish and maintain comprehensive security programs designed to address security risks and to cease misrepresenting their privacy or security.

TORT

Tort cases for data security breaches have thus far not been very successful. Most cases have been dismissed for failing to state a cognizable injury.

WHAT CONSTITUTES A PRIVACY HARM?		
THEORY OF HARM	**INJURY IN FACT (STANDING)**	**COGNIZABLE HARM**
Increased risk of identity theft	Most courts reject. See, e.g., *Amburgy v. Express Scripts, Inc.*, 671 F. Supp. 2d 1046 (E.D. Mo. 2009); *Key v. DSW, Inc.*, 454 F. Supp. 2d 684 (S.D. Ohio 2006).	No court has yet recognized as a cognizable harm.
	But at least one court recognized this theory. *Krottner v. Starbucks Corp.*, 628 F.3d 1139 (9th Cir. 2010).	
Credit monitoring expenses	Most courts reject.	Most courts reject, except for one case by the First Circuit. *Anderson v. Hannaford Bros. Co.*, 659 F.3d 151 (1st Cir. 2011).
Emotional distress	Most courts reject emotional distress alone without an accompanying physical or financial injury.	Most courts reject emotional distress alone without an accompanying physical or financial injury.
Lost benefit of the bargain (overpayment for services)	Courts have rejected this theory when plaintiffs have failed to establish adequate evidence. See, e.g., *McLoughlin v. People's United Bank, Inc.*, 2009 WL 2843269. But cases can be successful where plaintiffs can establish this injury. See, e.g., *Doe 1 v. AOL, LLC*, 719 F.Supp. 2d 1102 (N.D. Cal. 2010).	At least one court has held that if plaintiffs can provide evidence of signing up for services and paying fees based upon promises of security, then they can establish a legally cognizable harm. See *Doe 1 v. AOL, LLC*, 719 F.Supp. 2d 1102 (N.D. Cal. 2010).

Loss of intrinsic value of data property	Most courts reject, but some courts have expressed vague receptivity to this theory. See, e.g., *Claridge v. RockYou, Inc.*, 785 F. Supp. 2d 855 (N.D. Cal. 2011) (noting that PII can constitute "valuable property" exchanged for defendant's promise to employ reasonable security).	Some courts have been receptive to this theory. See, e.g., *Claridge v. RockYou, Inc.*, 785 F. Supp. 2d 855 (N.D. Cal. 2011); *Rowe v. UniCare Life & Health Ins. Co.*, 2010 WL 86381 (N.D. Ill. 2010) (rejecting motion to dismiss but noting that plaintiff's proof of this claim was quite dubious).
Increased risk of junk mail	All courts have rejected thus far. See, e.g., *Bell v. Acxiom Corp.*, 2006 WL 2850042 (E.D. Ark. 2006).	All courts have rejected thus far. See, e.g., *Bell v. Acxiom Corp.*, 2006 WL 2850042. But in a spyware case, one court held that burdening of resources and loss of functionality could constitute a cognizable injury. *Sotelo v. Direct Revenue, LLC*, 384 F.Supp. 2d 1219 (N.D. Ill. 2005).
Time and effort expended to deal with the breach	All courts have rejected thus far. See, e.g., *Holmes v. Countrywide Fin. Corp.*, 2012 WL 2873892 (W.D. Ky. 2012).	All courts have rejected thus far. See, e.g., *In re Hannaford Bros. Co. Customer Data Security Breach Litigation*, 4 A.3d 492 (Me. 2010).

DATA DISPOSAL

Numerous states have laws that require a business to destroy personal information in a safe and effective fashion once it will no longer retain it.

State Data Disposal Statutes

AK	Alaska Stat. § 45.48.500
AZ	Ariz. Rev. Stat. § 44-7601
AR	Ark. Code Ann. § 4-110-104
CA	Cal. Civ. Code § 1798.81
CO	Colo. Rev. Stat. § 6-1-713
CT	Conn. Gen. Stat. Ann. § 42-471
GA	Ga. Code § 10-15-2
HI	Haw. Rev. Stat. § 487R-2
IL	20 ILCS 450/20
IN	Ind. Code § § 24-4-14-8, 24-4.9-3-3.5(c)
KS	Kan. Stat. Ann. § 50-7a03
KY	Ky. Rev. Stat. § 365.725
MA	Mass. Gen. Laws Ch. 93I, § 2
MD	Md. Code, Comm. Law § 14-3507
MI	MCL § 445.72a
MO	Mo. Stat. § 288.360
MT	Mont. Code Ann. § 30-14-1703
NV	Nev. Rev. Stat. § 603A.200
NJ	N.J. Stat. § 56:8-162
NY	N.Y. Gen. Bus. Law § 399-H
NC	N.C. Gen. Stat. § 75-64
OR	Ore. Rev. Stat. § 646A.622
RI	R.I. Gen. Laws § 6-52-2
SC	S.C. Code § 37-20-190
TX	Tex. Bus. & Com. Code. Ann. § 72.004
UT	Utah Code Ann. § 13-44-201
VT	9 Vt. Stat. Ann. § 2445
WA	Wash. Rev. Code § 19.215.020
WI	Wisc. Stat. § 134.97

Illustrative statutes include:

California, Cal. Civ. Code § 1798.81
Requires a business to take all reasonable steps to destroy or arrange for the destruction of a customer's records within its custody or control that contain personal information and that are no longer to be retained by the business. Destruction is by (1) shredding, (2) erasing or (3) otherwise modifying the personal information in those records to make it unreadable or undecipherable through any means.

Illinois, 20 ILCS 450/20

Covers the public sector alone. Requires the Department of Central Management Services or any other authorized agency that disposes of surplus electronic data processing equipment by sale, donation or transfer to implement a policy mandating that computer hardware be cleared of all data and software before disposal by sale, donation or transfer.

New York, N.Y. Gen. Bus. Law § 399-H

Prohibits a business, firm, partnership, association, corporation or business person from disposing of a record containing personal identifying information unless it does any of the following: "a. shreds the record before the disposal of the record; or b. destroys the personal identifying information contained in the record; or c. modifies the record to make the personal identifying information unreadable; or d. takes actions consistent with commonly accepted industry practices that it reasonably believes will ensure that no unauthorized person will have access to the personal identifying information contained in the record."

Texas, Tex. Bus. & Com. Code Ann. § 72.004

Requires a business disposing of a business record that contains personal identifying information of a customer of the business to "modify, by shredding, erasing, or other means, the personal identifying information so as to make the information unreadable or undecipherable." Provides that a business is considered to comply with this law if it contracts with a person engaged in the business of disposing of records in accordance with these statutory requirements.

Washington, Wash Rev. Code 19.215.020

Requires an "entity" to "take all reasonable steps to destroy or arrange for the destruction of personal financial and health information and personal identification numbers issued by government entities in an individual's records within its custody or control when the entity is disposing of records that it will no longer retain."

FOR FURTHER REFERENCE

Treatises

Chris Hadnagy, *Social Engineering: The Art of Human Hacking* (2010)
A thorough overview of the techniques fraudsters use to trick people.

Ronald Weikers, *Data Security and Privacy Law* (2014)
2200-page treatise on data security and privacy law.

Books

Anupam Chandler et al., eds., *Securing Privacy in the Internet Age* (2008)
An insightful set of essays focusing on a variety of proposals to heighten privacy and data security, whether through the common law, statutory reforms or the market.

Kevin Mitnick, *Ghost in the Wires: My Adventures as the World's Most Wanted Hacker* (2012)
Engaging stories about how hackers can con people into providing access to computer networks.

Bruce Schneier, *Liars and Outliers: Enabling the Trust that Society Needs to Thrive* (2012)
A sociological examination of trust and security.

Bruce Schneier, *Schneier on Security* (2008)
Sage wisdom from a leading security expert on security technology and policy.

Bruce Schneier, *Secrets and Lies: Digital Security in a Networked World* (2004)
A practical—yet also philosophical—guide to data security that focuses on the big picture as well as the key details.

P.W. Singer & Allan Friedman, *Cybersecurity and Cyberwar: What Everyone Needs to Know* (2014)
In an FAQ format, this book discusses cybersecurity with many stories and anecdotes.

Articles and Other Sources

Andrea M. Matwyshyn, ed., *Harboring Data: Information Security, Law, and the Corporation* (2009)
Offering a range of multidisciplinary and international perspectives on the evolving landscape of data security.

Privacy Rights Clearinghouse, *Chronology of Data Security Breaches,* www.privacyrights.org/data-breach
A comprehensive searchable database of data security breach incidents from 2005 to the present.

Sasha Romanosky, David Hoffman & Alessandro Acquisti, *Empirical Analysis of Data Breach Litigation*, 11 J. Empirical Legal Stud. 74 (2014)
The article empirically explores data breach litigation. Despite the fact that the law is strongly against plaintiffs in data breach class actions, about 50% of cases settle. A firm is 3.5 times more likely to be sued when data breach causes individuals financial harm, but 6 times lower when the firm provides free credit monitoring. There were 86 different types of causes of action in the cases they studied, the most common being State Unfair Business Practice statutes, the federal Fair Credit Reporting Act, breach of contract, negligence, the federal Privacy Act, and the privacy torts.

Paul M. Schwartz & Edward J. Janger, *Notification of Data Security Breaches*, 105 Mich. L. Rev. 913 (2007)
Advocating greater automatic protection for consumers, clearer consumer notification, coordinated sharing of information about data incidents among affected organizations and heightened oversight of the decision by breached entities whether to inform consumers or other entities.

Andrew B. Serwin, *Poised on the Precipice: A Critical Examination of Privacy Litigation*, 25 Santa Clara Computer & High Tech. L.J. 883 (2009)
An examination of trends in privacy litigation involving data security breaches.

Daniel J. Solove & Woodrow Hartzog, *The FTC and the New Common Law of Privacy*, 114 Colum. L. Rev. 583 (2014)
Argues that "the FTC's privacy jurisprudence is functionally equivalent to a body of common law." Companies look to these agreements as a quasi-common law for determining best practices, and the structures of these FTC agreements amount to a common law equivalent—and one that is amenable to study.

CHAPTER 11

Education Privacy

ESSENTIAL POINTS

- Student education records are protected by the Family Educational Rights and Privacy Act (FERPA), but this statute lacks a private cause of action, decreasing the effectiveness of enforcement.

- Although FERPA is the primary federal statute protecting education records, other federal statutes also are applicable such as the Protection of Pupil Rights Act (PRPA), the Individuals with Disabilities Education Act (IDEA) and the National School Lunches Act (NSLA), among others.

- Students have Fourth Amendment privacy rights on public school campuses against unreasonable search or seizure. But courts tend to be deferential to school officials, so student rights are limited.

- Numerous states are enacting statutes forbidding educational institutions from requesting social media account information from students or prospective students.

STUDENT RECORDS

Family Educational Rights and Privacy Act (FERPA)
20 U.S.C. § 1232g (1974)

Primary Function: To protect the privacy of student education records.

Applies to: "Education records," which are "those records, files, documents, and other materials which contain information directly related to a student; and are maintained by an educational agency or institution." 20 U.S.C. §1232g (a)(4)(A). FERPA covers only records and information from records, not information generally. The personal knowledge and observations of educators that are not part of an education record are not covered by FERPA.

Ownership of Rights: FERPA rights initially belong to the parents/guardians of a student. When a student *either* turns 18 *or* attends an institution of postsecondary education (an "eligible student"), FERPA rights transfer from the parents to the student. At the college level, FERPA rights always belong to the student, regardless of age.

Rights: FERPA provides parents/guardians or eligible students with the following rights:

1. To review the student's education records
2. To correct any inaccuracies or misleading information in those records
3. To control certain disclosures of the information in those records
4. To file a complaint with the U.S. Department of Education in the event of a violation of the above rights

Notice: Each year, schools must inform parents or eligible students of their rights under FERPA.

Opt Out: Unless a parent or eligible student opts out, a school may release to the public "directory information" designated by the school, such as the student's name, address, telephone numbers, birth date, major, activities and sports, dates of attendance, degrees and awards received and certain other data. 20 U.S.C. § 1232g(b)(5).

Opt In: Schools generally cannot disclose other information from a student's education records without the written consent of a parent or "eligible student."

Exceptions: Schools may (but are not required to) disclose information without consent in a number of cases, such as to school officials with legitimate educational interests, to the parents of a student who is their dependent for federal tax purposes, to "appropriate parties" in the event of a threat to health or safety, to other schools to which a student is transferring or has transferred, in connection with financial aid, to comply with a judicial order or subpoena, to organizations conducting studies on behalf of the school and in several other circumstances. *FERPA Regulations*, 34 C.F.R. § 99.31.

Law Enforcement Records: Records that are both created and maintained by a separate law enforcement unit of a school (either commissioned police or public safety) at least in part for law enforcement purposes are not considered "education records" and are not subject to FERPA protections.

Treatment Records: These records are the medical or psychological records of a student 18 years or older who is being treated by a physician, psychiatrist, psychologist or other related professional or paraprofessional. 34 C.F.R. § 99.3. They are not considered "education records" as long as they are not shared with others not involved in the student's treatment.

Enforcement: FERPA authorizes the secretary of education to take any "appropriate actions to enforce" FERPA, potentially including the termination of all education-related federal funding, if a school fails to comply with the statute. 20 U.S.C. § 1232g(f). The Department of Education's Family Policy Compliance Office (FPCO) oversees the enforcement of FERPA. See 34 C.F.R. § 99.60(b). Before the FPCO takes action, an individual must file a complaint against a school. The FPCO then investigates and if the school is found in violation of FERPA, the FPCO recommends specific steps that the institution must take to comply. If the school fails to comply, then enforcement actions may be taken.

FERPA Regulations (2011), 34 C.F.R. § 99.3: The regulations define two previously undefined terms in FERPA in order to expand the sharing of student personal data. FERPA permits access to student personal data—without consent —to "authorized representatives" of state or federal "education programs." The new regulations expand both definitions to allow a myriad of types of third parties to access student data.

Leading Cases

Owasso Independent School District v. Falvo, 534 U.S. 426 (2002)
"Education records" under FERPA does not include student homework or classroom work while in the hands of students. Teachers can have students in the class grade each other's papers or exams or see each other's homework.

Gonzaga University v. Doe, 536 U.S. 273 (2002)
A university contacted the state agency for teacher certification to inform the agency about allegations of sexual misconduct on the part of a university student applying to become an elementary school teacher. The allegations of misconduct were later recanted. The student sued the school under 42 U.S.C. § 1983, alleging a violation of FERPA. The Court held that FERPA could not be enforced by a private right of action under § 1983. However, state common law and some other privacy rights continue to be enforceable by private action.

United States v. Miami University, 294 F.3d 797 (6th Cir. 2001)
A student newspaper sought disciplinary records from a university. The Ohio Supreme Court held that the records fell within the Ohio Public Records Act, which mandated disclosure. Upon learning the school planned to disclose the records, the U.S. Department of Education intervened and filed a complaint in federal court. Ultimately, the Sixth Circuit concluded that disciplinary records are "education records" under FERPA and the statute bars their disclosure.

Protection of Pupil Rights Amendment (PPRA)
20 U.S.C. § 1232h (1978)

Primary Function: To protect the privacy of students in surveys, medical exams and marketing programs.

Surveys: Provides an opt-in and opt-out right depending upon the kind of information involved:

1. *Opt in*—written parental consent required when conducting a survey involving information about politics, mental health, sex, illegal activity, income and other sensitive information.

2. *Opt out*—required for any surveys involving other kinds of information. 34 C.F.R. § 98.

Medical Examinations: Provides an opt-out right for any medical exam that involves exposure of private body parts or incision, insertion or injection into the body. No right to opt out if the exam is necessary to protect the immediate health or safety of a student, for hearing, vision or scoliosis, or is required by law. 34 C.F.R. § 98.

Marketing: If the school (or a contractor) collects, discloses or uses personal data from students for marketing purposes, parents or eligible students must be given the right to opt out. 34 C.F.R. § 98.

No Child Left Behind Act (NCLB)
20 U.S.C. §§ 1232f-j, 7908 (2001)

Primary Function: In addition to many other provisions, mandates that schools provide military recruiters with the names, addresses and telephone numbers of secondary students.

Opt Out: Parents can ask schools to withhold their child's name, address and telephone listings from military recruiters. 20 U.S.C. § 7908.

Individuals with Disabilities Education Act (IDEA)
20 U.S.C. § 1400 (1975)

Primary Function: In addition to many other provisions, IDEA has privacy protections for students involved in special education. Many of these protections are identical to those in FERPA, but there are some differences, explained below.

Destruction of Data: When information about children with disabilities is no longer needed, agencies maintaining it must inform their parents. The parents can request that it be destroyed. *IDEA Regulations,* 34 C.F.R. § 300.573.

Public Notice: State educational agencies must provide public notice about the collection of personally identifiable information and a summary of their privacy policies. 34 C.F.R. § 300.561.

Privacy Official: State educational agencies must have an official responsible for ensuring that the privacy of personally identifiable information is properly maintained and officials handling such information are properly trained. 34 C.F.R. § 300.572.

National School Lunch Act (NSLA)
42 U.S.C. § 1758(6) (1946)

Primary Function: In addition to many other provisions, the NSLA mandates that the names of children participating in the National School Lunch Program must remain confidential.

Applies to: Any person "directly connected with the administration or enforcement" of a school lunch program or federal education program, or state health or education program. 42 U.S.C. § 1758(6)(A)(i).

Enforcement: A person "who publishes, divulges, discloses or makes known in any manner, or to any extent not authorized by Federal law (including a regulation), any information obtained under this subsection shall be fined not more than $1,000 or imprisoned not more than 1 year, or both." 42 U.S.C. § 1758(6); regulation at 7 C.F.R. § 245.8.

Jeanne Clery Disclosure of Campus Security Policy and Campus Crime Statistics Act (Clery Act)
20 U.S.C. § 1092(f) (1990)

Primary Purpose: Mandates disclosure of college and university campus crime statistics and security policies.

Disclosures of Sex Offenses: "Both the accuser and the accused must be informed of the outcome of any institutional disciplinary proceeding brought alleging a sex offense." *Clery Act Regulations,* 34 C.F.R. § 668.46(b)(11)(vi)(B). (Such disclosures are also expressly permitted by FERPA.)

Other Regulations

Gainful Employment Rule (2011)
20 U.S.C. § 1002

This rule, which seeks to determine whether education at postsecondary schools leads to gainful employment, will use income data from the Social Security Administration.

Other Statutes

Beyond the statutes listed above, many schools might be subject to other federal statutes:

Children's Online Privacy Protection Act (COPPA): Applies if a school has a website "directed to children" or with "actual knowledge that it is collecting personal information from a child." 15 U.S.C. § 6502(a)(1).

Electronic Communications Privacy Act (ECPA): Applies if a school engages in certain kinds of electronic surveillance (e.g., audio surveillance and surveillance of electronic communications). 18 U.S.C. §§ 2510-2522.

Computer Fraud and Abuse Act (CFAA): The CFAA criminalizes all "unauthorized access" to any kind of computer with Internet access. Because there is no exception for school officials, anytime a school official searches a student-owned computer without consent, it could constitute a CFAA violation. 18 U.S.C. § 1030.

Health Insurance Portability and Accountability Act (HIPAA): In some limited circumstances, some school records might be regulated under the HIPAA Privacy Rule. But any records that are either "education records" or "treatment records" under FERPA—which is to say virtually all health-related records that a school may have about its students—are exempt from HIPAA. *HIPAA Privacy Rule,* 45 C.F.R. § 160.103.

STATE LAWS

Student Data Collection, Use, and Disclosure

Alabama: State Board of Education Policy (2013)
In October 2013, the Alabama State Board of Education adopted a new policy on student data that allows the state to share student data with the federal government only in aggregate form. The policy also calls on school districts to adopt their own policies on the collection and sharing of student data.

California, Student Online Personal Information Protection Act (2014)
New law restricting companies from selling or disclosing personal information about students from kindergarten through high school. The statute specifically targets operators of Internet web sites, online services, online applications, or mobile applications. These companies are prohibited from knowingly engaging in targeted advertising to students or their parents, from using covered information to amass student profiles, from selling students' information, or from disclosing covered information. The law also requires an operator to implement and maintain reasonable security procedures and practices appropriate to the nature of the covered information.

Georgia, Executive Order (2013)
Executive Order prohibiting the state from collecting or sharing personally identifiable data on students and prohibiting student data from being collected for the development of commercial products or services.

Iowa, Executive Order (2013)
Student data in Iowa should be collected in accordance with state and federal privacy laws and only aggregate student data is to be provided to the federal government.

Texas, H.B. 2268 (2013)
Texas law enforcement officials must obtain a warrant before accessing email and other communications content.

Social Media Account Access

Numerous states are enacting statutes forbidding educational institutions from requesting social media account information from students or prospective students. Some examples are below.

Louisiana, Personal Online Account Privacy Protection Act (2014)

This law prohibits educational institutions, such as primary and secondary schools and universities, from requiring students or prospective students from disclosing authorizing information to personal online accounts. The educational institution may place conditions, however, on the use of the school's equipment or online services.

Illinois, Right to Privacy in the School Setting Act (2013)

This law prohibits post-secondary educational institutions from requiring students or their parents or guardians to provide passwords or other account information in order to gain access to a student's account or profile on social networking websites. The law does not prohibit a covered school from monitoring use of the school's equipment or services and does not include email within the meaning of "social networking website." An elementary or secondary school may request or require account information when there is reasonable cause to believe the account contains evidence that the student violated a school rule or policy, but the school must notify the student and his or her parents or guardians.

New Mexico, Senate Bill 422 (2013)

This law prohibits post-secondary educational institutions from requesting or requiring students or potential students to provide passwords in order to gain access to a social networking website account or profile. Post-secondary educational institutions are further prohibited from taking adverse action against a student or potential student for refusing to grant access to a social networking website account or profile.

Oregon, S.B. 344 (2013)

This bill prohibits a public or private educational institution from requiring, requesting or otherwise compelling a student or prospective student to disclose or to provide access to a personal social media account.

STUDENT SPEECH AND EXPRESSION

Student speech and expression can be invasive of privacy or constitute harassment or cyberbullying. In certain circumstances, the First Amendment limits the ability of schools to discipline students for such speech.

First Amendment and On-Campus Speech: Students have First Amendment rights on campus. *Tinker v. Des Moines Sch. Dist.,* 393 U.S. 503 (1969). These rights, however, are limited, as school officials have discretion to discipline students for the "use of vulgar and offensive terms." *Bethel Sch. Dist. No. 403 v. Fraser,* 478 U.S. 675 (1986). Speech that is "reasonably viewed as promoting illegal drug use" can be punished when at a school event. *Morse v. Frederick,* 551 U.S. 393 (2007). "Educators do not offend the First Amendment by exercising editorial control over the style and content of student speech in school-sponsored expressive activities." *Hazelwood Sch. Dist. v. Kuhlmeier,* 484 U.S. 260 (1988).

The First Amendment and Off-Campus Speech: Schools have much less ability to respond to off-campus speech. Only when the speech causes a "substantial disruption of or a material interference with school activities" does the school have the power to sanction a student under the First Amendment. The "substantial disruption" test comes from *Tinker.*

Anti-Bullying Laws: Many states have passed anti-bullying laws that address cyberbullying—the use of the Internet or electronic devices to attack another student with insults, harassment or invasion of privacy.

State Anti-Bullying Laws

AR	Ark. Code Ann. § 6-18-514
CA	Cal. Educ. Code §§ 32260
DE	Del. Code Ann. tit. 14, § 4112D
FL	Fla. Stat. § 1006.147
ID	Idaho Code ann. § 18-917A
IL	720 Ill. Comp. Stat. Ann. 5/12-7.5
IN	Ind. Code § 20-30-5.5-3
IA	Iowa Code § 280.28
KS	Kan. Stat. Ann. § 72-8256
MD	Md. Code Ann., [Educ.] § 7-424.1
MN	Minn. Stat. § 121A.0695
NE	Neb. Rev. Stat. § 79-2,137
NJ	N.J. Stat. Ann. § 18A:37-15
OK	S.B. 1941
OR	Or. Admin R. 581-022-1140
PA	24 Pa. Cons. Stat. Ann. § 13-1303.1-A
RI	R.I. Gen. Laws § 16-21-26
SC	S.C. Code Ann. § 59-63-120
UT	Utah Code § 53-A-11a-102
WA	Wash. Rev. Code § 28A.300.285

SEARCHES AND SURVEILLANCE

Fourth Amendment

The Fourth Amendment protects student privacy at public schools, but warrants and probable cause are not required for school officials to engage in searches. Searches are justified when there are "reasonable grounds" that they will reveal evidence of a crime or a violation of school policy. At private schools, searches are governed primarily by contract and state common law privacy principles.

Leading Cases

New Jersey v. T.L.O., 469 U.S. 325 (1984)
Students have Fourth Amendment rights at school. Warrants and probable cause are not required. A search is justified "when there are reasonable grounds for suspecting that the search will turn up evidence that the student has violated or is violating either the law or the rules of the school.

Vernonia School District v. Acton, 515 U.S. 646 (1995)
Mandatory drug testing of student athletes is constitutional under the Fourth Amendment. Athletes have a "reduced expectation of privacy," and the search was relatively unobtrusive. The school has a compelling interest in combating illegal drug use.

Board of Education v. Earls, 536 U.S. 822 (2002)
Mandatory drug testing of all students participating in any extracurricular activity is constitutional under the Fourth Amendment. Students in extracurricular activities have a reduced expectation of privacy. The school demonstrated that it had reason to address illegal drug use.

Safford Unified School Dist. No. 1 v. Redding, 129 S. Ct. 2633 (2009)
Although school officials had reasonable suspicion to search a student's backpack and outer clothing for illegal drugs, requiring a student to expose private parts beneath underwear and bras went beyond the permissible scope of the search. There was no "indication of danger" from the drugs or reason to suspect the student was hiding them in her underwear.

SELF-REGULATORY MEASURES

Student Privacy Pledge (2014)

Drafted by the Future of Privacy Forum, this pledge involves companies declaring that they will refrain from selling information on K-12 students, refrain from using students' data to target them with advertisements; and refrain from compiling personal profiles of students unless authorized by schools or parents. Although not contractually binding, this pledge creates a public commitment for the companies of the kind that could lead to enforcement actions by the FTC should these privacy promises be violated.

FOR FURTHER REFERENCE

Treatises

Mary A. Lentz, *Campus Security for Public and Private Colleges and Universities* (2010)
Detailed discussion of FERPA and related statutes.

Mary A. Lentz, *School Security* (2010)

Steven McDonald, ed., *The Family Educational Rights and Privacy Act: A Legal Compendium* (2d ed. 2002)
Useful collection of background material, articles, interpretative material and sample policies and forms. Includes a detailed annotated bibliography.

James A. Rapp, *5 Education Law* (2010)
Comprehensive treatment of the law of educational records and related legal issues. Available online through Lexis-Nexis.

LeRoy Rooker, *American Association of Collegiate Registrars and Admissions Officers (AACRAO) 2012 FERPA Guide* (2012)
Comprehensive overview of FERPA with quiz questions, sample forms, and FPCO letters.

Articles and Other Sources

Darryn Cathryn Beckstrom, *State Legislation Mandating School Cyberbullying Policies and the Potential Threat to Students' Free Speech Rights*, 33 Vermont L. Rev. 283 (2008)
Examines state cyberbullying laws and their free speech implications.

Lynn M. Daggett, *FERPA in the Twenty-First Century: Failure to Effectively Regulate Privacy for All Students,* 58 Cath. U. L. Rev. 59 (2008)
A detailed overview and critique of FERPA.

Family Policy Compliance Office (FPCO) Website,
http://www2.ed.gov/policy/gen/guid/fpco/index.html
Contains guidance about FERPA and PRPA.

Joel Reidenberg et al., *Privacy and Cloud Computing in Public Schools,*
Fordham Center on Law and Information Policy (2013)
This study examines how school districts address privacy when they transfer student information to cloud computing service providers. To conduct this study, Fordham's Center on Law and Information Policy selected a national sample of school districts from every geographic region of the country and requested from each selected district all of the district's cloud service agreements, notices to parents, and computer use policies for teachers.

Richard Salgado, *Protecting Student Speech Rights While Increasing School Safety: School Jurisdiction and the Search for Warning Signs in a Post-Columbine/Red Lake Environment,* 2005 BYU L. Rev. 1371 (2005)
Addresses the issue of how schools can combat off-campus threats and online bullying.

CHAPTER 12

Employment Privacy

ESSENTIAL POINTS

- The Fourth Amendment applies to searches by the government that affect public- or private-sector employees. The "special needs" doctrine applies only when the government is the employer; that is, to public-sector employees.

- The constitutional right of informational privacy, as articulated in *Whalen v. Roe*, applies to government searches but not those by private-sector employers.

- Many kinds of searches and surveillance by private-sector employers will not run afoul of privacy laws if the employers obtain employee consent beforehand. Even where employers have threatened to terminate employees if they do not consent, the consent has been deemed valid.

- The Electronic Communications Privacy Act (ECPA) applies not only to government and law enforcement officials, but to private parties as well. Its jurisdiction extends to employers that monitor employee telephone and e-mail communications and Internet use. Obtaining employee consent beforehand typically exempts most instances of electronic surveillance of employees from ECPA's restrictions.

- The National Labor Relations Act (NLRA) ensures that employees (whether unionized or not) can engage in "concerted activity" to discuss workplace conditions and terms and conditions of employment. According to the National Labor Relations Board (NLRB), which enforces the NLRA, overly broad social media policies that restrict employee expression on social media can chill protected activity under the NLRA.

SEARCHES

Government Employees: Fourth Amendment

When government employers engage in searches of government employees for non–law enforcement purposes, the Fourth Amendment "special needs" doctrine merely requires the search to be "reasonable." No warrant or probable cause is needed.

O'Connor v. Ortega, 480 U.S. 709 (1987)
Government employees have a reasonable expectation of privacy at the workplace. They can expect privacy as to items they bring to work. They have limited expectations of privacy in their office depending upon the context. Based on the "special needs" doctrine, the Fourth Amendment does not require government employers to obtain a warrant or have probable cause to carry out a search. The search only needs to be "reasonable … under all the circumstances."

National Treasury Employees Union v. Von Raab, 489 U.S. 656 (1989)
Drug testing at the workplace for noncriminal purposes falls under the "special needs" doctrine. The constitutionality of workplace drug tests is evaluated by balancing the interference with privacy against the government interest in testing.

Skinner v. Railway Labor Executives' Ass'n, 489 U.S. 602 (1989)
Mandatory drug testing for railroad employees involved in railroad accidents is reasonable under the Fourth Amendment. Because railroads are a highly regulated industry, employees have minimal privacy expectations. The government has a compelling interest in preventing accidents from drug impairment.

Chandler v. Miller, 520 U.S. 305 (1997)
A drug-testing requirement for candidates for public office violates the Fourth Amendment. Ordinary law enforcement methods are sufficient to prevent drug use, and candidates are subject to relentless scrutiny.

Private Sector Employees: Fourth Amendment

In the private-sector employer context, employees are protected by the Fourth Amendment if they have a reasonable expectation of privacy in their offices, desk drawers or computers. If it is the government alone doing the searching, employees have full Fourth Amendment protection. The government needs a warrant and probable cause to search when the employee has a reasonable expectation of privacy. The "special needs" doctrine does not apply because the government is not the employer.

Since the employer owns (and often exercises common authority over) employee offices and computers, the employer can consent to the search. If the employer cooperates, the search is valid under the consent exception to the Fourth Amendment. The consent exception does not apply in the case of searches by government employers, since the government cannot consent to its own search.

Leading Cases

Mancusi v. DeForte, 392 U.S. 364 (1968)
A person can have a reasonable expectation of privacy in an office at a private-sector workplace. "[C]apacity to claim the protection of the amendment depends not upon a property right in the invaded place but upon whether the area was one in which there was a reasonable expectation of freedom from governmental intrusion."

United States v. Ziegler, 474 F.3d 1184 (9th Cir. 2007)
The FBI directed a search of the computer of an employee at a private-sector company. "[I]n the private employer context, employees retain at least some expectation of privacy in their offices." But the employer had common authority over the employee's computer and could give valid consent to search it as well as the employee's office.

Leventhal v. Knapek, 266 F.3d 64 (2d Cir. 2001)
An employee has a reasonable expectation of privacy as to his office computer when he doesn't share it with others, nobody else has regular access to it and his employer does not engage in the practice of routine computer searches.

United States v. Simons, 206 F.3d 392 (4th Cir. 2000)
An employee lacks a reasonable expectation of privacy as to his workplace computer when the employer's Internet use policy states that the company will monitor employees' Internet use.

Searches and Surveillance by Private-Sector Employers

Employee Consent: Many searches and types of surveillance by private-sector employers will not run afoul of privacy laws. At-will employees can consent to very invasive searches and surveillance as a condition of employment. *Jennings v. Minco Technology Labs,* 765 S.W.2d 497 (Tex. Ct. App. 1989).

Public Policy: Some limits exist on the kind of searches that the law permits employers to carry out. In some states, terminating an at-will employee for not submitting to invasive searches or surveillance will be in violation of public policy. *Borse v. Piece Goods Shop,* 963 F.2d 611 (3d Cir. 1992) (holding that "dismissing an employee who refused to consent to urinalysis testing and to personal property searches would violate public policy if the testing tortiously invaded the employee's privacy").

In some states, not only is tort law a source of public policy, but constitutional law is as well—even though it does not ordinarily apply to the private sector. *Hennessey v. Coastal Eagle Point Oil Co.,* 609 A.2d 11 (N.J. 1992).

State Constitutional Protections: Some state constitutions apply to everyone, not just to the government. The California Supreme Court has held that the right to privacy in the California Constitution "creates a right of action against private as well as government entities." *Hill v. NCAA,* 865 P.2d 633 (Cal. 1994). To assert a claim for invasion of one's constitutional right to privacy, a plaintiff in California must establish: (1) a legally protected privacy interest, (2) a reasonable expectation of privacy under the circumstances and (3) conduct by the defendant that constitutes a serious invasion of privacy. Once a plaintiff establishes these three elements, the defendant may prove that the invasion of privacy is justified because it furthers "legitimate and important competing interests." *Id.*

State Statutes: Some states have enacted laws prohibiting certain kinds of searches and surveillance in the workplace. For example, Conn. Gen. Stat. § 31-48b(b) prohibits an employer from "recording or monitoring the activities of his employees in areas designed for the health or personal comfort of the employees or for safeguarding of their possessions, such as rest rooms, locker rooms or lounges." Such laws cannot be contracted around, even by unions. *Cramer v. Consolidated Freightways, Inc.,* 255 F.3d 683 (9th Cir. 2001) (en banc) (union cannot agree in collective bargaining agreement to allow employer to engage in surveillance prohibited by criminal law).

QUESTIONING AND TESTING

Fourth Amendment

The Fourth Amendment will generally not limit "mere questioning" by government employers even when questions demand "highly personal private information." *Greenawalt v. Indiana Department of Corrections*, 397 F.3d 587 (7th Cir. 2005).

Constitutional Right to Information Privacy

The constitutional right to information privacy was first identified in *Whalen v. Roe*, 429 U.S. 589 (1977). See Chapter 6. Courts have held that it protects against government employers making unwarranted disclosures of employee information. See, e.g., *American Federation of Government Employees v. HUD*, 118 F.3d 786 (D.C. Cir. 1997) ("the employees could cite no case in which a court has found a violation of the constitutional right to privacy where the government has collected, but not disseminated, the information."). The constitutional right to information privacy does not restrict public employers from asking background check questions involving private matters. *National Aeronautics and Space Administration v. Nelson*, 131 S.Ct. 746 (2011).

The government must provide appropriate safeguards for the information it collects from employees or else it will violate the constitutional right to information privacy. "Safeguards against disclosure of private material have been held to be adequate when there exists a statutory penalty for unauthorized disclosures; when there exist security provisions to prevent mishandling of files coupled with an express regulatory policy prohibiting disclosure, and in a unique situation when, even absent an explicit statutory or regulatory policy, the record supported the conclusion that those officials with private information would not disclose it." *Fraternal Order of Police, Lodge No. 5 v. City of Philadelphia*, 812 F.2d 105 (3d Cir. 1987).

Employee Polygraph Protection Act (EPPA)
29 U.S.C. §§ 2001–2009 (1988)

Primary Function: To regulate the use of polygraphs by private-sector employers.

Applies to: Private-sector employers. Specifically exempts government employers.

Limitations on Polygraph Testing: : Private-sector employers cannot require employees to submit to polygraph examinations. 29 U.S.C. § 2002.

Exception—Investigations: Employers can require employees to submit to polygraphs when "the test is administered in connection with an ongoing investigation involving economic loss or injury to the employer's business, such as theft, embezzlement, misappropriation or an act of unlawful industrial espionage or sabotage" and the employer "has a reasonable suspicion that the employee was involved in the incident or activity under investigation." 29 U.S.C. § 2006(d).

Exception—Security Services: Employers who engage in security services are exempt if they protect government interests or "currency, negotiable securities, precious commodities or instruments or proprietary information." 29 U.S.C. § 2006(e). When polygraphs are used under these exceptions, the test or the refusal to take the test cannot be the sole basis of any adverse employment action. 29 U.S.C. § 2007(a). Polygraph examiners cannot ask questions concerning beliefs regarding religion, racial matters, politics, sexual behavior or union activities. 29 U.S.C. § 2007(b). Disclosure of polygraph information to people authorized by the examinee, the employer or pursuant to a court order. 29 U.S.C. § 2008.

Enforcement: : Violations will result in a civil penalty of up to $10,000. The secretary of labor may bring an action to obtain restraining orders and injunctions to require compliance with the EPPA. Employers who violate the EPPA are liable to employees or prospective employees for legal and equitable relief including reinstatement, promotion and payment of lost wages and benefits. 29 U.S.C. § 2005.

Preemption: The EPPA does not preempt state law. About half of the states regulate the use of polygraphs by statute.

Americans with Disabilities Act (ADA)
42 U.S.C. §§ 12112 *et seq.* (1990)

Primary Function: To protect the rights of people with disabilities, and in doing so, regulate how employers can conduct medical examinations.

Applies to: Government and private-sector employers. A "disability" is defined as "a physical or mental impairment that substantially limits one or more of the major life activities of such individual." 42 U.S.C. § 12102.

Pre-Employment: The ADA treats pre-employment and post-employment examinations and inquiries differently. Employers are prohibited in conducting medical examinations or inquiries to determine if the individual has a disability or the "nature and severity of such disability." But the employer "may make pre-employment inquiries into the ability of an applicant to perform job-related functions." 42 U.S.C. § 12112(d).

Post-Hiring: Employers are prohibited from conducting medical examinations or inquiries to determine if the individual has a disability or the "nature and severity of such disability" unless there is a job-related reason "consistent with business necessity." 42 U.S.C. § 12112(d)(4). Drug testing is not considered a "medical examination" under the ADA. 42 U.S.C. § 12114(d).

Occupational Safety and Health Act (OSHA)
29 U.S.C. § 654 *et seq.* (1970)

OSHA provides a right of employees to access their medical records maintained by their employers. This includes questionnaires and results of examinations. 29 C.F.R. § 1910.1020 (e)(2)(ii)(A). Employers must avoid disclosing the names of employees suffering an injury to an "intimate body part," "resulting from a sexual assault," relating to mental illness, or involving "HIV infection, hepatitis, or tuberculosis," among other things. 29 C.F.R. § 1904.29(b)(7).

Genetic Information Nondiscrimination Act (GINA)
42 U.S.C. § 2000ff *et seq.*

GINA prohibits employers from discriminating on the basis of genetic information. It also prohibits employers from demanding or buying an employee's genetic information. 42 U.S.C. § 2000ff-1(b). There are a few very limited exceptions. The law also has a provision requiring confidentiality of any genetic information maintained by the employer. 42 U.S.C. § 2000ff-5.

State Employment Testing and Inquiry Laws

Many states restrict certain forms of employment testing and questionnaires. For example, Wisconsin prohibits employers from requiring employees or applicants to undergo HIV testing. Wisc. Stat. Ann. § 103.15(2). Massachusetts prohibits employers from asking prospective employees about arrests not leading to conviction, misdemeanor convictions or any prior commitment to medical treatment facilities. Mass. Gen. Laws ch. 151B § 4(9). A number of states restrict genetic testing. Cal. Govt. Code § 12940(o); Conn. Gen. Stat. Ann. § 46a-60(11) (A); Del. Code Ann. tit. 19, § 711(e); N.Y. Exec. Law § 296.19 (a)(1).

State Criminal Background Check "Ban the Box" Laws

More than 10 states and many localities have passed "Ban the Box" laws and ordinances. The term "Ban the Box" originated in a campaign by various advocacy groups to stop the check box on hiring applications asking applicants about whether they have a criminal record. Examples of recent laws include:

D.C. Fair Criminal Record Screening Amendment Act (2014)
Restricts employers from using criminal background checks during the application process. Once employers make a conditional employment offer,

they are then permitted to consult criminal background check information. Employers "cannot make any inquiry or require an applicant to disclose or reveal any criminal conviction until after making a conditional offer of employment." Conditional offers may be withdrawn for a "legitimate business reason" and must be reasonable. When such an offer is withdrawn, applicants can request all records considered by the employer. There is no private right of action, but people can file complaints with the DC Office of Human Rights. Penalties range between $1000 to $5000, with half going to the complaining individual. Exemptions include courts, the federal government, when any law requires consideration of criminal history, or when the position involves "direct care to minors or vulnerable adults."

Illinois Job Opportunities for Qualified Applicants Act (2014)
Employers with 15 or more employees may not inquire about the criminal history of an applicant until the applicant has been selected for an interview and notified about such selection. For hiring without interviews, inquiries into criminal history cannot occur until after a conditional employment offer is made. Exemptions include public-sector employers as well as when laws exclude employees with criminal convictions from certain jobs. No private right of action, and first offenses receive a warning. Subsequent violations are punished with fines.

San Francisco Police Code Article 49 and Administrative Code Article 12 (2014)
Employers with 20 or more employees within the City are prohibited from inquiring into or considering arrests that did not lead to conviction, expunged or voided convictions, juvenile justice system convictions, convictions older than 7 years, among other things. "Inquiry" is defined as "any direct or indirect conduct intended to gather information from or about an applicant." Convictions older than 7 years or unresolved arrest can be considered if they have "a direct and specific negative bearing on that person's ability to perform the duties or responsibilities necessarily related to the employment position." Notice must be provided to an applicant or employee before the employer takes adverse action based upon conviction history.

Rhode Island Fair Employment Practices Law (2014)
Employers of 4 or more people are restricted from inquiring into the criminal backgrounds of applicants prior to the first interview. The law applies to both private sector and government employers.

EMPLOYEE ACCESS TO THE COMPUTER NETWORK

United States v. Nosal, 676 F.3d 854 (9th Cir. 2012) (en banc)
A former employee who accessed confidential information from his employer's databases did not exceed "authorized access" under the CFAA. Circuit courts remain split on this issue.

United States v. Rodriguez, 628 F.3d 1258 (11th Cir. 2010)
An employee violated the CFAA by using his employer's computer for nonbusiness purposes because his employer had clearly told him not to do so.

There is currently a major circuit split on the issue in the cases above.

SURVEILLANCE AND MONITORING

Electronic Communications Privacy Act (ECPA)

ECPA applies not only to government and law enforcement officials, but also to private parties. Thus, employers are subject to the restrictions of federal electronic surveillance law. However, three notable exceptions to electronic surveillance law are relevant to the employment context:

- The Wiretap Act and SCA do not apply when one party to a communication consents to the interception or access.

- When employers are the providers of the communications service, they are exempt from the Wiretap Act or SCA if they are acting in a way necessary to render the service or protect the rights or property of the service.

- The Wiretap Act does not apply when an employer uses certain intercepting devices "in the ordinary course of [the employer's] business." The device must be furnished to the employer by the provider of the communication service.

Employers must be careful to monitor employees as they have set forth in their policies. For example, in *Watkins v. L.M. Berry & Co.*, 704 F.2d 577 (11th Cir. 1983), an employer promised employees that it would not monitor personal calls, but it ultimately ended up listening in on an employee's call about a new job. The court held that the employer exceeded the scope of what was told to the employee.

Leading Case

Quon v. City of Ontario, 130 S.Ct. 2619 (2010)
Despite the police department's official general Internet use policy, which prohibited use for personal benefit, the department had an informal policy of allowing personal uses of department-supplied pagers so long as employees paid for the extra usage. The department monitored an employee's personal use of the pager, and the employee alleged a violation of the Fourth Amendment. The court assumed for the purposes of argument that the employee had a reasonable expectation of privacy and held that the search was reasonable because it was "motivated by a legitimate work-related purpose" and was "not excessive in scope."

What Every Employer Must Know to Comply with ECPA

1. Clearly notify employees of the monitoring policy.

2. Putting employees on notice of the policy is typically sufficient to establish consent under ECPA.

3. We recommend using computer login screens where users need to accept the terms of the monitoring. This creates the most unambiguous consent.

EMPLOYMENT PRIVACY LAW: PUBLIC vs. PRIVATE SECTOR

TYPE OF PROTECTION	PUBLIC SECTOR	PRIVATE SECTOR
Fourth Amendment	Searches must be reasonable under the circumstances. *O'Connor v. Ortega.* This is determined by balancing the invasion of privacy against the government's interest.	No Fourth Amendment restrictions on employer searching. The Fourth Amendment protects employees from government searches of their offices, but not if the employer permits the government to engage in the search.
Constitutional Right to Informational Privacy	Government employers must avoid unwarranted disclosures of employee personal data and provide appropriate safeguards to the information it collects from employees.	When private employer collects information from employees, it does not implicate this constitutional right due to lack of state action.
State Constitutional Law	State constitutions will also regulate the government employers of that state.	Most state constitutions do not apply to the private sector. There are some exceptions (e.g., California).
Breach of Contract	If privacy is promised by employers in a contract, then an employee would have a cause of action for a breach.	
Privacy Torts	Employers can violate the privacy torts, but the employer can make consenting to certain kinds of searches and surveillance conditional on employment.	

TYPE OF PROTECTION	PUBLIC SECTOR	PRIVATE SECTOR
Wrongful Termination in Violation of Public Policy	Employers cannot terminate an employee for refusing to consent to a privacy invasion in violation of public policy. The sources of public policy can include tort law, constitutional law and criminal law.	Employers cannot terminate an employee for refusing to consent to a privacy invasion in violation of public policy. Since constitutional law does not apply to private sector employers, most courts hold it can't be a source of public policy. But in some states, courts have held that the constitution can serve as a source of public policy against private-sector employers. In many instances, tort law can be contracted around, but criminal law cannot.
Federal Electronic Surveillance Law	Government and private-sector employers must follow the requirements of federal electronic surveillance law.	
State Electronic Surveillance Law	State government and private-sector employers must follow the requirements of state electronic surveillance law. Some courts have found that ECPA preempts stricter requirements, but the matter is not settled.	

EMPLOYER SOCIAL MEDIA POLICIES AND PRACTICES

National Labor Relations Act (NLRA)

In a series of three memos issued in 2011 and 2012, the National Labor Relations Board (NLRB) acting general counsel describes many NLRB investigations and cases involving social media issues. These materials reveal that employer social media policies will run afoul of the NLRA, 29 U.S.C. §§ 151–169, when they are overbroad and could be construed as chilling employee discussion about the terms and conditions of employment with other employees via social media. The third memo in this series provides specific examples of different employer policies and rules, both acceptable and unacceptable.

- First Report on Social Media Cases, Office of the General Counsel, NLRB, Memorandum OM 11-74 (August 18, 2011).

- Second Report on Social Media Cases, Office of the General Counsel, NLRB, Memorandum OM 12-31 (January 24, 2012).

- Third Report on Social Media Cases, Office of the General Counsel, NLRB, Memorandum OM 12-59 (May 30, 2012).

The NLRA and Social Media Policies

The NLRA ensures that employees (whether unionized or not) can engage in "concerted activity" under the NLRA § 7 to complain about workplace conditions and other issues pertaining to the terms and conditions of employment. Broad social media policies that restrict disparaging or vulgar comments run afoul of § 7 if they can be construed as potentially extending to concerted activity. According to the NLRB memoranda and actions, such policies are overbroad and can chill concerted activity.

The NLRA does not prohibit:

• Restricting individual outbursts by employees that are not part of concerted activity with other employees

• Insulting people or the company, or revealing confidential information that does not pertain to the terms and conditions of employment

Leading Cases

Costco Whole Corporation and United Food and Commercial Workers Union, **Local 371, 358 NLRB No. 106 (2012)**
The NLRB concluded that Costco violated Section 8 of the NLRA by maintaining a social media policy that prohibited employees from electronically posting statements that "damage the Company … or damage any person's reputation." This language would tend to chill employees' exercise of their Section 7 rights, which protect a range of collective activities.

Karl Knauz Motors, Inc. d/b/a Knauz BMW and Robert Becker.
Case 13–CA–046452 (2012)
Salesperson at a car dealership allowed the 13-year old son of a customer to sit in the driver's seat of a car. An accident occurred where the car ran over the customer's foot and ended up in a pond. Another sales person took photos and posted them to Facebook and said: "This is your car. This is your car on drugs." The employee who posted on Facebook was

fired. The NLRB concluded that this post did not relate to protected activity, and the firing did not violate the NLRA. However, the employer's social media policy which prohibited being "disrespectful" or "using profanity or other language which injures the image or reputation of the Dealership" was overbroad. The policy was missing a disclaimer that NLRA-protected speech was not prohibited by the policy.

Hispanics United of Buffalo, Inc. and Carlos Ortiz. Case 03–CA–027872 (2012)

Five employees were fired for making comments on Facebook responding to a co-worker's criticisms about their job performance. The NLRB concluded that the speech involved protected activity under the NLRA and that the employees were improperly fired.

Three D, LLC (Triple Play), 361 NLRB No. 31 (2014)

Several employees at a non-union employer—a bar and restaurant—posted comments to a Facebook post by a former employee criticizing the employer for a tax withholding issue among other things. Some current employees and others commented on post, including a statement that the employer believed to be defamatory. One employee called the employer an "asshole." One employee hit the Like button. The employee who called the employer an "asshole" and the employee who "Liked" the post were fired. The NLRB concluded that the comment and Like were related to the post about the tax issue, which involved workplace terms and conditions. Just because there is a comment or a Like does not mean that these employees endorse everything in a discussion thread. The employer's social media policy prohibiting "engaging in inappropriate discussions about the company, management, and/or co-workers" was too vague and chilled employee NLRA rights.

Hoot Winc, LLC d/b/a/ Hooters of Ontario Mills, Case No. 31-CA-104872 (2014)

NLRB deemed employer confidential information policy overbroad and chilling of Section 7 activity. Employer policy prohibited unauthorized disclosure of "sensitive Company operating materials or information" that "includes but is not limited to, recipes, policies, procedures, financial information, manuals or any other information in part or in whole as contained in any Company records." Some of this information could involve employment terms and conditions, and there was no exemption in the policy for protected activities.

Lily Transportation Corp., Case CA-108618 (2014)

Confidentiality policy that prohibited the disclosure of "confidential information, including Company, customer information and employee information maintained in confidential personnel files," was overbroad because information about wages and other matters involving terms and conditions of employees could be included. Social media policy that employees refrain from "disparaging, negative, false or misleading" information about the company" failed to make clear the zone of NLRA-protected speech.

Durham School Services, L.P., 360 NLRB No. 85 (2014)
Employer, a company operating school busses, had a social media policy requiring employees to keep "communication with coworkers … professional and respectful, even outside of work hours" and threatened to punish employees who share with the public "unfavorable" information about the company, its employees, or customers. This policy was overbroad and failed to define what "respectful" or "unfavorable" information was, and risked chilling NLRA-protected speech.

Laurus Technical Institute, 360 NLRB No. 133 (2014)
Employer policy prohibited "gossip about the company, an employee, or customer." The policy defined gossip as "[n]egative or untrue or disparaging comments" about others or "repeating" a "rumor" or "information that can injure a person." The NLRB deemed the policy overbroad and ambiguous.

Professional Electrical Contractors of Connecticut, Inc., Case No. 34-CA-071532 (2014)
Employer policy prohibiting "using personal computers in any manner that may adversely affect company business interests or reputation" was overbroad because it failed to exclude NLRA-protected activities.

Employer Access to Employee Social Media Accounts

Numerous states are enacting statutes forbidding educational institutions from requesting social media account information from employees or prospective employees. Some examples are below.

Illinois Right to Privacy in the Workplace Act (H.B. 3782) (2012)
Prohibits employers from requiring employees or applicants to provide access to their social media website accounts.

Louisiana Personal Online Account Privacy Protection Act (2014)
Prohibits employer from requesting or requiring employees or applicants to give information such as account names or passwords giving access to a personal online account. This statute explicitly does not extend to information necessary to operate devices or online services provided by the employer, nor prohibit an employer from searching public information on an employee's or

applicant's online account. Inadvertently obtaining account information does not create liability, but an employer may not act upon, keep or in any way distribute such information. The law extends a similar framework to the university-student relationship.

Maryland's User Name and Password Privacy Protection and Exclusions (S.B. 433) (2012)

Restricts employers from demanding that employees or applicants provide information to allow an employer access to a "personal account or service."

New Hampshire Use of Social Media and Electronic Mail (2014)

Barring employers from requesting or requiring employee or applicant login information, requesting that an employer add contacts or change settings to a personal account, or disciplining employees accordingly. Inadvertently obtaining account information does not create liability, but an employer may not act upon, keep or in any way distribute such information. The act does not explicitly restrict employers from monitoring provided services and equipment, or conducting investigations under requirements of state and federal statutes.

Utah, Internet Employment Privacy Act, H.B. 100 (2013)

Enacting protections for personal Internet accounts. The Act includes provisions such as permitting or prohibiting certain actions by an employer and providing a private right of action.

Wisconsin Senate Bill 223 (2013)

As a condition of employment, employees may not require employees to provide access to a personal Internet account, or discriminate against an employee refusing to give such information. Employers are also prohibited from refusing to hire an applicant because the applicant will not disclose information to gain access to a personal Internet account. Exceptions apply when the employee uses a device or service at least partially provided for by the employer. An employer may request to view a personal Internet account during an investigation following a reasonable belief that the employee transferred the employer's proprietary information. Under such circumstances, however, the employer can only request to view the account, not require the information to access the account.

FOR FURTHER REFERENCE

Treatises

Matthew W. Finkin, *Privacy in Employment Law* (4th ed. 2013)
Analysis of the law of privacy in the employment context with coverage of
recent developments such as employer access to applicant and employee social
media accounts.

Robert Sprague, *ed. Workplace Data: Law and Litigation* (2013)
Analysis of legal issues relating to "electronically stored information"
relating to employees with a special focus on discovery issues.

Miriam H. Wugmeister & Christine E. Lyon, editors, *Global Employee
Privacy and Data Security Law* (2d ed. 2011)
Focusing on how global privacy and security laws create obligations
within the employment context.

Articles and Other Sources

Corey A. Ciocchetti, *The Eavesdropping Employer: A Twenty-First Century
Framework for Employee Monitoring, 48* American Business L. J. 285 (2011)
Surveys the patchwork of federal and state laws regulating employment
privacy and proposes a sliding-scale framework for when and how
employers should conduct monitoring of employees.

Lothar Determann & Robert Sprague, *Intrusive Monitoring:
Employee Privacy Expectations Are Reasonable in Europe, Destroyed
in the United States,* 26 Berkeley Tech. L. J. 979 (2011)
Comparison of EU and U.S. privacy in the workplace. Conclusion is that
the U.S. offers minimal to no protection in situations where there is not a
preexisting basis for an expectation for privacy. With few exceptions, U.S.
employers can routinely deploy contracts and notice strategies that lead
employees waive privacy rights.

Matthew W. Finkin, *Menschenbild: The Conception of the Employee
as a Person in Western Law,* 23 Comp. Lab. L. & Pol'y 577 (2002)
Interesting comparison between U.S. law and EU civil law systems in
how they handle employee privacy rights.

Pauline T. Kim, *Privacy Rights, Public Policy, and the Employment
Relationship,* 57 Ohio St. L.J. 671 (1996)
Argues that the privacy torts can serve as a source of public policy limiting
an employer's ability to terminate employees who refuse to be subjected to
privacy intrusions.

Paul A. Secunda, *Privatizing Workplace Privacy,*
88 Notre Dame L. Rev. 277 (2012)
Discusses the U.S. Supreme Court's Fourth Amendment decision in
City of Ontario v. Quon and argues that public-sector workers should
have greater privacy protections than private-sector workers.

Paul A. Secunda, *Blogging While (Publicly) Employed:*
Some First Amendment Implications, **47 Louisville L. Rev. 679 (2009)**
Examining the First Amendment free speech rights of public-sector
employees who use social media.

William J. Stuntz, Implicit Bargains, *Government Power,*
and the Fourth Amendment, **44 Stan. L. Rev. 553 (1992)**
Provides a thoughtful defense of the Fourth Amendment special
needs doctrine in the government employment context.

CHAPTER 13

International Privacy Law

ESSENTIAL POINTS

- Since the Universal Declaration of Human Rights (1948), there has been a global effort to define internationally relevant and binding privacy norms.

- The phrase "data protection law" is the favored terminology for information privacy law outside of the United States.

- A number of international organizations have joined in the effort to shape and create privacy law, both international and domestic. Leading international entities involved in this process include the Organisation for Economic Co-operation and Development (OECD), the Council of Europe, the European Court of Human Justice, numerous entities of the European Union and the Asia-Pacific Economic Cooperation (APEC).

- The EU Data Protection Directive establishes common rules for data protection among member states of the European Union. It also forbids data transfers to countries outside of the EU that lack "adequate protection" for personal data.

- The EU considers the U.S. generally to lack adequate protection for personal information. However, companies that participate in the Safe Harbor arrangement are considered to provide adequate protection. In addition, international data transfers can take place through contractual arrangements or the establishment of binding corporate rules.

Data Protection and Information Privacy: A Note on Terminology

In the United States, information privacy law is the area of law concerned with the collection, use and disclosure of personal information. In most of the rest of the world, this same area of law is termed "data protection law." This usage is followed in many English-speaking countries, including the United Kingdom.

WORLDWIDE PRIVACY RIGHTS AND GUIDELINES

Universal Declaration of Human Rights (1948)

The United Nations General Assembly adopted the Universal Declaration of Human Rights on December 10, 1948. Article 12 explicitly protects "privacy," but a number of other parts of the declaration are relevant to information privacy.

Article 1: "All human beings are born free and equal in dignity and rights."

Article 3: "Everyone has the right to life, liberty and security of person."

Article 8: "Everyone has the right to an effective remedy by the competent national tribunals for acts violating the fundamental rights granted him by the constitution or by law."

Article 12: "No one shall be subjected to arbitrary interference with his privacy, family, home or correspondence, nor to attacks upon his honor and reputation. Everyone has the right to protection of the law against such interference or attacks."

Article 19: "Everyone has the right to freedom of opinion and expression; this right includes freedom to hold opinions without interference and to seek, receive and impart information and ideas through any media and regardless of frontiers."

OECD Privacy Guidelines (1980)

The Organisation for Economic Co-operation and Development (OECD) is a group of 34 leading industrial countries concerned with global economic and democratic development.

OECD MEMBER COUNTRIES		
Australia	Hungary	Poland
Austria	Iceland	Portugal
Belgium	Ireland	Slovak Republic
Canada	Israel	Slovenia
Chile	Italy	Spain
Czech Republic	Japan	Sweden
Denmark	Korea	Switzerland
Estonia	Luxembourg	Turkey
Finland	Mexico	United Kingdom
France	Netherlands	United States
Germany	New Zealand	
Greece	Norway	

The 1980 OECD Guidelines establish eight key principles for the protection of personal information:

1. *Collection Limitation:* Data should be collected lawfully with the individual's consent.

2. *Data Quality:* Data should be relevant to a particular purpose and be accurate.

3. *Purpose Specification:* The purpose for data collection should be stated at the time of the data collection and the use of the data should be limited to this purpose.

4. *Use Limitation:* Data should not be disclosed for different purposes without the consent of the individual.

5. *Security Safeguards:* Data should be protected by reasonable safeguards.

6. *Openness Principle:* Individuals should be informed about the practices and policies of those handling their personal information.

7. *Individual Participation:* People should be able to learn about the data that an entity possesses about them and to rectify errors or problems in that data.

8. *Accountability:* The entities that control personal information should be held accountable for carrying out these principles.

The 2013 Guidelines add additional concepts to the original eight key principles. These include:

- *National privacy strategies:* While effective laws are essential, the strategic importance of privacy today also requires a multifaceted national strategy coordinated at the highest levels of government.

- *Privacy management programs:* These serve as the core operational mechanisms through which organizations implement privacy protection.

- *Data security breach notification:* This provision covers both notice to an authority and notice to an individual affected by a security breach affecting personal data.

The Influence of the OECD Guidelines

Some of the major laws and regulations influenced by the OECD Guidelines are:

- U.S. Cable Communications Policy Act of 1984

- Australia's Privacy Act of 1988

- New Zealand's Privacy Act of 1993

- South Korea's Act on the Protection of Personal Information Managed by Public Agencies of 1994

- Asia-Pacific Economic Cooperation (APEC) Privacy Guidelines of 2004

UN Guidelines for the Regulation of Computerized Personal Files (1990)

Adopted by a resolution of the General Assembly on December 1, 1990, the guidelines set up 10 principles concerning minimum guarantees of national legislations:

1. *Principle of lawfulness and fairness:* Information about persons must not be collected or processed in unfair or unlawful ways or used in ways contrary to the principles of the Charter of the United Nations.

2. *Principle of accuracy:* Files are to be kept as complete as possible and persons responsible for them are to conduct regular checks on the accuracy and relevancy of data.

3. *Principle of purpose-specification:* The purpose that a file is to serve and its use in terms of that purpose should be specified, legitimate and, once established, receive publicity or be brought to the attention of the affected party.

4. *Principle of interested-person access:* Ensures the right of access to information and right to have corrections made in the case of unlawful, unnecessary or inaccurate entries.

5. *Principle of nondiscrimination:* Subject to exceptions made under Principle 6, data must not be compiled if it is likely to cause unlawful or arbitrary discrimination. Information that can fall into this category includes data "on racial or ethnic origin, colour, sex life, political opinions, religious, philosophical and other beliefs as well as membership of an association or trade union."

6. *Power to make exceptions:* Departures from Principles 1 to 4 are permitted only if necessary "to protect national security, public order, public health or morality, as well as, inter alia, the rights and freedoms of others." Departures from Principle 5 are subject to these same requirements as well as the limits prescribed by the International Bill of Human Rights and the other relevant instruments for human rights and the prevention of discrimination.

7. *Principle of security:* Appropriate measures must be taken to protect files against natural and human dangers.

8. *Supervision and sanctions:* The law in every country must designate an authority "to be responsible for supervising observance of the principles set forth above."

9. *Transborder data flows:* Information should be able to circulate freely between two countries that offer comparative legislative safeguards for the protection of privacy. In the absence of "reciprocal safeguards," a country may not restrict circulation of information "unduly" and may do so "only in so far as the protection of privacy demands."

10. *Field of application:* The principles are to apply to all public and private computerized files as well as, subject to appropriate adjustments, to manual files.

EUROPE

European Convention on Human Rights (ECHR)
Article 8—The Right to Respect for Private and Family Life (1950)

The ECHR: The ECHR protects a wide range of civil and political rights. It was adopted in 1950, shortly after the Universal Declaration of Human Rights of the United Nations. The ECHR was drafted under the auspices of the Council of Europe, an international organization, which currently has 47 European states as members.

Article 8: The ECHR explicitly guarantees a right to privacy in its Article 8, which states:

1. Everyone has the right to respect for his private and family life, his home and his correspondence;

2. There shall be no interference by a public authority with the exercise of this right except such as is in accordance with the law and is necessary in a democratic society in the interests of national security, public safety or the economic well-being of the country, for the prevention of disorder or crime, for the protection of health or morals or for the protection of the rights and freedoms of others.

European Court of Human Rights: The Council's European Court of Human Rights has an important role in interpreting the key reference texts of the council. It bears the ultimate role of enforcing and interpreting the ECHR. This tribunal has decided a series of important cases concerning media invasions of privacy, the activities of the police and security agencies, the issuing of identity papers, monitoring of communications by employers and other privacy topics.

Leading Cases

P.G. & J.H. v. United Kingdom, 44787/98 ECHR (Sept. 25, 2011)
Article 8's protection of private life can be affected by measures that occur "outside a person's home or private premises." One element, although not necessarily a conclusive factor, is "a person's reasonable expectations as to privacy." Yet, the ECHR also found that "files gathered by security services on a particular individual fall within the scope of Article 8 even where the information has not been gathered by any intrusive or covert method." Specifically, Article 8 was implicated "once any systematic or permanent record comes into existence" of monitoring a public scene through technological means, such as closed circuit television.

Von Hannover v. Germany, 59320/00 ECHR (June 24, 2004)

Princess Caroline of Monaco sued German magazines for publishing photographs of her. The ECHR found that "the decisive factor in balancing the protection of private life against freedom of expression should lie in the contribution that the published photos and articles make to a debate of general interest." The photos in this case "made no such contribution" because the applicant exercised no official function and the photos and articles related exclusively to details of her private life.

Copland v. United Kingdom, 62617/00 ECHR (March 7, 2007)

Collection and storage of personal information related to an individual's telephone, as well as her e-mail and Internet usage, without her knowledge, implicated Article 8 rights. Such an "interference" with Article 8 must be carried out "in accordance with the law" under Article 8(2), European Convention on Human Rights. There is a need, therefore, for a domestic law that regulates such activity, and such a law must also "be compatible with the rule of law" and its requirements.

Mosley v. United Kingdom, 48009/08 ECHR 774 (May 10, 2011)

Holding that this case concerned "a flagrant and unjustified invasion of the applicant's private life" and that "there is a distinction to be drawn between reporting facts—even if controversial—capable of contributing to a debate of general public interest in a democratic society, and making tawdry allegations about an individual's private life." The ECHR found that Article 8 of the Convention on Human Rights did not require a prenotification requirement before news stories regarding a person's private life were published.

Von Hannover v. Germany (no. 2), 40660/08 and 6064/08 ECHR (Feb. 7, 2012)

Affirming decisions of the Federal Court of Justice and Federal Constitutional Courts regarding publication in Germany of photographs of Princess Caroline of Monaco. The ECHR held that the national courts "carefully balanced the right of the publishing companies to freedom of expression against the right of the applicants to respect for their private life." In the judgment of the ECHR, the key parts of the analysis of the national courts concerned whether the photos had "contributed to a debate of general interest" and "the circumstances in which the photos had been taken.

Axel Springer v. Germany, 39954/08 ECHR (Feb. 7, 2012)

Finding German courts were not justified in ordering an injunction blocking publication of certain information "reporting on the arrest and conviction of a well-known actor for a drug-related offence." The ECHR concluded that the courts' interference with the "freedom of expression" protected by Article 10 of the Convention lacked a "reasonable relationship of proportionality" between the resulting restrictions and "the legitimate aim pursued."

Von Hannover v. Germany (no. 3), 8772/10 ECHR 835, (Sept. 19, 2013) Holding that the German Federal Court of Justice's refusal to grant an injunction prohibiting any further publication of von Hannover's photograph did not violate Article 8 of the Convention. The ECHR found that the German court sufficiently took the ECHR's rulings into consideration when balancing the right to respect for private life against the right to freedom of expression. Given that it lies in the discretion of the Member States to ensure the rights given by Article 8, the ECHR declared that the German court's rulings did not constitute a breach of von Hannover's privacy rights as enshrined in Article 8. The ECHR also accepted the German court's findings that the photographs contributed to a debate of general interest.

Council of Europe Convention on Privacy
ETS No. 108 (1981)

Background: Throughout the 1980s, the most important European-wide agreement regarding the processing of personal information was the Council of Europe's Convention for the Protection of Individuals with Regard to Automatic Processing of Personal Data (Convention). This document is a European treaty opened for signature in 1981 and one to which 46 nations have acceded. It was the first legally binding international instrument in the field of data protection law. Among the countries where the Convention has recently entered into force are Austria (2012), the Ukraine (2011), Monaco (2009), and Armenia (2008).

Minimum Standards: The convention is a "non-self-executing treaty." Its standards do not directly impose binding norms on signatory nations. Its requirement is for signatory nations to establish domestic data protection legislation that give effect to the convention's principles and provide a common core of safeguards for the processing of personal information. Domestic statutory standards can, in turn, exceed those basic safeguards. As Article 11 of the convention states, domestic law can "grant data subjects a wider measure of protection than that stipulated in this convention."

Data Quality: The convention's common protective core contains a number of elements. Among the most important is the Article 5 requirement of "data quality." This term captures a number of concepts relating to FIPs. In its broadest sense, data quality requires that personal information be "stored for specified and legitimate purposes and not used in a way incompatible with those purposes." Moreover, the concept of data quality limits the processing of personal data to circumstances that are "adequate, relevant and not excessive in relation to the purposes for which they are stored."

Access and Correction: Beyond data quality, the convention calls for individual rights permitting a person access to and an ability to correct personal data. Domestic law also is to provide judicial remedies for violations of these rights.

EU Data Protection Directive
Council Directive 95/46 (1995)

Primary Function: To facilitate the free flow of personal data within the EU by establishing an equally high privacy level in all EU member states. The directive establishes obligations for the processors of personal data and rights for the affected party. It also created the Article 29 Working Party.

Reasons for Its Creation: The directive was viewed as necessary because European integration both increased the sharing of data among member states and generated new demands for personal information within separate member states. The directive was also viewed as necessary because of divergences among the statutory protections among EU countries with national data protection legislation.

Harmonizing: The Data Protection Directive establishes common rules for data protection among EU member states. It is a "harmonizing" directive that requires member states to enact national legislation that reflects its principles. See Articles 5 and 24.

Key Terms: The directive relies on the following key terms:

1. *"Personal data"*—data about any "identified or identifiable natural person"

2. *"Data subject"*—the person to whom the data pertains

3. *"Processing of personal data"*—"any operation or set of operations… performed upon personal data" in a wide variety of means (collection, use, disclosure, storage, retrieval, erasure)

4. *"Controller"*—any person, business, organization or government entity that "determines the purposes and means of the processing of personal data"

5. *"Processor"*—any person or entity that processes data for the controller

Article 3—Exception for Law Enforcement and National Defense: The directive contains a broad exemption for data processing relating to law enforcement and national defense. Its Article 3(2) states that the directive will not apply "in any case to processing operations concerning public security, defence, state security ... and the activities of the state in areas of criminal law."

Article 7—Criteria for Making Data Processing Legitimate: The directive permits the processing of personal data only under certain circumstances. These are when (1) a data subject has given his consent, (2) to fulfill a contract, (3) to meet a legal obligation of the controller of the data, (4) to protect a vital interest of the data subject, (5) to carry out a task in the public interest or (6) to fulfill a legitimate interest pursued by the controller or by a third party "except where such interests are overridden by the interests for fundamental rights and freedoms of the data subject which require protection under Article 1(1)."

Article 8—Special Protection for Sensitive Data: Article 8 provides for special treatment of data that is particularly sensitive for data subjects. Thus, it restricts the processing of certain categories of personal data, namely, information "revealing racial or ethnic origin, political opinions, religious or philosophical beliefs, trade-union membership and the processing of data concerning health or sex life." There are a number of explicit exceptions to this rule. Moreover, member states may, for reason of "substantial public interest," make further exceptions to the ones explicitly found in Article 8. The commission must be notified of all such further derogations.

Articles 10 & 11—Notice: These articles set out the kinds of notice to be provided to the data subject when information is collected directly from him and when it is not collected from a third party.

Article 12—Access and Correction: The data subject has a right of access to certain information from the data controller as well as an ability to correct, erase or block information that does not comply with the directive.

Article 15—Restrictions on Automated Decisions: Subject to certain exceptions, the directive establishes a right for "every person not to be subject to a decision which produces legal effects concerning him or significantly affects him and which is based solely on automated processing of data intended to evaluate certain personal aspects relating to him, such as his performance at work, creditworthiness, reliability conduct, etc." Article 15(1). The exceptions provided are (1) when the decision "is taken in the course of entering into or performance of a contract" and there are "suitable measures to safeguard ... legitimate interests" of the data subject or (2) when the processing "is authorized by a law which also lays down measures to safeguard the data subject's legitimate interests." Article 15(2).

Article 17—Data Security: Member states must provide "appropriate technical and organizational measures" of data security.

Articles 22 & 23—Individual Remedies: Article 22 requires member states to provide for a "judicial remedy for any breach of the rights guaranteed him by the national law applicable to the processing in question." Article 23 further requires member states to provide that "the controller" of the data in question provide compensation to "any person who has suffered damage as a result of any act incompatible with the national provisions adopted pursuant to this directive."

Article 25—Adequacy Standard for International Data Transfers: A transfer of personal data is only permitted to a non-EU member state that has "an adequate level of protection." Article 25(1). The directive states: "The adequacy of the level of protection afforded by a third country shall be assessed in the light of all the circumstances surrounding a data transfer operation or set of data transfer operations." Article 25(2). There has been a formal finding at the EU level that the laws of the United States generally do not provide adequate protection. The Article 29 Working Group (for more on this entity, see below) has stated that the "current patchwork of narrowly focused sectoral laws and voluntary self-regulation in the U.S. is not adequate." Article 29 Working Group, Opinion 1/99.

Article 28—National Supervisory Authorities: Each member state must establish one or more public authorities to monitor the application of the laws and regulations adopted pursuant to the directive. The directive states: "These authorities shall act with complete independence in exercising the functions entrusted to them." Article 28(1). Member states are to consult with the supervisory authorities when creating the rules and regulations for the protection of individuals' rights with regard to data processing. Article 28(2).

Articles 29 & 30—Working Party: The directive created a new institution of data protection on the European level. It calls this entity the "Working Party on the Protection of Individuals with Regard to the Processing of Personal Data" (Working Party). Each member state is to designate a representative for the Working Party. This entity has "advisory status" and is to "act independently." Article 29(1). In Article 30, the directive sets out the numerous tasks of the Working Party.

Leading Case

Criminal Proceedings Against Bodil Lindqvist, European Court of Justice, 11/6/2003

The posting of information on a website constituted a "processing" of personal data within the sense of the Data Protection Directive. Without the data subject's permission, such personal information could not be posted, that is, made subject to "processing." The European Court of Justice also found that member states could enact data privacy protections beyond the areas that the directive had specified so long as no provision of European Community law precluded such action.

Google Spain v. AEPD, C-131/12 (May 13, 2014)

The European Court of Justice (ECJ) required that Google remove from its search results links to a 1998 newspaper article about his foreclosed house. According to the ECJ, under what has become known as the "right to be forgotten," EU citizens have a right to the deletion of certain personal data under the EU Data Protection Directive. Operators of search engines must remove links to third party webpages when such links violate people's fundamental privacy rights.

A Leading German Case on Search Engines

Google Autocomplete, German Federal Court of Justice
BGH VI ZR 269/12 (May 14, 2013)

In May 2013, Germany's Federal Court of Justice found that Google's Autocomplete function was capable of violating an individual's personality rights and that an autocomplete suggestion was Google's own content. The Federal Court of Justice held that although the operator of a search engine was not generally required to check Autocomplete suggestions in advance for privacy violations, it did have responsibility once it acquired knowledge of a legal violation of a right to personality. In such case, search engines were required to prevent their software from generating a result that would lead to the privacy violation.

EU Proposed Legislation

European Commission, Proposal for a Regulation of the European Parliament and of the Council on the protection of individuals with regard to the processing of personal data and on the free movement of such data (General Data Protection Regulation) (Jan. 25, 2012)

Includes high penalties for violations, a new and narrower definition of "consent," a requirement for most businesses with more than 250 employees to have a privacy officer, data breach notification requirements, and a "right to be forgotten." The proposed regulation also contains protections against decisions based exclusively on "automated processing" and extra safeguards for sensitive data. Within the EU, the proposed regulation has been controversial for the fashion in which it increases the power of the commission and takes power away from the member states and national data protection commissions. It does so through the creation of a "consistency mechanism" and by a grant of power to the commission to issue a wide range of "delegating" and "implementing" acts.

On March 12, 2014 the Parliament voted in favor of the proposed regulation. The Parliament, the Council of the European Union and the Commission will now negotiate a final text for the Regulation. Once adopted, the Regulation will establish a unified data protection law for Europe and be immediately and directly enforceable within all Member States.

Important aspects of the proposed regulation include;

Limits on Data Processing
Data may only be processed if, and as long as, the purposes of the processing could not be fulfilled by other means. There is a requirement of data minimization, meaning data has to be adequate, relevant, and limited to the minimum necessary in relation to the purposes for which the data is processed."

The Right to Erasure
Right to obtain erasure of personal data from the data controller where legitimate interests of controller are overridden by the individual's privacy rights. Data controller is responsible for taking all reasonable steps to inform third parties who are processing the personal data that a request for erasure has been made.

Stricter Consent
The Proposed Regulation heightens the consent requirement by shifting the burden of proof to a controller to show that individuals agreed to the processing of their personal data.

Limits on Processing of Sensitive Data and Automated Decision-making
Reinforces the Directive's concept of consent by placing "the burden of proof" on a "controller" to show that individuals agree to the processing of their personal data.

Monetary Fines
High penalties for violations are set out in Article 79. In the version of the Draft Regulation adopted by the European Parliament's Committee on Civil Liberties, Justice and Home Affairs, for example, fines can amount to up to 5 percent of a company's worldwide turnover or $100 million Euros, whichever is greater.

Consistency Mechanism

The Proposed Regulation creates a new institution, the European Data Protection Board (EDPB), which provides a forum for national supervisory authorities. It also grants great power to the commission to issue a wide range of "delegating" and "implementing" acts.

The US-EU Safe Harbor Arrangement (2000)

The EU has never found the U.S. to provide an adequate level of protection and would be unlikely to do so. As a result, the U.S. Department of Commerce and the EU Commission negotiated a Safe Harbor Arrangement. Organizations in the U.S. can voluntarily agree to adhere to the Safe Harbor principles for privacy and publicly attest to such adherence. These organizations are viewed as meeting the EU Directive's "adequacy" standard for information privacy. As a consequence, international transfers of information from companies in the EU may take place with organizations that are compliant with the Safe Harbor.

Safe Harbor Principles

There are seven Safe Harbor principles. Companies that enter into the arrangement must follow all seven:

1. **Notice**

2. **Choice**
   Both opt out and opt in are permitted under different circumstances.

3. **Onward Transfers (Transfers to Third Parties)**
   Transfer is permitted only if there will be adequacy of protection by a third party.

4. **Security**

5. **Data Integrity**
   Personal information must be relevant for purposes for which it is to be used. It must be reliable for intended use, accurate, complete and current.

6. **Access**

7. **Enforcement**

European Commission, *Restoring Trust in EU-US Data Flows* (November 2013)
On November 27, 2013, the European Commission released a number of reports on the functioning of the EU-US Safe Harbor as well as the PNR agreement and Terrorist Finance Tracking Program. It called for actions in six areas: (1) swift adoption of the EU's data protection reform; (2) improving the Safe

Harbor; (3) strengthening data protection safeguards in the law enforcement area; (4) using the existing Mutual Legal Assistance and Sectoral agreements to obtain data; (5) addressing European concerns in the on-going U.S. reform process; and (6) promoting privacy standards internationally.

Regarding the Safe Harbor, the European Commission issued thirteen recommendations. These pertain to the need to make the Safe Harbor Framework more transparent, to embed Alternative Dispute Resolution mechanisms in the Framework, to increase enforcement and audits of the Safe Harbor, and to make clear the circumstances under which U.S. authorities may access EU personal data. It called on relevant U.S. authorities to respond to these recommendations and remedy these issues.

EU Parliament Votes Non-Binding Resolution to Suspend Safe Harbor (March 2014)

In March 2014, the EU Parliament passed a resolution calling for "immediate suspension" of the Safe Harbor Framework. It did so because of its view that the Safe Harbor did not adequately protect European citizens. This resolution does not affect the current validity of the Framework, which is negotiated by the European Commission. It also called for Parliament to withhold consent to any Transatlantic Trade and Investment Partnership (TTIP) with the U.S. unless such a deal fully respected EU fundamental rights to data protection.

FTC Enforcement of the Safe Harbor Agreement

In January 2014, the FTC settled Safe Harbor charges with twelve companies. According to the FTC, these companies had deceptively claimed that they held current certifications under the Safe Harbor. In three of the complaints, the FTC alleged that the companies had also deceptively claimed certifications under the U.S.-Swiss Safe Harbor. Among the companies settling with the FTC were two teams in the National Football League, a provider of P2P file sharing, and a DNA testing lab.

Leading Case

In the Matter of Google, Inc. (FTC 2011)

Google Buzz violated the FTC Act and Safe Harbor by suggesting that Gmail users could choose whether to join Buzz, but then enrolling some people who had not wanted to join Buzz in certain Buzz features. The FTC required Google to institute a "comprehensive privacy program." This was the first case involving a Safe Harbor violation and the requirement that a company develop a comprehensive privacy program.

In re Google, Inc. (FTC 2012)

Google agreed to pay a $22.5 million fine to the FTC based on the charge that, in violation of its promises, it placed a tracking cookie on the computers of Safari users. This practice violated the October 2011 settlement with the FTC that Google not misrepresent the extent to which it provided users control over their data.

FTC Enforcement of the Safe Harbor Agreement (FTC 2014)
In January 2014, the FTC settled Safe Harbor charges with twelve companies. According to the FTC, these companies had deceptively claimed that they held current certifications under the Safe Harbor. In three of the complaints, the FTC alleged that the companies had also deceptively claimed certifications under the U.S.-Swiss Safe Harbor. Among the companies settling with the FTC were two teams in the National Football League, a provider of P2P file sharing, and a DNA testing lab.

Schrems v. Data Protection Commissioner, IECH 310 (Irish High Court, June 18, 2014)
Assessing a claim that the Snowden revelations demonstrated that there is "no effective data protection regime in the United States" and that, therefore, the Safe Harbor did not provide "adequate" data protection. The litigant would have the Data Protection Commissioner of Ireland exercise his statutory authority and stop Facebook Ireland from transferring any personal information to its parent company in the U.S. The Irish High Court found that the Safe Harbor agreement, which authorized these transfers, was a matter of EU law and pre-empted Irish data protection law. As a matter of EU law, the Irish Court then certified these issues to the European Court of Justice: did the Snowden revelations and the entry into force of Article 8 of the Charta of Human Rights require re-evaluation of (1) the 1995 EU Directive on Data Protection and (2) the 2000 Commission decision that the Safe Harbor provided adequate data protection?

Other Safe Harbor Arrangements

U.S.-Swiss Safe Harbor Framework (2009)
Follows the same approach as the Safe Harbor with the EU. A U.S. organization that self-certifies under the U.S.-Switzerland Safe Harbor Framework is viewed as providing "adequate protection" under Swiss data protection law. As in the EU-U.S. Safe Harbor, these Safe Harbor principles require safeguards concerning: (1) notice, (2) choice, (3) onward transfers, (4) access, (5) security, (6) data integrity and (7) enforcement. The Department of Commerce has issued a list of Frequently Asked Questions (FAQs) to supplement these Safe Harbor principles. It has also published a handbook, U.S.-Swiss Safe Harbor Framework, Guide to Self-Certification (March 2012).

Positive Adequacy Determinations by the EU Commission

Adequacy determinations of the EU (with the date of the finding):

- Andorra (October 2010)
- Argentina (June 2003)
- Australia: Passenger Name Records Agreement (June 2008)
- Canada (December 2001)
- Bailiwick of Guernsey (November 2003)
- Bailiwick of Jersey (May 2008)
- The Faeroe Islands (March 2010)
- Isle of Man (April 2004)
- Israel (January 2011)
- New Zealand (December 2012)
- Switzerland (July 2000)
- United States: Passenger Name Records Agreement (December 2000)
- United States: Safe Harbor Principles (December 2000)
- Uruguay (August 2012)

The Safe Harbor Agreement supplies an adequate level of data protection for U.S. companies that comply with its requirements. The United States has also concluded a Passenger Names Record Agreement with the EU. This agreement permits the transfer of a broad range of information about passengers on flights from EU Member States to U.S. airports to be transferred to the U.S. Department of Homeland Security. Australia has reached a similar agreement to permit a transfer of information about passengers on flights to the Australian Customs and Border Protection Service.

The United States has never formally sought an adequacy determination from the European Commission for its entire legal system, as opposed to the more limited EU recognition of the Safe Harbor Principles and Passenger Name Records Agreement. This reticence is likely due, according to Christopher Wolf, "because of the well-understood outcome: request denied." Christopher Wolf, *Delusions of Adequacy?*, 43 Washington Univ. J. L. & Policy 227, 229 (2013).

Source: European Commission, Frequently Asked Questions Relating to Transfers of Personal Data from the EU/EEA to Third Countries, at http://ec.europa.eu/justice/policies/privacy/docs/international_transfers_faq/international_transfers_faq.pdf

Model Contractual Clauses

The EU has approved two sets of model contractual clauses. If a company in a nonmember state follows either of the model contractual clauses, it is deemed to have "adequate protection" under the EU Directive on Data Protection. The first set of model contractual clauses was approved by the EU in 2001. The second set of model contractual clauses was approved by it in 2003.

Binding Corporate Rules (BCRs)

BCRs can be used instead of model contract clauses as a means to meet the "adequacy" test. If a company chooses to use them, the BCRs must be uniform throughout the entire organization. The EU has set the following requirements for BCRs:

- BCRs must be enforceable by "data subject."

- BCRs must indicate a clear duty of cooperation with data protection authorities in the EU.

- In principle, the approval of a BCR must come from each data protection authority (DPA) in each of the countries from which data are to be transferred. The Working Party has developed a so-called standard application for approval of a BCR, and a procedure for filling out a single copy of a form, which can be submitted to the "lead DPA" for approval. The Article 29 Working Party has developed a multifactor test for determining the lead DPA.

Discovery from EU Member Nations in U.S. Litigation

Strict data protection laws in Europe may conflict with U.S. discovery rules. Civil discovery in the U.S. tends to be largely managed by the parties to litigation and proceeds under a broader test that permits more material to be discoverable than is usual in civil law jurisdictions. A European company's transfer of certain personal data to the U.S. might violate European privacy law.

The **Restatement (Third) of Foreign Relations Law § 442(1)(c)** provides a set of factors for U.S. courts in deciding the permissibility of ordering information sought for production that is located in a foreign country:

> the importance to the investigation or litigation of the documents or other information requested; the degree of specificity of the request; whether the information originated in the United States; the availability of alternative means of securing the information; and the extent to which noncompliance with the request would undermine important interests of the United States, or compliance with the request would undermine important interests of the state [or country] where the information is located

In *Volkswagen, A.G. v. Valdez*, **909 S.W. 2d 900 (Tex. 1995)**, the Texas Supreme Court rejected a finding of the trial court ordering discovery of documents from Volkswagen that were located in Germany. It found that the trial court abused its discretion in failing to balance the competing interests of the parties and in disregarding German law in its entirety. The Texas Supreme Court applied the Restatement (Third) of Foreign Relations Law § 442. Among its findings was that production of the document would violate German privacy law and bear little importance to the litigation.

Directive on Privacy and Electronic Communications (E-Privacy Directive) Directive 2002/58/EC (2002) (Amendments 2009)

Primary Function: To protect "the right to privacy in the electronic communication sector." Like the Data Protection Directive, it seeks to harmonize the regulations in the member states in order to ensure an equivalent level of protection in them.

Confidentiality and Security: Requires member states to ensure the confidentiality of communications through their national legislation. It requires providers of telecommunication services to protect the security of their systems and services.

Opt Out: The directive permits the use of information in the terminal equipment of a user, as through cookies, only if the user is provided with clear and comprehensive information about the purpose of the processing and is given a chance to opt out.

Opt In: The directive directs member states to permit unsolicited telephone calls, e-mails and faxes only when the affected party has provided opt-in consent.

Exceptions: The directive does not apply to issues concerning "public security and defence, state security and criminal law." These issues are regulated through the EU Data Retention Directive (see below).

Cookies and the 2009 Amendments: The EU amended the E-Privacy Directive in 2009 to make cookies subject to prior user consent following the provision of "clear and comprehensive information" to the affected party. It forbids the placing of cookies without such consent with an exemption for cookies "strictly necessary in order for the provider of an information society service explicitly requested by the subscriber or user to provide the service."

EU Data Retention Directive Directive 2006/24/EC (2006)

Primary Function: The Data Retention Directive requires member states to enact laws that mandate storage of telecommunications information "for the investigation, detection, and prosecution of crime." Under the Data Retention Directive, member nations of the European Union are to enact statutes that require providers to store certain telecommunications data. Article 1(1) of the directive provides: "This directive aims to harmonise Member States' provisions concerning ... the retention of certain data which are generated or processed by them, in order to ensure that the data are available for the purpose of the investigation, detection and prosecution of serious crime, as defined by each Member State in its national law."

Limits on Data Retention: The directive mandates retention of certain specified categories of information "for periods of not less than six months and not more than two years from the date of the communication." Article 6.

Leading Cases

Decision of Federal Constitutional Court, 1 BvR 256/08, 1 BvR 263/08, 1 BvR 586/08 (March 2, 2010)
In Germany, the Federal Constitutional Court ruled that parts of the German statute enacted pursuant to the directive violated the German constitution, the Basic Law. The Constitutional Court found that the statute's technical conditions for the data storage were not secure enough, that the statute did not clearly establish legal norms for the use of the stored data, and that the statute could "cause a diffusely threatening feeling of being under observation that can diminish an unprejudiced perception of one's basic rights in many areas." In the current form of the law, "such retention represents an especially grave intrusion" into the constitutional rights of citizens. It required the immediate deletion of the personal telecommunications data already collected and for amendments to the law that would provide stricter conditions for the use and storage of such information.

ECJ, Joined Cases C-293/12 and C-594/12—*Digital Rights Ireland* and *Seitlinger and Others* (April 8, 2014)
On 8 April 2014, the European Court of Justice declared the Data Retention Directive 2006/24/EC (2006) invalid. It held that it did not meet the principle of proportionality. The Data Retention Directive lacked sufficient safeguards to protect the fundamental rights of respect for private life and of protection for personal data. The Court also found that data retention generally served a legitimate and general interest by protecting public security and would be permissible if subject to clear and precise conditions.

European Data Protection Supervisor (EDPS)

The EDPS is an independent supervisory authority that protects personal data and privacy in EU institutions and entities. It does so through:

• Oversight of the EU administration's processing of personal data

• Advising the EU on policies and legislation that affect privacy

• Cooperating with other international authorities with the goal of ensuring "consistent data protection"

NORTH AMERICA

Canada

Charter of Rights and Freedoms (1982)
The Canadian Charter of Rights and Freedoms does not contain an explicit right to privacy, but Sections 7 and 8 serve to protect privacy.

Section 7: Everyone has the right to life, liberty and security of the person and the right not to be deprived thereof except in accordance with the principles of fundamental justice.

Section 8: Everyone has the right to be secure against unreasonable search or seizure.

Leading Cases:

Hunter v. Southam, Inc., [1984] 2 S.C.R. 145
Section 8 of the charter only protects against violations of reasonable expectations of privacy.

Regina v. Plant, [1993] 3 S.C.R. 281
Factors for determining the existence of a reasonable expectation of privacy include "the nature of the information, the relationship between the appellant and the Commission, the place and manner of the search and the seriousness of the offence under investigation."

R. v. Chehil, 2013 SCC 49 (2013)
Use of a properly deployed drug detection dog is a search that is reasonable based merely on "reasonable suspicion." Because dog sniffs are minimally intrusive, narrowly targeted, and can be highly accurate, these searches may be conducted without prior judicial authorization.

Even though indicia like a dog's past performance and the risk of cross-contamination can be relevant to determining a dog's reliability, no specific evidentiary requirements will apply mechanically to every case. The prosecution does not have to prove that the dog is infallible, just as it does not have to prove that an informer's tip is infallible.

R. v. Vu, 2013 SCC 60 (2013)
The privacy interests at stake when computers are searched require that these devices be treated, to a certain extent, as a separate place. Therefore, police must obtain a specific search warrant to search a computer; police must satisfy the authorizing justice that reasonable grounds exist to believe that any computer they discover will contain the information things for which they are searching.

R. v. Telus Communications Co., 2013 SCC 16 (2013)

Canada's Supreme Court found police were required to comply with rules regarding interception set out in the Criminal Code if they want to secure the prospective and continuous production of text messages from a mobile carrier. It found that the police cannot merely obtain a general warrant but must obtain an intercept order and comply with the conditions needed to intercept voice communications if they want to copy text messages.

Privacy Act (1985)

Limits the collection, use and disclosure of personal information by federal government institutions. Vests powers in the Privacy Commissioner to receive and investigate complaints, initiate an investigation and make findings and recommendations. Grants a private right of action only in relation to a refusal by a government institution to provide individual access to his or her personal information held by the government.

Personal Information Protection and Electronic Documents Act (PIPEDA) (2000)

PIPEDA regulates all private-sector entities that collect personal information on Canadians and personal information used in connection with any commercial activity. PIPEDA is based on the OECD Privacy Guidelines and, more directly, the Canadian Standards Association (CSA) Model Code for the Protection of Personal Information, which articulates 10 privacy principles. PIPEDA's Schedule 1 reprints most of the CSA Model Code.

PIPEDA's 10 Privacy Principles
(from the CSA Model Code)

1. Accountability
Responsibility for data transferred to others; must have point person for PIPEDA compliance.

2. Identifying Purposes
Purposes for data use must be articulated when collected.

3. Consent
Consent requirements and opt-out rights.

4. Limiting Collection
Data collection limited to that necessary for purposes. No deceptive collection.

5. Limiting Use, Disclosure and Retention
Data use limited to purposes of collection. Data no longer needed must be deleted.

6. Accuracy
Data must be kept accurate.

7. Safeguards
Must protect data security.

8. Openness
Privacy policies must be transparent and understandable.

9. Individual Access
People are entitled to know about the data gathered about them and can challenge accuracy of it.

10. Challenging Compliance
People can complain to an organization about failures to comply with PIPEDA.

PIPEDA requires that the individual must consent prior to the collection, use or disclosure of personal data. It also incorporates the OECD's purpose specification principle, security safeguard principles, openness principle, accountability principle and data quality principle, among others. Under PIPEDA, the Privacy Commissioner of Canada has the power to investigate citizen complaints and to conduct audits.

PIPEDA has provisions that acknowledge the federalistic structure of Canada. It permits a province's privacy law to displace it only when the provincial privacy law is "substantially similar" to it. PIPEDA does not contain an explicit benchmark regarding the meaning of "substantial similarity," but assigns an important task to the national privacy commissioner in making this determination. In a report to parliament, the privacy commissioner stated that, in the view of his office, substantial similarity means "equal or superior" to PIPEDA "in the degree and quality of privacy protection provided." Privacy Commissioner of Canada, *Report to Parliament Concerning Substantially Similar Provincial Legislation* (2001).

The EU Commission issued a decision in December 2001 that found PIPEDA to provide an adequate level of protection.

Canada's Anti-Spam Law (CASL) (2010)

Scope: Canada's Anti-Spam Law (CASL) prohibits electronic spam, alterations of transmission data and installation of certain computer programs on another person's computer.

It also prohibits the use of false or misleading representations in an email for the promotion of products or services (Section 52.01 of the Competition Act), collection of personal information by means of unauthorized access to computer systems, and the unauthorized compiling of lists of electronic addresses (Section 7.1 of PIPEDA)

In addition to commercial e-mail, CASL also regulates spyware, malware and botnets. As a result, it regulates more areas than the CAN-SPAM Act in the U.S.

Enforcement: CASL's regulatory scheme also includes strong administrative monetary penalties and a private right of action. According to CASL's clause 21(1), every person who contravenes this statute's clauses 7 to 10 is liable for an administrative monetary penalty. Clauses 7 to 10 refer to sending unsolicited commercial electronic messages; altering transmission data; installing computer programs; and aiding, inducing, procuring or causing to be procured any of the former actions. The maximum penalty for such violation is $1 million in the case of an individual, and $10 million in the case of an organization.

CASL also provides for a private right of action that enables a person affected by an act or omission that constitutes a contravention of the statute's clauses 7 to 10 to obtain an amount equal to the actual amount of the loss or damage suffered, or expenses incurred, and statutory damages for the contravention.

Regulations and Guidelines for Canada's Anti-Spam Law (2012)

The Canadian Radio-television and Telecommunications Commission (CRTC) is the main regulatory agency responsible for pursuing administrative penalties for violation of CASL. The act also gives it authority to issue regulations and guidelines regarding compliance with the act.

In March 2012, the CRTC issued its final regulations for CASL. These regulations set out the information that an organization must include when it requests consent for receiving commercial e-mail. In October 2012, the CRTC released two sets of guidelines regarding CASL.

The first, CRTC 2012-548, specifies the kinds of identification that a message gives regarding the sender and gives examples of acceptable mechanisms for subscribers to unsubscribe from mailings as well as the kinds of consent requests that are acceptable.

The second guideline, CRTC 2012-548, is perhaps the most important of these documents. It expresses a negative opinion on "toggling," a set of practices involving pre-checked boxes. In toggling, the person whose consent is being sought must *uncheck* the box to indicate that she does not consent. Toggled boxes generally are considered to provide "opt-out consent." The second guideline states, "The Commission considers that in order to comply with the express consent provisions under the Act, a positive or explicit indication of consent is required. Accordingly, express consent cannot be obtained through opt-out consent mechanisms." As a result, express consent under CASL must be through opt-in. In this regard, CASL will set stricter requirements than CAN-SPAM does in the U.S.

Common Law Torts

Canada recognizes only one of the Warren and Brandeis privacy torts, that of intrusion upon seclusion (see below). Other Canadian torts have been applied to protect privacy, and Canada recognizes the breach of confidence tort in the UK and a few other commonwealth countries. *Lac Minerals v. Int'l Corona Res. [1989]*, 2 S.C.R. 575.

Jones v. Tsige, 2012 ONCA 42 (Jan. 18, 2012)

The Court of Appeal for Ontario recognized the U.S. privacy tort of intrusion upon seclusion—intentionally intruding upon a person's seclusion or solitude, or into his private affairs.

Provincial Privacy Laws

• Alberta Personal Information Protection Act, S.A. 2003, c. P-6.5 (2004)

• British Columbia Privacy Act, R.S.B.C. 1996, ch. 373 (1968)
  – Personal Information Protection Act, S.B.C. 2003, ch. 63 (2004)

• Manitoba Privacy Act, C.C.S.M. ch. P125 (1970)

• Newfoundland and Labrador Privacy Act, R.S.N.L. 1990, ch. P-22 (1990)

• Quebec Charter § 5
  – Quebec Civil Code §§ 35-40
  – Quebec Act, R.S.Q., ch P-39.1 (1993)

• Saskatchewan Privacy Act, R.S.S. 1978, c. P-24 (1978)

Mexico

Constitution

Article 16 provides privacy protection to one's person, family, home, documents and possessions, as well as communications.

Federal Data Protection Act (FDPA) (2010)

The act is an omnibus law, following the EU model, that requires a lawful basis for collecting, processing and disclosing personal information. Unlike the EU model, however, the statute embodies the "habeas data" concept embraced by several South and Latin American countries—the individual to whom the data refers is treated as a "data owner" with legal rights, such as those of access, that derive from this status. For more on habeas data, see the box at right. The Federal Data Protection Act of Mexico also creates a supervisory authority, the Federal Institute of Access to Information and Data Protection.

The Federal Institute is granted strong powers to hear objections to data processing practices and issue decisions to protect the rights granted by the Federal Data Protection Act.

Other Statutes

Mexico has many federal laws related to privacy, addressing government records, marketing, credit reporting and electronic surveillance.

SOUTH AMERICA

Argentina

Constitution of the Argentine Nation

Article 43 provides for a right to "habeas data." A person can "obtain information on the data about himself and their purpose, registered in public records … or in private ones."

Law for the Protection of Personal Data (2000)

Argentina was the first country in South America to adopt a comprehensive data protection law. The law is based on the EU Data Protection Directive, several provisions of the Argentina constitution and earlier national laws. Among its measures are rules of procedure that permit "habeas data" as a judicial remedy. The Argentina data protection law also prohibits international transfers of personal information to countries without adequate protection. In June 2003, the Commission of the European Community decided that Argentina provides an adequate level of protection for personal data.

Habeas Data

The concept of "habeas data" is common among South and Latin American countries. Habeas data is a special judicial measure that permits any person to know the content and purpose of the data pertaining to her in public records or in certain private records. Habeas data is a novel concept from the late 1980s, first introduced in the Constitution of Brazil. It is a legal mechanism that permits an individual to find out what information is held about her and to gain certain traditional information privacy rights with respect to that data.

Brazil

Constitution
The constitution of Brazil explicitly protects privacy in its Article 5. It also contains a constitutional right to habeas data.

Privacy Statutes
Brazil lacks any omnibus information privacy law. It does contain some sectoral privacy laws. These include a consumer protection law (1990) that regulates personal data recordkeeping and a federal law (1996) that regulates wiretapping.

The proposed Data Protection Bill (2011) has yet to be enacted; the draft legislation follows the EU model. It requires consent prior to transfer as well as breach notification. It also contains a requirement of consent for the transfer of personal data outside Brazil. The draft legislation establishes a Data Protection Authority with the power to issue sanctions and requires opt-in consent for processing of sensitive personal data.

MIDDLE EAST

Dubai

Data Protection Law (2004)
One of the seven emirates of the United Arab Emirates, Dubai is an important business hub in the Middle East. In 2007, it amended its Data Protection Law (2004) and strengthened it in various ways, including the creation of an independent Office of Commissioner of Data Protection.

Israel

Protection of Privacy Act (PPA) (1981)
The PPA applies to both public and private entities. It requires certain databases to be registered with the government. The PPA also establishes an office, the Israeli Law, Information, and Technology Authority (ILITA), that plays the central role in overseeing the PPA's database registration provisions. In an opinion from December 1, 2009, the Article 29 Working Party found that Israeli data protection law provides an "adequate level" of data protection in the sense of the EU Data Protection Directive. The EU Commission will take this finding into regard as it makes its own decision on this issue.

Other Statutes
Israel's Basic Law on Human Dignity protects privacy of the home and one's papers and belongings. Israel also has a law that protects the privacy of digital

information (Computer Law of 1995) and that regulates credit reporting (Credit Data Service Law of 2002).

ASIA

Japan

Constitution
Article 13 provides a "right to life, liberty, and the pursuit of happiness." In 1963, the Supreme Court held that this provision protects a right to privacy.

Personal Data Protection Act (PDPA) (2005)
This omnibus privacy law requires businesses to provide information to an individual about how they use, store and process her personal data. It also limits disclosures of data to third parties unless they meet a set of statutory conditions. Such disclosures can be made pursuant to a law or ordinance; when necessary for the protection of human life, safety or property and it is difficult to obtain the consent of the individual; when necessary to improve public hygiene and promote the health of children and it is difficult to obtain the individual's consent; and when cooperation is necessary for certain government activities and consent of the individual would hinder achievement of that purpose.

China

China does not have an omnibus privacy law. Its civil law does protect against harm to reputation, and its criminal law protects against those who violate "rights of communication freedom."

China's Several Provisions on Regulation of the Order of Internet Information Service Market (2011)
Regulates entities providing "Internet information services" by restricting them from providing personal information to third parties without consent or collecting data not necessary to provide services. Requires notice to users, security safeguards and notices of harmful data disclosures to the telecommunications authority.

Hong Kong

Personal Data Ordinance (1997)
The ordinance regulates the public and private sectors. This law created an oversight authority, the Office of the Privacy Commissioner for Personal Data.

Hong Kong Personal Data (Privacy) Amendment Ordinance (2012)

Updates the 1996 ordinance to provide notification and consent for the use, transfer or sale of data for direct marketing, requirements for contracts for outsourcing, and other provisions. The Ordinance provides for strong penalties. For the transfer of personal data to third parties, it permits a maximum penalty of HK$ 1,000,000 and imprisonment for 5 years. For other direct marketing contraventions, it allows a maximum fine of HK$ 500,000 and imprisonment for 3 years.

Other Statutes

Hong Kong has also enacted sectoral protections for employment data (2001) and consumer credit data (2003).

Singapore

Personal Data Protection Act ("Singapore PDPA") (2012)

The Act follows the general structure of the EU-Data-Protection Directive. The Singapore PDPA's rules regarding the transfer of data also follow the provisions set out in the EU-Directive, so that the standard of protection in the receiving country is of crucial importance. Unlike the EU model, however, it contains no extra definition for sensitive data and most provisions do not apply to business information. Regardless of its size, organizations subject to the Singapore PDPA must designate a data protection officer. Currently there is no requirement for an organization to register its use of personal information with the data protection authority. The PDPA also establishes a national Do Not Call (DNC) Registry to allow individuals to register their telephone numbers and to opt out of receiving marketing phone calls, mobile text messages and faxes from organizations.

South Korea

Personal Information Protection Act (PIPA)(2011)

South Korea enacted an omnibus data protection law in 2011 as well as sectoral laws, such as the "IT Network Act" or "Act on Real Name Financial Transactions and Guarantee of Secrecy." Among Asian countries, South Korea is now considered to offer the strictest privacy laws. It is also an example of an Asian country following the EU model of data protection legislation. Key concepts under the PIPA include a requirement of prior consent and an obligation that data processors reveal the purpose of processing, using, and collecting of data.

All organizations must also register with the Minister of Public Administration and Security and appoint a data protection officer. If a data subject accuses a data processor of non-compliance, the burden of proof rests with the data processor. This requirement is intended to forces companies to keep detailed records of their data processing to prove compliance. Penalties in case of non–compliance consist of imprisonment or fines of up to 100 million Won, which is approximately $ 92,000.

Under the IT Network Act, a service provider must notify the Korean Communications Commission (the "KCC") or the Korea Internet & Security Agency (the "KISA") if it discovers a breach or intrusion of data security. A service provider must analyze the cause of the intrusion and prevent it from being spread. Individuals can withdraw their consent to data processing and transfers at any time.

India

Constitution
Article 21 protects a right to privacy as a component of the right to "personal liberty." In 1964, the Supreme Court held that this provision encompassed a right to privacy. *Kharak Singh v. State of UP*, (1964) 1 SCR 332.

Statutory Protections
India also has sectoral privacy protections for financial transactions (Public Financial Institutions Act of 1993), communications (Telegraph Act of 1885) and telecommunications (Common Charter of Telecom Services).

India's Information Technology Rules (April 2011)
The full title of these regulations is "the Information Technology (Reasonable security practices and procedures and sensitive personal information) Rules, 2011." In these regulations, India defines the information that constitutes "sensitive data" under the act and spells out the circumstances under which these data may be collected. It also requires organization and corporations to develop clear privacy policies concerning how they handle user information.

Philippines

Data Privacy Act (2012)
The Data Privacy Act is a consolidated data privacy legislation that follows both the EU model and the APEC framework. The Act mandates that all personal information controllers comply with a set of requirements before processing or other activities may take place. It includes some of Asia's toughest sanctions for privacy violations. Among its penalties, the statute permits fines and prison sentences for first time breaches, ongoing liability of controllers for personal information sent offshore or provided to third party processors, and the deportation of foreigners who breach the Act.

EUROPE, NON-EU COUNTRIES

Russia

Constitution of the Russian Federation
Article 23 protects "the right to privacy, to personal and family secrets and to protection of one's honor and good name." It also protects privacy of communication. Article 24 forbids collecting, using or disclosing personal information without consent. Article 25 protects privacy of the home.

Law on Personal Data (2006)
Omnibus privacy law that restricts private-sector information gathering without consent and provides rights regarding government records.

Russia's Cross-Border Data Transfer Rules (2011)
Amendments to Russia's data protection law created new rules on the cross-border transfer of personal data. It permits this transfer to countries that are parties to Europe's Convention for the Protection of Individuals with regard to Automatic Processing of Personal Data (1981). It also authorizes the Russian Federal Service for Oversight of Communications, Information Technology and Mass Media (the Russian Data Protection Agency) to approve a "whitelist" of approved data transfer countries that are not parties to the convention. On this approved list are to be those countries that provide adequate protection of personal data. The amendments also permit a cross-border transfer if the data subject consents to the transmission.

Other Statutes
Russia has a law protecting against the interception of electronic communications (Communications Law of 2003).

APEC Privacy Framework (2004)

Origin: Ministers of nations that form the Asia-Pacific Economic Cooperation (APEC) adopted the Privacy Framework in 2004. The APEC Privacy Framework seeks to enable multinational businesses to implement uniform approaches to the use of personal data. The resulting guidelines strongly reflect the OECD Privacy Guidelines.

Advisory Only: Unlike the EU Data Protection Directive, the APEC Framework does not mandate that member states enact its principles into law. The APEC Framework is advisory only.

APEC Privacy Framework's 9 Principles

The nine principles of the APEC Privacy Framework are:

1. Preventing Harm
2. Notice
3. Collection Limitation
4. Use of Personal Information
5. Choice
6. Integrity
7. Security Safeguards
8. Access and Correction
9. Accountability

Accountability: One of the most interesting of these principles is that of accountability. The APEC Framework states that organizations that process information should be "accountable for complying with measures that give effect" to its principles. In its commentary to this principle, the APEC Framework further observes:

> Efficient and cost effective business models often require information transfers between different types of organizations in different locations with varying relationships. When transferring information, personal information controllers should be accountable for ensuring that the recipient will protect the information consistently with these Principles when not obtaining consent. Thus, information controllers should take reasonable steps to ensure the information is protected, in accordance with these Principles, after it is transferred.

The idea of accountability has proven influential at the international level. The idea is that accountable privacy requires processes tailored to the specific risks of the data risk at hand. For an example of the influence of this concept, the Article 29 Working Group in 2010 called for a "statutory accountability principle" as a way to help move data protection from theory to practice. Article 29 Data Protection Working Party, Opinion 3/2010 on the Principle of Accountability, at 3. Accountability concepts involve data controllers implementing "appropriate and effective measures" that are "scalable"—that is, proportionate to the risks involved. As the Working Party discussed this concept, "the types of measures should be coherent with the risks represented by the data processing and the nature of data."

APEC MEMBER NATIONS		
Australia	Japan	Russia
Brunei Darussalam	Malaysia	Singapore
Canada	Mexico	South Korea
Chile	New Zealand	Taiwan
China	Papua New Guinea	Thailand
Hong Kong	Peru	United States
Indonesia	Philippines	Vietnam

AUSTRALIA

Constitution
The constitution lacks an express provision protecting the right to privacy.

Privacy Act (1988)
The act establishes 11 privacy principles. These principles are known as the National Privacy Principles (NPPs). The Office of the Privacy Commissioner is responsible for the administration of the Privacy Act. The Privacy Act establishes limits on transfers to another country. A 2000 law amended the original Privacy Act to expand it from the public sector to the private sector as well. The act established a "co-regulatory" scheme. Companies can apply to the privacy commissioner to substitute their own privacy practices if they are "overall equivalent" to the NPPs. Further exemptions are possible for "small businesses" and employment records. Data can readily be transferred abroad because any restrictions that do apply are not strictly written.

FOR FURTHER REFERENCE

Treatises

Gert Brüggemeier et. al (eds.), *Personality Rights in European Tort Law* (2010)
Mapping the landscape of tort privacy law in different European countries and drawing comparisons with the U.S.

Simon Chesterman, ed., *Data Protection Law in Singapore* (2014)
A series of essays exploring Singapore's Personal Data Protection Act (2012) and other aspects of privacy law in Singapore. Essays also explore Malaysia's Data Protection Law and draws comparisons with other Asian jurisdictions.
Axel von dem Bussche & Markus Stamm, Data Protection Law

in Germany (2013)
Concise treatise on the Federal Data Protection Act and its requirements. Coverage of issues such as customer and supplier data protection, employee data protection, and international transfer of personal data.

Lothar Determann, *Determann's Field Guide to International Data Privacy Compliance* (2012)
A concise and practical guide to the many dimensions of international privacy law.

Gilles Dutertre, ed., *Key Case-law Extracts: European Court of Human Rights* (2003)
Extensive selection of decisions of the European Court of Human Rights in its Article 8 cases.

Françoise Gilbert, *The Global Privacy and Security Law Reference* (2009)
3000-page treatise covering 66 countries; updated three times each year.

Rosemary Jay, *Data Protection Law and Practice* (2007)
Leading guide to the UK's Data Protection Act and relevant case law.

Christopher Kuner, *European Data Protection Law: Corporate Compliance and Regulation* (2d ed. 2007)
Examines European data protection law as it relates to legal compliance issues for companies.

Christopher Kuner, *Transborder Data Flows and Data Privacy Law* (2013)
Examining the transfer of personal data across national borders under data protection law. Coverage includes the EU and other global regulatory regimes, such as the APEC Privacy Framework, Organization of American States, and World Trade Law.

Barbara McIsaak et al., *The Law of Privacy in Canada* (rev. ed. 2006)
Multivolume treatise on all aspects of Canadian privacy law.

Chris Millard, ed., *Cloud Computing Law* (2013)
A wide-reaching examination of the European law of cloud computing, including the issues of public sector cloud procurement and the privacy of personal data in clouds.

Stephanie Perrin et al., *The Personal Information Protection and Electronic Documents Act: An Annotated Guide* (2001)
Concise one-volume guide to Canada's PIPEDA.

Eduardo Ustaran, editor, *European Privacy: Law and Practice for Data Protection Professionals* (2012)
Detailed guide to EU privacy law.

Articles and Other Sources

Kenneth A. Bamberger and Deirdre K. Mulligan, *Privacy in Europe: Initial Data on Governance Choices and Corporate Practices*, 81 Geo. Wash. L. Rev. 1529 (2013)
The authors examine the ground-level practices of corporations and other private entities and make suggestions to policymakers in the EU.

Colin J. Bennett, *Regulating Privacy: Data Protection and Public Policy in Europe and the United States* (1992)
Important early study about differences in policy approaches to privacy in Europe and the U.S. Argues that the American experience demonstrates "the enormous problems associated with enforcing data protection standards without a commission or some other agency whose sole responsibility is privacy."

Colin J. Bennett & Charles D. Raab, *The Governance of Privacy: Policy Instruments in Global Perspective* (2006)
Study of development of global privacy standards finds that while their overall level is being "traded up"—that is, improved—nonetheless, surveillance practices may not be reduced.

Francesca Bignami, *European Versus American Liberty: A Comparative Privacy Analysis of Antiterrorism Data Mining*, 48 B.C. L. Rev. 609 (2007)
Examination of comparative regulations for data mining in the EU and the U.S. arguing that the Bush administration's warrantless surveillance program at the NSA would be illegal in Europe and might be legal under the then applicable U.S. law.

David H. Flaherty, *Protecting Privacy in Surveillance Societies: The Federal Republic of Germany, France,* Canada, and the United States (1989)
Classic account of the role of data protection agencies in Europe and the development of information privacy there and in North America.

Francoise Gilbert, *European Data Protection 2.0, 28 Santa Clara Computer & High Technology* L.J. 815 (2012)
Analyzes the regulation and argues that the proposed reform document will create "more obligations for companies, and more rights for individuals."

Serge Gutwirth et al., eds., *Reinventing Data Protection?* (2009)
Strong and up-to-date collection of essays looking at a wide variety of
different issues in EU data protection.

Dennis D. Hirsch, *Going Dutch? Collaborative Dutch Privacy Regulation
and the Lessons It Holds for U.S. Privacy Law,* 2013 Mich. St. L. Rev. 83 (2013)
Argues that the Dutch model of collaboration between regulators and
industry in rule drafting offers an effective solution to the challenges of
crafting effective privacy law. US policymakers can learn from the 20-plus
years of Dutch experience using this collaborative model.

Christopher Kuner, *The European Commission's Proposed
Data Protection Regulation, 11 PVLR 1* (Feb. 6, 2012)
Explores how the proposed regulation would change existing EU privacy
law. In Kuner's judgment, "[S]ome of its specific innovations seem misguided.
… And while there is a need for more stringent enforcement of the law
and more harmonized enforcement powers, the combination of ill-defined
offenses and huge mandatory fines raises basic questions of fairness."

Christopher Kuner et. al, *The Proposed EU Data Protection Regulation
Two Years Later, 13 PVLR 1* (Jan. 6, 2014)
Analyzing the current status of the Proposed Regulation with attention
to the amendment adopted by the European Parliament and on progress
made in the Council of the EU towards enactment of this document.

Abraham L. Newman, *Protectors of Privacy* (2008)
Political scientist explains why nations in the EU adopted comprehensive
information privacy statutes and why the U.S. has taken a narrowly focused
sectoral approach. Also explains why the EU approach, and not the U.S.
approach, has been broadly adopted throughout the world.

Paul Ohm, *Sensitive Data, 88 S.Cal. L. Rev. --* (forthcoming 2015)
Developing a taxonomy for defining sensitive data based on a concept of
"information that can be used to enable privacy or security harm when
placed in the wrong hands."

Joel Reidenberg, *The Data Surveillance State in Europe and the
United States,* 49 Wake Forest L. Rev. 583 (2014)
US law has generally focused on access restraints for government to obtain
privately held information, ignored the collection and storage of data.
In contrast, the EU focuses more on restricting the collection and retention
of data and less on government access. This article recommends stricter
retention limits combined with stronger access controls, increased
transparency of government access to personal information, and personal
liability of government officials for overreaching.

Joel R. Reidenberg, *Resolving Conflicting International Data Privacy Rules in Cyberspace*, 52 Stan. L. Rev. 1315 (2000)
Development of models of different strategies for developing international cooperation and achieving a high level of privacy protection for personal information in international data transfers.

Ira Rubinstein, *Big Data: The End of Privacy or a New Beginning?*, 3 Int'l Data Privacy L. 74 (2013)
Europe is presently considering a General Data Protection Regulation that would replace the aging Data Protection Directive. The Proposed Regulation creates new individual rights and imposes new accountability measures on organizations that collect or process data. But the Big Data tsunami is likely to overwhelm these reform efforts. Thus, this article argues that a supplementary approach should use codes of conduct. In particular, the article stresses that regulators should encourage businesses to adopt new business models premised on consumer empowerment by offering incentives such as regulatory flexibility and reduced penalties.

Ira Rubinstein, Gregory Nojeim & Ronald Lee, *Systematic Government Access to Personal Data: A Comparative Analysis*, 4 Int'l Data Privacy L. (2014)
Drawing on the analysis of the law and practices in 13 countries in an earlier volume of this journal, this article develops both (1) a descriptive framework for comparing national laws on surveillance and government access to data held by the private sector, and (2) a normative framework based on factors derived from constitutional and human rights law. The article calls for a robust, global debate on the standards for government surveillance premised on greater transparency about current practices.

Paul M. Schwartz, *The EU-U.S. Privacy Collision: A Turn to Institutions and Procedures*, 126 Harv. L. Rev. (2013)
Exploring the path that the U.S. has taken in its information privacy law and the reasons for the relative lack of American influence on worldwide information privacy regulatory models. This Article also analyzes the likely impact of the Proposed Data Protection Regulation and how it may destabilize the current privacy policy equilibrium.

Paul M. Schwartz, *Information Privacy in the Cloud*, 161 U. Pa. L. Rev. 1623 (2013)
Comparative analysis of U.S. and EU privacy regulations of cloud services and the current uncertainty around many established privacy doctrines, including the definition of personal information and jurisdiction issues. Identifying weaknesses in how both systems regulate cloud companies and developing proposals for both legal systems.

Paul M. Schwartz & Karl-Nikolaus Peifer, *Prosser's Privacy and the German Right of Personality*, 98 Calif. L. Rev. (2010)
Contrasts German and U.S. tort privacy law and finds considerable similarities as well as significant differences regarding a relatively higher protection of celebrity identity in Germany and lesser post-mortem protection for the tort of right of appropriation.

Paul M. Schwartz & Daniel J. Solove, *Reconciling Personal Information in the United States and European Union*, 102 Cal. L. Rev. 877 (2014)
The privacy law of the US and EU greatly differ in their definitions of personal information. The US approach is narrow and inconsistent, while the EU approach is overly broad. Schwartz and Solove propose a tiered risk-based approach to bridge the gaps between US and EU privacy law—"PII 2.0"—which focuses on whether data identifies a person, whether the data is identifiable, or whether there is a minimal risk that the data is identifiable. The article suggests that more Fair Information Practice Principles (FIPPs) be applied the risk of identification increases.

Peter P. Swire & Robert E. Litan, *None of Your Business: World Data Flows, Electronic Commerce, and the European Privacy Directive* (1998)
Path-breaking early study of the European Data Protection Directive and its possible impact on commerce.

James Q. Whitman, *The Two Western Cultures of Privacy: Dignity versus Liberty*, 113 Yale L.J. 1151 (2004)
Argues that deep-seated cultural and legal differences in Europe and the United States have led to an approach to privacy centered on personal dignity in the former and individual liberty in the latter.